For Gretchen
With best regards,

Jimmy Carter

GLEANINGS FROM
AN UNPLANNED LIFE

Gleanings from an Unplanned Life

An Annotated Oral History

JAMES L. BUCKLEY

INTERCOLLEGIATE STUDIES INSTITUTE

WILMINGTON, DELAWARE

2006

Cataloging-in-Publication Data

Buckley, James Lane, 1923–

    Gleanings from an unplanned life : an annotated oral history / by James L. Buckley. — 1st ed. Wilmington, DE : ISI Books, 2006, c2005.

    p. ; cm.

    ISBN-13: 978-1-933859-11-8
    ISBN-10: 1-933859-11-3

    Includes excerpts from: Oral history transcripts of the Historical Society of the District of Columbia Circuit, Oral History Project.

    1. Buckley, James Lane, 1923– —Interviews. 2. Judges—United States—Interviews. 3. Lawyers—United States—Interviews. 4. Circuit courts—Washington (D.C.)—Biography. I. Title.

KF8745.B834 A3 2006   2006929553
347.73/14092—dc22   0610

Published in the United States by:
Intercollegiate Studies Institute
Post Office Box 4431
Wilmington, DE 19807-0431

Interior design by Sam Torode

Manufactured in the United States

To my wife Ann,
whose good-natured, tolerant love
has made this unplanned life possible

A memior (of sorts) for my grandchildren
(and children, who will probably never ask their
father the questions I never asked mine).

CONTENTS

Introduction

I WAS BORN in an elevator in New York City's Women's Hospital in the early hours of March 9, 1923. That was the first of a series of unplanned, unanticipatable events that have shaped my life. It was also a rather unceremonious way to enter the world. I wouldn't have entered it at all, however, had it not been for an allergy gene that caused my paternal grandfather, who was beset by asthma, to abandon Canada for the starker landscape of south Texas. At least it seems unlikely that my father would have courted my New Orleans mother if he had been reared in Canada.

I grew up in a small rural community located in the northwest corner of Connecticut beyond commuting range from anywhere. I loved the life there; and while bobbing around the Pacific as a naval officer in World War II, I decided on a career as a country lawyer. After four years learning the trade at a New Haven law firm in preparation for a move to the country, I was lured away by my father and found myself working for a family business headquartered in New York City. Then through a series of wildly improbable circumstances, beginning with the decision of my brother Bill to run for the office of mayor of New York City on the strict understanding that he could not win, I have found myself among the very few who have served in high positions in all three branches of the federal government; in my case, as a senator, an under secretary of state, and, most recently, as an appellate judge.

1

It is thanks to that last position that I now find myself the subject of an oral history commissioned by The Historical Society of the District of Columbia Circuit. It is part of the society's ongoing program to record the lives of judges who have served in that circuit through extended, in-depth interviews conducted by volunteer members of the District of Columbia Bar. The resulting oral histories are then made available to historians and the general public in both recorded and transcribed form. I was particularly fortunate in the society's choice of Wendy White as my interviewer. Ms. White brought her skills as a first class litigator to the task. She was intelligent, highly personable, and curious about all aspects of my life; and in the course of her interviews, she was able to tease out details and memories that I could never have exhumed on my own.

As a result, I have been able to use the oral history as the framework for the following narrative of a largely unplanned life. I have deleted portions of little interest to non-lawyers and made minor editorial revisions of the original text, which is on file with the Historical Society and the Library of Congress and may be viewed on the society's website, and have italicized the substantive additions and commentary (the "annotations"). I cannot vouch for the complete accuracy of my recollections, but I believe they are accurate in essence if not in detail.

FIRST INTERVIEW

Forebears, Family, Childhood

WW: Today is August 14, 1995. This is Wendy White from Shea & Gardner, and I'm here with Judge James L. Buckley of the United States Court of Appeals for the District of Columbia Circuit. We are here as part of the D.C. Oral History Project, and this is our first session. We are starting at about 2:15 p.m. Eastern Daylight Time. I start with the only question that sounds like a deposition question, which is, why don't you tell us your full name and where you live.

JLB: OK. James Lane Buckley. My address is 4980 Quebec Street N.W. in the District of Columbia. I actually live in these chambers.

WW: This is where you spend all your time?

JLB: Yes.

WW: Well, I haven't had any trouble finding you here. What's your date of birth?

JLB: March 9, 1923.

WW: You are married?

JLB: Married.

WW: And your wife's name is Ann?

JLB: Ann

WW: What was her maiden name?

JLB: Ann Frances Cooley.

WW: And you have six children.

JLB: Right

WW: And what are their names?

JLB: The oldest is Peter; next is James (we call him Jay); Priscilla; William (we call him Bill); David; and Andrew (Andy).

WW: We are going to talk in a little bit about your wife and your family; but to begin I would like to go back in time and start, if you will, by talking about your grandparents—either what you know of them or knew about them and where they were from. Let's find out more about them. Do you want to start with your paternal grandparents?

JLB: OK. My grandfather was named John Buckley and his wife, Mary Ann, formerly Mary Ann Langford. They grew up in a rural area of Canada and emigrated to Texas shortly after their marriage. My grandfather had asthma, and somebody persuaded him that Texas was where he should go for relief. My grandparents moved at first to a place called Washington-on-the-Brazos, which is the site of the Texas Declaration of Independence. I think the town has since disappeared. My father was born there. He was their third child. Within a year or two after that they moved to a very dry, tiny town in south Texas—San Diego, which is the seat of Duval

4

County. Apparently my grandfather had all the virtues except that of making money. But he ended up as the successful reform candidate for sheriff of Duval County. He died about 20 years before I was born.

WW: About what year was it when he came to Texas?

JLB: My father was born in 1881 so my grandparents moved to Texas before then.

WW: What was he doing in Canada?

JLB: He grew up there — his family were farmers.

WW: What part of Canada — eastern or western?

JLB: The Province of Ontario, near Hamilton.

WW: His wife Mary Ann was also from Hamilton?

JLB: Not from Hamilton, but from some town nearby.

WW: And did they get married young or old or who knows?

JLB: Somebody knows. I have a cousin who has taken an interest in these things, and if it is of critical importance to you, I could probably find out.

Thanks to information assembled by two of my cousins, I can report the following about my Canadian forebears. My paternal grandfather, John Buckley, was born in 1848 in what is now Burlington, Ontario, of parents who had emigrated from County Cork, Ireland, in 1845. John's father was Anglican and his mother Catholic. According to a story my father used to tell us, when his Buckley grandparents were newly wed and were watching an Orangemen's parade in Ireland, his grandfather struck a man who had insulted his wife for being a Catholic with such force that his grandfather had to be kept in jail for several days while it was determined whether he should be tried for murder. The man survived, and my father's paternal grandparents were free to move to Canada where religious passions were less threatening. My grandmother Mary Ann Langford's parents had emigrated to Canada from County Limerick, Ireland, in 1830 and owned a pub in Oakville, Ontario. Her father was also an Anglican who had married a Catholic. My grandparents were married in Oakville in 1872 and moved to Texas a few years later with their first-born children, John and Priscilla.

WW: So they got married and they decided to leave Canada for health reasons. Do you think that's why they left?

JLB: Apparently my grandfather had very bad allergy problems, and the gene has passed on for many generations.

WW: Is it in this chambers?

JLB: Yes, but I'm grateful for it; otherwise I might not be an American citizen.

WW: Did you know your paternal grandparents?

JLB: I knew my grandmother slightly. The last time I saw her was when I was five. She lived in Texas, we lived in Connecticut. We visited her at Christmas. My grandfather died in 1904.

WW: And how about your mother's parents—where did they come from?

JLB: My mother's father was born in New Orleans, her mother was born in Port Gibson, Mississippi.

WW: I didn't know you had all these southern roots.

JLB: Although I was born in New York City and grew up in New England, I am culturally southern.

WW: We will talk about that when we get to your political career. What was your mother's father's name?

JLB: Aloysius Steiner.

WW: And her mother, your grandmother?

JLB: Maiden name was Wassem.

WW: And her first name was?

JLB: Marie Louise.

WW: What did Aloysius Steiner do in New Orleans?

JLB: He was the secretary-treasurer of what was then this country's largest wholesaler of sugar refining equipment.

WW: You know, when you live in Washington and everybody practices law, it's really wonderful to hear about people who do real things that matter in this world. Was this a family business?

JLB: No. I knew that he was a financial officer, but I only learned the nature of the business when I went to New Orleans about five years ago to visit the last survivor of my parents' generation, an uncle who had just turned 80, and he told me. For whatever reason, when I was growing up, I never thought to ask what my grandfather did.

WW: Did you know either of them?

JLB: I knew my grandmother. She had lived in New Orleans, and we would visit occasionally. The last time I saw her was when I was about 13. She spent a month with us in Connecticut. My grandfather died three or four years before I was born.

WW: Was your mother born in New Orleans?

JLB: Yes.

WW: Do you have any memories of stories told about your grandparents or what their lives were like? Did your parents talk about their parents?

JLB: Not all that much. My father had some stories that were possibly apocryphal, but I don't recall his having said anything much about how they lived.

WW: Do you know what kind of people they were, what was important to them?

JLB: Character and their faith. Apparently my father's father was principled, honest, courageous, and taciturn. His mother was a strong and devout individual. That is all I can say about them.

WW: In your father's generation?

JLB: There were six children, the oldest of whom died when he was 17 or 18.

WW: What were their circumstances?

JLB: They were among the poor in a poor town. It was a town of 2,200 of whom 2,000 were Mexican. There was no electricity, and their water was delivered by burro from the town well.

WW: And how do you know that? Did you talk to your father about it?

JLB: My Uncle Claude told me. I visited my uncle after my father died and he started reminiscing a bit.

WW: It's interesting how often you learn about your parents much later in life and from relatives not your parents.

JLB: I am just appalled that I never thought to ask a lot of questions.

WW: I think that is very common and it is not until later that you ever think to ask. If you were to ask me all these questions, I wouldn't know many of the answers either.

JLB: And, of course, not having known my grandparents. But my children knew their grandmothers very well. They knew both of their grandmothers.

WW: Do you have pictures of your grandparents?

JLB: I have a picture of my father's father on the wall in the other room. A cousin of mine sent it to me. It was taken in front of the courthouse in San Diego about 100 years ago and shows a dozen court-related men, including Sheriff John Buckley. I have titled it "The agents of law and order in Duval County." Duval County is famous in Texan history. Famous for its corruption. That's where Lyndon Johnson won his Senate primary race by getting 110 people to vote from the grave in alphabetical order. According to a professor at the University of Texas, my grandfather was one of them; he voted 40 years after his death.

WW: Now, was John Buckley a political man? Did he run for sheriff? Do you have to be a political character to become sheriff?

JLB: Well, I guess it depends on the circumstances. He was an unsuccessful sheep rancher. I think he tried selling hardware at some point. Whatever it was, it never quite worked. But apparently he was enormously respected, if one believes obituaries. An article in a Corpus Christi paper reporting his death said that he was greatly respected for his character and integrity, and that people came to his funeral from all over. He was also brave. San Diego was not a very peaceful town, but he rarely carried a gun—he had one but didn't carry it, and that was considered significant in those days. How did we get into this?

WW: I wanted to know whether he was political?

*"Agents of Law and Order," San Diego, Texas, ca. 1895.
Sheriff John Buckley, middle row right.*

JLB: Oh political—I just don't know. What got me into the character bit is that he ran as a reform candidate. He may have been persuaded to run, so he may not have been a political man otherwise, he may have been just a very respected person. There was a family called Parr that was very powerful in Duval County, and he opposed their candidate. Apparently my grandfather may have been elected by virtue of the fact that we are Catholic and most of the non-Mexicans were Protestants. If you go to church, you get to know fellow congregation members. He became very close to the Mexican community. When he was sheriff, he became very unpopular with a lot of "Anglos" because he sympathized with the Mexicans and tried to protect them.

WW: Well, I'm looking of course for your political roots.

JLB: His election was challenged—it went all the way to the Supreme Court of Texas. He was declared the winner a year after the election.

WW: What was the basis for the challenge, do you have any idea?

JLB: I've got the documents somewhere.

In order to flesh out my paternal grandfather's story and to convey something of the flavor of the San Diego my father grew up in, I quote at length from a letter that my Uncle Claude wrote some years ago to my cousin Edmund Buckley, who has assumed the mantle of family historian:

"My Father and Mother were natives of Canada. They were born and raised in a rural community somewhere near Hamilton, Ontario. My sister Priscilla and my brother John (who died in San Diego at the age of 18) were born in that community. . . . Shortly after Priscilla's birth, my Father contracted a bad case of asthma, which became chronic and serious. He and his family left this cold country and migrated to Texas and settled in the old town of Washington in Grimes County, a town which was the first capital of the Republic of Texas. As this country was a low coastal one, wet, and teeming with malaria, his ailment worsened. He just had to find a new place to live. . . . A friend got him to move down to the San Diego country, a somewhat desert land on which thrived only the stunted mesquite and the cactus. This happened in the later eighteen-seventies [actually, the early 1880s, as my father was born in Washington in 1881]. He became engaged in the mercantile business. . . . Then he was elected Sheriff of Duval County [in 1890] and served in that office all through the eighteen-nineties.

"My Father was an unusual man. He was honest, fearless, unassuming, and uncommunicative. At that time San Diego . . . had about 200 Americans and 2,000 Mexicans. The American Colony, if I may call it that, was most cosmopolitan. The six main merchants of the town were from France, Canada, Germany, England, Poland, and Spain. The town carpenter was directly from Scotland. The one and only hotel, the Marinet, was French owned. Two of the town's prominent stockmen were from Ireland. The chairman of the School Board was from Ohio and the principal from Colorado. With one or two exceptions, all school teachers were Mexicans. The town's wool and cotton buyers were Frenchmen. San Diego's richest citizen, *Norman G. Collins, was from Minnesota. At the time of his death he owned 27 ranches in Southwest Texas. . . . Among the Mexican citizens were some very high class folks from Camargo and Monterrey, Mexico. The town doctors were a Frenchman and a Spaniard.*

"The town itself and the county and the whole Southwest were wild and wooly. They abounded in law breakers of all types and kinds. The worst of these were the cow thieves and the smugglers, the latter were a mean bunch who made a living by smuggling tequila from Mexico to San Antonio and other points in Texas. Their direct route from Rio Grande City to San Antonio came right through San Diego. They carried the tequila in goat skins which they tied to their saddles. At times as many as twenty smugglers traveled together. Then there were the gunmen among the Americans and Mexicans of the town. My Father had to deal with all the elements. He rarely toted a pistol. He carried one only when traveling in the country. And he never used a holster. He stuck the pistol inside his trousers at the waist and on the left side. He didn't smoke and he rarely indulged in liquors. Several attempts were made to assassinate him, but each one was foiled. He had bitter enemies, particularly among the low white trash of the town. They even went to the extreme of having him indicted by a federal grand jury in San Antonio for aiding and abetting a revolution against the United States and Mexico. This revolution was initiated by one Catarino Garza of Palatio Blanco, a little community some twenty miles south of San Diego. And the revolution was intended solely to oust Porfirio Diaz from the presidency of Mexico. As Garza was a close friend and political follower of my Father, the latter's enemies had him indicted for aiding and abetting this revolution. The indictment was later dismissed and quashed. Garza was able to enlist some three hundred Mexicans throughout the counties of Duval, Starr, and Zapata. The U.S. had to send in soldiers to put down the revolution. I saw Garza only once and that was when he made a political speech in favor of my Father at a torchlight gathering one night in the main plaza of San Diego. I remember that he had two pistols on him and that he was heckled from time to time during his speech. It looked for a while that shooting might start.

"My Father was defeated in 1900 for Sheriff. After that and until his death he became a sheep buyer and annually shipped thousands and thousands of sheep to Kansas City. He died in Rockport in 1904 from a cerebral hemorrhage."

WW: What an interesting story. Was religion an important part of your grandfather's life?

JLB: I suspect so.

WW: And your grandmother? Were all four of your grandparents Catholic, raised as Catholic?

JLB: All four of mine were, although only one of my great-grandfathers was. Both of my father's grandfathers were Protestant, as was one of my mother's.

Grandmother Buckley and her children: Priscilla, Claude, Edmund, Eleanor, and my father, William.

WW: You said that your father had five siblings?

JLB: He had five siblings, of whom I knew four. Two sisters and two brothers.

WW: Who were they and what were they like?

JLB: The eldest was Priscilla Buckley, a maiden aunt, wonderful sense of humor, and formidable character. The other sister, who was the next to the youngest in the family, was Eleanor. She was quiet, and very beautiful. And also unmarried. Then my two uncles, Uncle Edmund and Uncle Claude. They both started out as lawyers, as did my father, and then one of them stayed in the law and the other became an entrepreneur in various fields. Both stayed in Texas, via Mexico—that's another story.

WW: Via Mexico? Did they live in Mexico for a while?

JLB: My father developed a huge interest in Mexico when growing up, and after he emerged from the University of Texas Law School, he went to Mexico City and hung out a shingle. He grew up speaking absolutely fluent Spanish so he took whatever courses you had to take to qualify to practice in Mexico; and then, when oil was discovered in Tampico, he said, "Ah ha, this is my opportunity." Because he knew Mexican law and spoke English, he believed he could secure the legal business of oil companies who presumably would want to be represented by somebody who knew his way around and understood the people. So he moved his shingle to Tampico and then invited his two brothers to join him. That is how the three of them ended up in Tampico practicing law.

WW: Is this before you were born?

JLB: Before I was born.

WW: And did they marry—Edmund and Claude?

JLB: Yes.

WW: Did they raise families?

JLB: Yes.

WW: And where did they end up after Mexico—in Texas?

JLB: One of them, Uncle Claude, ended up in San Antonio and the other one in Austin.

WW: And are they still there? Are they alive?

JLB: They are dead. They were born in the 1880s.

WW: But did you know either of them?

JLB: Yes, but not well. Uncle Edmund died of lung cancer, and I'm trying to think if it was immediately after World War II or immediately before the war. I think immediately after the war. Uncle Claude died when he was 90.

WW: Do you keep up with any of the families?

JLB: Yes, with some of my cousins—but not as well as I would like. I find them a great group. When I went to a court-sponsored training course in San Antonio on how to use a word processor and LEXIS and things of that nature, I had a splendid time with four cousins who live there.

WW: And there is one other sibling—was there a child who died young?

JLB: Yes, John.

WW: Was he the oldest?

JLB: He was the oldest son—he was born in Canada.

WW: And where is your father in the pecking order?

JLB: He was number three.

WW: What's your father's name?

JLB: William.

WW: OK. Now let's go over to your mother's family and do the same thing. How many sisters and/or brothers did your mother have?

JLB: She had two sisters and one brother.

WW: Why don't you tell me about them.

JLB: OK. The brother was about 11 or 12 years younger than the youngest of the three girls. My mother was the oldest.

WW: What was your mother's name?

JLB: Aloïse. Her name was adapted from her father's, Aloysius, whose father and grandfather were named Alois, so the name, or variations of it, seem to carry on.

WW: And is this a longtime New Orleans family?

JLB: Her father was the first one born in New Orleans. That was in 1855. Her grandfather and great-grandfather immigrated from Switzerland in the 1840s.

WW: And the next generation?

JLB: My mother, the oldest, was born in 1895. Then the next child was Vivian and she married Marion Lombard, a doctor in the U.S. Public Health Service who was sent to New Orleans before we entered the First World War because of a typhus or yellow fever epidemic. New Orleans used to have all of the tropical diseases sooner or later; anyway, that's how she met him. He stayed in the service, which meant she ended up living everywhere in the United States. She in turn produced a bunch of my first cousins. Then the other sister, Aunt Inez. . . . Incidentally, they were tiny people—about five feet tall. My mother was about five feet and a half. Not five and a half feet—five feet and half an inch.

WW: That's how tall I am. So you didn't get your tall genes from this side of the family. Your tall genes did not come from your mother.

JLB: Well, her mother was five feet eight; her father was five feet five. Her mother's father was six feet five.

WW: Well, maybe you did. I take that back.

JLB: Aunt Inez also married a doctor, but a doctor who was a New Orleans native and stayed there. Claude Perrier was his name.

WW: And are they still in New Orleans? Do you have cousins in New Orleans?

JLB: Oh yes, I do. My parents' generation is gone now, the last survivor being my mother's brother, Jimmy, who died two years ago.

WW: And you said he was much younger than the other three.

JLB: Yes.

WW: What did he do?

JLB: He was with a finance company of some kind.

WW: You said your father grew up in these poor world Texas circumstances—what about your mother?

JLB: Prosperous. You know, not rich but comfortable.

WW: Was it a prominent family in New Orleans—a well-known family in New Orleans?

JLB: No. Not that I know of, but socially very acceptable in a socially conscious city.

*My mother's family: from the left, Josephine Wassem (her aunt),
Vivian (sister), my mother (age 14), her grandmother Wassem,
father, mother, and sister Inez.*

WW: And how did they get to New Orleans from Switzerland, do you know?

JLB: It puzzles me. I just don't understand what would cause people to go from a Swiss climate to there, but apparently there were others. There was a German-speaking community in New Orleans, and it was a Catholic city. My mother's paternal forebears came from Switzerland's Catholic German-speaking canton, St. Gallen. But to go from Switzerland to the fever swamps of New Orleans was to me surprising.

WW: Very surprising. That's right. I did not realize that New Orleans had a significant German community.

JLB: Well, there were some; and my Lutheran great-grandfather Henry Wassem, who lived in Mississippi, had also started out in New Orleans.

A word about my mother's forebears who, I fear, are overshadowed in this chronicle by my father's. My mother's Swiss ancestors lived in the city of Bergt in the Canton of St. Gallen. In 1845, my great-great-grandfather Alois Steiner, his wife, and their seven children (including great-grandfather Alois) packed up and, for whatever reason, moved all the way to New Orleans. A hundred and forty years later, while my wife and I were driving through Switzerland, I decided to snoop out the ancestral neighborhood. On entering the canton, I located a phone book and checked the listings for Bergt. I found over a dozen Steiners, including at least two Alois Steiners. When we entered the town itself, on a late cold and rainy Saturday afternoon, it became immediately apparent why our branch of the family might have chosen to leave. Bergt proved to be the only Swiss municipality I have ever seen that seemed totally devoid of charm.

That still leaves the mystery of their decision to move to a hot and humid New Orleans. But there they settled, and by the time my mother came along, the family was a respected part of the New Orleans bourgeoisie and its members were fully accepted by the old French families that had settled the city. (When my mother was growing up, many of her schoolmates still spoke French at home.) I have little feel for my grandfather other than that he was a quiet, gentle man of a studious bent. He read voraciously, always with a dictionary at his side. He was a short man—a few inches shorter than his wife, in fact—which explains why no family picture shows them both standing or both sitting. He was a pillar of the church, as evidenced by his name engraved in marble as a member of the building committee responsible for the construction of Mater Dolorosa Church, on Carrollton Avenue, where my parents were married. The only anecdote about him that comes to mind is that when he was a boy, he absented himself from school to witness the hanging of the traitor who revealed the location of the chain across the Mississippi that was supposed to protect New Orleans from attack by the Yankees. I dismiss, as apocryphal, my mother's claim that he was descended from William Tell.

Grandfather Steiner was first married in 1883, to a Mary Margaret Sporl, by whom he had four children, two of whom were stillborn. Within six or seven years, his wife and surviving children had all died. He subsequently married Marie Louise Wassem, of Port Gibson, Mississippi. How a quiet 39-year-old 5' 5" widower managed to woo and capture the heart of a lively 23-year-old 5' 8" woman remains an enigma. We know from an entry in my grandfather's diary, however, that they met in New Orleans at a card party and that a "mutual admiration for each other sprung up at once." The Wassems had New Orleans connections as my great-grandfather Henry Wassem and his father had immigrated there from Hesse, Germany, in the 1840s following the father's retirement as a sergeant in the Hessian army. Henry Wassem served in the Civil War and was wounded at Shiloh fighting for the Confederacy. He was eighteen at the time. As his origins suggest, he was a Lutheran; but before moving to Fort Gibson, he married Mary Ann Lee, a Catholic lady of mystery. It is known that she was born in St. Louis, Missouri, on August 16, 1847, and that she was orphaned a few years thereafter when her parents died of yellow fever while visiting New Orleans friends who subsequently took care of her. Family legend has it that she was a collateral member of THE Lee family of Virginia. Alas, a genealogist cousin is reasonably certain that she was the daughter of Irish immigrants. St. Louis baptismal records that might have identified her parents were destroyed by fire many years ago, but contemporary census records list only one Lee family in St. Louis at the time of her birth, so one must assume it was hers.

WW: So how did your parents meet? With such very different backgrounds?

JLB: My father was then getting on in years [*he was 36*], and I guess he was very anxious to meet a prospective bride. His brother Edmund had met one of my mother's sisters in Mexico, where she was visiting an uncle [*actually, a first cousin once removed*] whose father had moved there after the Civil War rather than take an oath of allegiance to the United States. He learned that there was a bevy of attractive Steiner sisters in New Orleans and suggested that my father call on them on a forthcoming trip to the city. So he did. There was a 14 year difference in my parents' ages. They were married four months later [*in December 1917*].

WW: Now that is an interesting story—and they were married in New Orleans? Well, tell me about what your father did as he grew up and what brought him to the point where he married your mother?

JLB: Well, he grew up as the son of the sheriff and played baseball and rode horses and things of that sort. He attended a tiny school that had an extraordinary teacher. The community was surprisingly cosmopolitan. It included French, German, and Irish families, and Virginians displaced by the Civil War, people with a fair amount of education who for whatever reasons ended up there, God knows why. In any event, the immediate goal on graduating from that school was to get a college education. My Aunt Priscilla and my father went to Austin, which is where the University of Texas is located, and they both went to work in the Texas land office translating Spanish deeds in order to raise the money for my father's tuition and living expenses. My aunt continued to do that until she retired many years later, but she helped finance the education of my father and their younger siblings. She herself never went to college.

WW: So Priscilla is the oldest. She did not go through the university herself but just worked to finance others?

JLB: That's right. She just worked to help.

WW: Did they all go?

JLB: The others all went. My father raced through college and law school in five years and then headed off to Mexico.

But not right away. According to records at the University of Texas, he received his law degree in 1905, served as quizmaster at the law school and was admitted to the Texas bar in 1906, and moved to Mexico in 1908.

WW: Had he ever been to Mexico?

JLB: Yes, he had been there several times—once selling soap. At another time he had the honor of serving as Pancho Villa's interpreter.

WW: There aren't a lot of people who can say that.

JLB: Villa called him Señor Ojos Azules. Mr. Blue Eyes.

WW: Your mother—who was 14 years younger and was growing up in New Orleans—what was her life like as she grew up?

JLB: Very social. She had been engaged a couple of times before she met my father; I know that.

WW: How do you know that?

JLB: She told us. Mother went to college for a year, but then had a nervous breakdown of some kind. Then came World War I. She volunteered for nursing, fainted dead away at the first sight of blood. Went to balls and so forth and then when she was 22, my father came along.

WW: So she was quite young?

JLB: He was 36 and she was 22.

WW: And they married four months later and where did they then move? Did they go back to Mexico?

JLB: Yes.

WW: Did she speak Spanish?

JLB: She spoke terrible Spanish fluently. Bad accent, utterly ungrammatical.

WW: But she picked it up.

JLB: She could say what she wanted to say. She could communicate and she could understand.

WW: Did your mother go to college?

JLB: Just one year.

WW: She never went back. So did they live in Mexico for long—what did they do next?

JLB: They lived in Tampico until 1920 or '21. Then my father achieved a signal honor. He became the first person against whom the president of Mexico invoked Article 33 of the Mexican Constitution. Article 33 empowers the president to expel "pernicious foreigners." [*I have since discovered that he was not the first to be so honored.*]

WW: Was he making too much money?

JLB: He was testifying here in Washington before the Senate Foreign Relations Committee as to why the United States should not recognize the current bandits in charge of Mexico. [*My father opposed recognition of the revolutionary regimes because of their persecution of the Church and their assaults on property rights.*]

WW: He was actually told he had to leave?

JLB: Oh, absolutely.

WW: Was there some formal proceeding?

JLB: No. The president had the authority. My father was told to get out.

Apparently that president, or succeeding ones, came to use that authority with such frequency that the subject of an Article 33 expulsion would be described as having been "thirty-threed." This in turn gave rise to the saying, in that violent period, that while pernicious foreigners were thirty-threed, pernicious Mexicans were thirty-thirtied.

WW: And I take it that at that time he had a successful practice?

JLB: He was successful. He had started representing various oil companies and ended up engaging in various land ventures, including real estate and oil exploration leases. These ventures proved very profitable.

WW: So let's talk about your brothers and sisters and who was born in Mexico. You were not born there.

JLB: No, I was not born there. None of us were born in Mexico although my oldest sister lived there as an infant. My oldest sister was born in New Orleans in 1918. My mother came up from Tampico for that purpose and then returned. My parents remained in Tampico until my father was expelled, which was before their second child was born.

WW: What is your oldest sister's name?

JLB: Aloïse.

WW: How many other siblings do you have?

JLB: There were ten of us. I am the fourth of ten. There are now seven.

WW: OK. Let's find out about your siblings.

JLB: Aloïse, the oldest, was five years older than I. She in turn had ten children. She died when she was about 45. She had some kind of brain hemorrhage.

WW: Leaving ten children. Did the other siblings have a relationship with her children in her absence? In other words, do you have a relationship and do your brothers and sisters have a relationship with them?

JLB: Some more than others. My brother John and I worked in New York with their father, Ben Heath, and they continued to spend summers in a converted barn on my family's place in Sharon, Connecticut; so several of us were in fairly close touch with them.

My family in 1939. Standing: JLB, Father, John.
Seated: Patricia, Aloïse, Priscilla, Bill, Carol,
Mother, Jane. On lawn: Maureen, Reid.

WW: Sometimes when a mother dies young, the rest of the family really dedicates a lot of time to these other children—and ten of them is a lot of work. Did your brother-in-law remarry?

JLB: Yes, he did. About five or six years after that.

WW: OK, that's your oldest sister.

JLB: The next in line is my oldest brother John, married with three children. He died in December of 1984. He was 62.

WW: What did he die of?

JLB: An abdominal problem.

WW: Where did he live?

JLB: He lived in Lakeville, Connecticut. He and I worked together, and we had an office in New York but also one in Sharon where we would work on Mondays and Fridays. We would go to New York Tuesday mornings and return Thursday evenings. Then comes my sister Priscilla. Priscilla is retired now. She is a journalist. After she graduated from Smith College in 1943, she went to work in New York City for the United Press radio division. After the war, she joined the UP's bureau in Paris. When my younger brother Bill started his magazine, *National Review*, he hauled her back to serve as its managing editor; and she continued as its managing editor until she retired about two years ago.

WW: So, she worked with your brother all those years.

JLB: She did not marry. And she has now retired to Sharon. And then comes your servant.

WW: We'll get back to you.

JLB: And after that comes my sister Jane who married Bill Smith. They lived in Calgary in Canada for a while. She has six children. They returned to Connecticut, to Sharon. She and Bill were later divorced, and she has remained single ever since. She lives in Sharon. Sharon, by the way, is a very small village. When we were growing up, Sharon had a population of about 1,600. That population has since exploded to 2,800.

WW: Does that include many of your cousins?

JLB: None of my cousins, no.

WW: All right, that's Jane.

JLB: After that comes brother Bill. He is married to a Canadian, Patricia Taylor. Their home is in Stamford, Connecticut, and they have an apartment in New York, where he edits his magazine, writes his columns, and does his television program. They have one child, a son who lives in Washington, D.C.

WW: Is your nephew a lawyer?

JLB: No, he's a writer. Lots of writing in the family. [*A great deal, in fact. Five members of my generation have made a living as writers or editors, and seven of us have had books and/or articles published commercially. The gene is at work in the next generation as well.*] Then we come to sister Patricia.

WW: So you have a sister and a sister-in-law named Patricia.

JLB: Right. Patricia married a fellow called Brent Bozell. She has ten children. You shake your head.

WW: It's amazing, amazing. What would you do if you ever had a family reunion and everybody came?

In 2002, a niece invited relatives to attend a midday party celebrating the 80th birthday of everyone's favorite aunt (and person), my sister Priscilla. No, not every-

one came. But 92 celebrants, consisting of four generations of blood relatives and their spouses, managed to make it. It was our first ingathering in almost 20 years, and probably our last.

JLB: This is a picture of my mother with 34 of her 50 grandchildren.

WW: Well, this is an impressive picture. It is mind-boggling. When you put together all of just your generation and their children, if you count it up, how many are there?

JLB: Seven of us are still living, and we have produced 50 children who, in turn, are producing their own. At the time of her death in 1985, my mother had 90 living descendants.

WW: That's an impressive effort, a very impressive effort. Great picture. OK; so Patricia has ten children as well, and she is still alive.

JLB: She is still alive; she lives in Washington, D.C. For a while she and her husband edited a magazine on Catholic subjects called *Triumph* which, as happens to most small magazines, eventually went under; and she now does editing work for a publishing company.

WW: Oh, so there are a lot of journalists.

JLB: Then we get to our youngest brother Reid. Reid has had two novels published. One of them was a second selection for the Book of the Month Club. It had about 750 pages.

WW: So it was hard to take to the beach.

JLB: He has done a lot of writing and lives in Camden, South Carolina, where my parents had maintained a winter home for many years. He has established a school there at which people, mostly executives, are taught how to present themselves, how to speak on their feet; and he writes articles and gives lectures on the side. And he is married and remarried.

WW: How many children do they have?

JLB: Four children by his first wife; one by the second marriage. He married a Spanish widow the second time around, and she has five children.

WW: OK.

JLB: Then we go to sister Maureen. Ten years younger than I. Maureen married a lovely man named Gerald O'Reilly, and she had five children. She died in her early 30s of a cerebral aneurism.

WW: And the youngest?

JLB: The youngest is Carol. Carol married and divorced twice and has four children. She is now living in Massachusetts, in Newburyport, which is near Boston.

WW: So what was it like growing up in a family of ten children?

JLB: Wonderful.

WW: That's a wonderful answer. There was probably something going on all the time. Did you take care of each other?

JLB: Yes. Mother claims that after four children there is very little incremental work. The discipline that I remember most when I was growing up was handed out by my brothers and sisters. When I got out of hand, they showed no mercy.

WW: Were there siblings with whom you were particularly close as you grew up?

JLB: Yes, my sister Priscilla. Large families have a tendency to break up into groups. I was the youngest of the oldest group. So my closest relationships were upstream rather than downstream.

WW: Were the age gaps evenly spaced or is there a break after you?

JLB: No break after me. My mother gave birth to 11 children in 20 years. One of them died two days after her birth. Difficulty breathing. So there was a gap there, but the real gap was between Maureen and Carol—five years.

WW: I admire her enormously. That's very hard work. So I know what your mother did with her time. But how did they end up in Connecticut? Where did they go after Mexico?

JLB: They went to New York, stopping on the way in New Orleans and Texas to catch their breath and, I guess, to collect whatever possessions escaped Mexico. By that time my father's principal assets were an absolute command of Spanish, an understanding of the Spanish legal system, and a demonstrated ability to develop intimate relationships with the foreigners among whom he lived—they respected him, he spoke their language, and he was very close to them. He had become intrigued by the oil business. Oil had been discovered in Venezuela by then, so he decided that what he wanted to do was to raise the money with which to form a company that would try to negotiate oil exploration concessions in that country. Where was the money? In those days it was in Wall Street. But he didn't want his children to live in New York City. For the first couple of years, my parents rented a house in Bronxville, New York, and then, somehow or other, my father found this remote Connecticut village, Sharon, which he thought was exactly right.

WW: Where is it?

JLB: On the New York border about 12 miles south of Massachusetts. It's in the northwest corner of Connecticut. It is about 95 miles north of New York City, so it's well beyond commuting range. My father would take the train into New York on Monday mornings and come back Friday afternoons. So we saw him on weekends.

WW: So your mother raised ten children essentially by herself with the other children helping.

JLB: With lots of help. We had a French governess and two Mexican nurses.

WW: And he had an apartment in Manhattan?

JLB: Yes.

WW: What was your father like?

JLB: A remarkable man. He was very shy with his children. He had a wonderful sense of humor, was very bright. Unlike certain of his sons, he had a wonderful memory for anecdotes. A man of great charm. And great intelligence. And great imagination. And great business courage. He had very strong principles.

WW: Which he communicated to his children. And what about your mother? What was she like and what was life like for her?

JLB: I gathered after I grew up that she had experienced some lonely times. But she was a lovely, lovely, lovely person. Wonderful with people. She was a woman of extraordinary faith, a deeply religious person. My father was too, but his was much more private.

WW: Was she active in the way she practiced religion? Did you go to Mass? Were you active in the Church as a family? Was she active in the Church?

JLB: Not active in the sense of being on this parish committee or that. But she went to church every day and had total faith in the Lord; and when she had problems, she would place them in His hands. She prayed energetically for any and all things. Her faith was a living, real thing for her.

WW: And she communicated that to her children.

JLB: Yes. She communicated the strength of her beliefs. But not all of her children were as graced as she was.

My parents were remarkable people by any objective standard. My father was intelligent, articulate, generous, witty, courtly, principled, inventive, and disciplined. But there was far more to him than the sum of those attributes, some magic ingredient that inevitably commanded the attention and respect of the movers of any community in which he settled, whether here or abroad. As a young man, for example, he had gained such prominence as an American practicing law in Mexico that in 1914, when U.S. forces occupied Vera Cruz, the American commander, General Funston, asked my 33-year-old father to serve as the city's civil administrator, an honor he declined because he strongly disagreed with Woodrow Wilson's policies towards Mexico. At the same time, he was held in such respect by the Mexicans that they invited him to serve as counsel to the Mexican delegation to the conference called by Argentina, Brazil, and Chile to mediate the differences between Mexico and the United States—an honor that he did accept. His was a quality I can best describe by reference to a story told about Yale president Richard

My parents in 1954. He would die in 1958, she in 1985.

Levin. It seems that at a meeting with alumni, a man who had checked his manners at the door asked Levin if he could explain why the current presidents of Yale, Harvard, and Princeton were all Jewish. Levin's response was, "We are cream. We rise to the top." My father was cream.

My mother's strengths and appeal were of a different kind and harder to describe—so difficult, in fact, that instead of trying and botching the job, I have included, as an appendix to this chronicle, the obituary that my brother Bill wrote for National Review. *It provides wonderful impressionistic glimpses of what she was like, but it falls short of explaining why she was so deeply and widely loved, or why so many turned to her when they had problems, or why she was the source of such fun for us as we were growing up and for the children we would later spawn. Nor does it describe the strength she was so often called upon to display when my father was fighting his lonely battles for corporate survival, or the competence she exhibited in managing her large and sometimes difficult household, or the qualities that caused her to be named mother of the year by a black Baptist church in Camden, South Carolina, or the uncanny way she had of making individuals of whatever age or background feel so utterly at home with her.*

I recall a conversation long ago, in Camden, with a young woman who knew both my parents well, one of the virtues of that unusual community being the ease with which the generations mingled. I remember her commenting at some length on what an extraordinary person each of them was. She ended by saying, "and, of course, none of you can match either one of them." And, of course, she was right.

WW: Were you born in New York?

JLB: Yes.

WW: And all your siblings after you, were they all born in New York?

JLB: All but two of them. My sister Maureen and my brother Reid were born in Paris.

WW: What were you doing in Paris at the time?

JLB: In 1929, my father concluded that he had it made, and now he was ready to do all those things you couldn't do when living in San Diego, Texas. So he took wife and, at that point, seven children to France; and a couple of months later, something called the Great Depression occurred—the crash. My brother John claims this is true—I'm not sure it is—that he was in my parents' bedroom one day when my father received a long distance telephone call. He turned to my mother and said, "Dear, how much money do you have in your purse?" She answered, "Oh, I've got 148 francs." He then said, "Well, that's all we have." That was a slight exaggeration, but in effect he had to go back to work and raise money in Europe. So we were stranded in Europe by the Depression.

WW: Do you remember that?

JLB: I don't. My brother John did. I was six years old at the time; he would have been nine.

WW: Do you remember any change in the family dynamic or your circumstances? At six you don't remember much, but sometimes you pick up the feeling of what's going on.

JLB: We were protected from vicissitudes.

WW: What happened?

JLB: Well, instead of spending six months or so abroad, we remained in Europe for another two and a half years.

WW: And what did your father do?

JLB: Raised money, to keep his company afloat. We returned in 1932. We spent the last nine months in England.

WW: Do you remember that? You were pretty little.

JLB: I remember some of it.

WW: Were you in school there?

JLB: Yes, in France and in England.

The school I attended in Paris, the Cours Marguerite, was my first although my oldest sister, Aloïse, had begun to teach me how to read before then (which may explain why my reading has always been excruciatingly slow). I don't recall having experienced any traumas at suddenly finding myself having to cope with a new language. All I know is that I soon found myself speaking French with total ease and playing with French boys in the Bois de Boulogne. Such trauma as I did experience with schools in that period was when we moved to England in the fall of 1931 and, at age eight, found myself deposited in an English boarding school along with my brother John. But children are resilient, and I quickly adjusted to the routine and to a curriculum which included introductory Latin and algebra and painfully detailed studies of English geography, county by county. I even took some pride in having been caned by the headmaster, Father Ritchie, for the sin of smuggling candy into my dormitory after a Sunday visit with my parents. The canes he used were made of bamboo grown on the premises and made limber with the oil used to treat cricket bats. And it was at this school, the Oratory Preparatory School, that I first became conscious of my fascination with birds.

WW: How's your French?

JLB: I wish it were great because my only daughter is married to a Frenchman who speaks no English. I can understand French quite well, but when I took a battery of aptitude tests on entering Yale, I found I was in the 30th percentile as far as an aptitude for foreign languages is concerned. I just can't grab the words and absorb them. I can get by in French, but I can't carry on a serious conversation.

WW: Did you learn at the time that you were there?

JLB: At ages seven, eight, and nine, I was trilingual. I absorbed idiomatic French at school in Paris. When I was very young, my father spoke to us in Spanish, and I had a Mexican nurse. So I spoke Spanish before I spoke English.

WW: That was to make sure that you always spoke Spanish, and did that work?

JLB: No. My French is better than my Spanish. But it worked for various members of my family who have a better native talent so that at least five or six of my brothers and sisters remain fluent in one or both of those languages. But I'm not one of them.

WW: What kind of impact did this have on your mother, this dramatic change?

JLB: Apparently there were some very hairy times on the corporate and financial fronts. Nevertheless, by the end of our stay in France, our family had grown to nine children, and we continued to have two Mexican nurses and a French governess.

WW: And that didn't change during this period?

JLB: My father went into debt. He had great confidence in his company's prospects and in his ability to raise the necessary money.

WW: Your mother had great confidence that it would all work?

JLB: She had great confidence in prayer. Oh! I forgot to mention one very important thing. We had a cow in Paris.

WW: Well, that's important, where did you keep the cow?

JLB: Some livery stable. Believe it or not, when we went to France, the home of Pasteur, you couldn't get pasteurized milk, so we drank something called Klim, which is milk spelled backwards. It was a powder that was mixed with water. It was just awful; and after seeing his children suffer for about a year, my father went to the Island of Jersey and bought himself a certified, disease-free Jersey cow.

WW: That says a lot about your family. Did you live in Paris, or did you live in one of the suburbs?

JLB: Two places. One was an apartment right in the heart of Paris, and the other one was a house on the edge.

WW: Do you have fond memories of that period?

JLB: Such memories as I have are fond, but I don't have many memories of Paris.

WW: And then you came back when you were about nine?

JLB: I was nine.

WW: Went back to Sharon?

JLB: Back to Sharon.

WW: Now, looking back on it, what were your father's circumstances at that time?

JLB: The bills were being paid, but it was touch and go as to whether the company would survive.

WW: I can't remember where we were. I think I was asking you about coming back, and you mentioned your father's business problems.

JLB: My father's company owned several large concessions in eastern Venezuela, where oil had not yet been discovered. The properties, however, had great geological interest. But if an exploratory oil company doesn't have any income, it must constantly find new sources of financing or negotiate a deal with a major oil company. My father would try to interest Standard Oil or some other corporation in investing X amount of dollars in exploratory drilling in order to earn an interest in a particular property, [*what is known in the oil world as a "farmout agreement"*]. This was a frantic, bankruptcy-around-the-corner type of existence, but his children were only peripherally aware of the pressures he was under.

WW: Is that right? Throughout this whole period, even as you grew up?

JLB: As we grew up we knew that there were some large problems. Mother would ask us to pray very hard that this or that deal would work out, but in the meantime we continued to have our piano lessons and this and that.

The "this and that" included instruction in a vast number of skills. At one time or another, my father arranged to have us exposed to ballroom and tap dancing, model boat making, fly fishing, carpentry, a stringed instrument (the mandolin in my case), as well as riding, tennis, and golf. It was part of his determination that we be given every opportunity to develop whatever talents or interests we might have. Shortly before he died, he remarked to my brother Reid that he had been able to give us every advantage but one: the experience of being poor. Because of my father's own experience with poverty, he understood both the value of money and the hard work and self-discipline required to earn it. But money was never his god, witness his willingness to abandon everything he had developed in Mexico rather than compromise important principles. He had been offered a reprieve by the president who succeeded the one who had expelled him but refused to return on the president's terms, which would have required him to remain silent on conditions in that country. Instead, he set out to rebuild his life.

I have often thought that God might have been answering my father's prayers for the welfare of his children when He allowed a major oil company executive to bribe a Venezuelan minister to repudiate an agreement he had made with my father. In those days, all the oil exported from the country was shipped out of Lake Maracaibo to refineries in the Caribbean and North America. My father had acquired land at the outlet of Lake Maracaibo that contained Venezuela's finest natural harbor. Under the agreement he had negotiated with the minister, he would make the land available for the construction of Venezuelan refineries in exchange for a fee of one cent (U.S.) for each barrel of oil processed by them. The benefits for Venezuela were obvious, as was the potential cost to the briber's employer, which owned a refinery on the nearby island of Aruba. The inflow, over

decades, of more than a million pennies a day into Buckley family coffers, how-
ever, could have been the ruination of at least some of us. As things have turned
out, we have been left well off, but not so well off that we haven't had to work. (On
reflection, I believe we would all have worked anyway. The net effect of our up-
bringing, which relied heavily on parental example, has been to produce ten ob-
servant Catholics who share a vigorous Puritan work ethic.)

There is a sequel to this story. My father was not a vengeful man, but he made
an exception in this case. He hired a journalist to come to Venezuela to write a
series of articles on its government, and he was able to place them with a
prominent New York newspaper. The leitmotif of the series was that while the
country's ruler, General Gomez, was an interesting rube of native cunning, the
brains of the regime were possessed by my father's nemesis. Before the series was
completed, the minister had been dismissed.

But I digress. Back to my childhood.

WW: So what was your life like; what did you do?

JLB: Well, I had my piano lessons.

WW: Was that important?

JLB: Not to me.

WW: Important to your mother?

JLB: Yes.

WW: I see. You don't now play the piano, I take it?

JLB: No.

WW: What else did you do?

JLB: I played, had friends, and had my Shetland pony.

WW: Did you ride?

JLB: Yes.

WW: Was that important to you?

JLB: It was important to me until I outgrew my pony and we began riding in horse shows. I had a very close friend who lived a mile away. He had a Shetland pony as well, and every day in the summertime we would meet and go on long rides together. We felt free. Sharon was strange — in this tiny town, there were about a dozen substantial houses along South Main Street, and these were owned by New York gentry who arrived in June right after school got out and stayed until after Labor Day. So we had a set of summer friends.

Sharon was a village of about 1,600 souls surrounded by a patchwork of working farms and woodlands in northwest Connecticut. That part of the state had been a major source of iron during the Revolutionary period and Sharon shared in the prosperity derived from its production and the small manufacturing industries that it spawned. These included, in the early part of the 19th century, the manufacture of a locally invented mousetrap that earned Sharon Valley the title of "Mouse Trap Headquarters of the Western World." Fortunately, the world (western or otherwise) did not beat a path to the inventor's door as Sharon's population peaked at around 2,600 during the 1830s. After the Civil War (for which it produced cannon balls), Sharon's economy and population went into a gradual decline. One consequence was that while Sharon has been endowed with a number of substantial and graceful homes built during the 18th and early 19th centuries, it was spared the blight of Victorian architecture. It was the quiet beauty of the village and its natural surroundings, and the availability of larger homes, that induced a handful of New York City families to spend their summers there. And it was this annual influx that caused Sharon to be divided between "summer" or "city people," who would arrive with their children, nurses, and maids in early June and depart after Labor Day, and "natives," who made their living there. These terms had sociological connotations, with the result that the two or three families, including ours, who remained in Sharon year round but sent their children to private schools and belonged to the then bare-bones Sharon Country Club, were regarded by the natives as "city people."

Given the small size of the village and the smaller size of the summer colony, my brothers and sisters and I would go around with no more than three or four boys and girls in any age group, and we made do with the pastimes of rural America before the days of television. For the more sophisticated among us (I was not one of them), life in Sharon could be boring. For the rest of us, it was a delight. Because it was hard to get into trouble in that kind of community, we enjoyed a great amount of freedom to wander about and amuse ourselves; and we had to amuse ourselves because there was no one else around to amuse us. So we would go fishing (with worms) in the various ponds and streams, play three-base softball and other games, wander through the woods, climb what we called mountains, swim in our pool or Mr. Hatch's pond and (in season) skate on it, once a couple of fathers had scraped away the snow. On Saturday nights we would go to the movies in the neighboring towns of Amenia, Lakeville, or Millerton. But summers offered something more, something utterly untypical of rural America. Sharon was within a forty-minute drive of Tanglewood and the Boston Symphony Orchestra's wonderful series of summer concerts. We would drive there, find a spot on the grass outside the shell, have a picnic supper, and then lie back on the grass listening to glorious sounds.

We were wonderfully innocent in those days. Of necessity, the girls tended to be tomboys, and we would wander around together without pairing up. There was no pressure to smoke, and no place to buy or sneak a drink even if any of us had ever given one a thought. And drugs? Unheard of. (When I arrived at Yale in the fall of 1940, a movie at an adventurous New Haven theater was featuring a film called Reefer Madness *which reportedly highlighted, in lurid detail, the hideous (but seductive) dangers of something called "marijuana," a substance I had barely heard of and couldn't have found if I had wanted to.)*

WW: Were you interested in sports?

JLB: No. We played softball, touch football, and things of that sort; but my interests were in birds and natural history.

WW: Were you a baseball fan?

JLB: No.

WW: Even as you grew up? Were you a Yankees fan?

JLB: Not really. I hate to admit that I was not a typical, red-blooded American boy.

WW: That answer surprises me. And how about politics? What kind of role did politics play in your life as you grew up?

JLB: My father was not a great fan of Franklin Delano Roosevelt. But then he was not a fan of many people in government. When growing up, I had no idea how he voted, or whether he voted. He and my mother obviously had 100 percent Democratic Party roots. But keep this in mind. When my parents were growing up, the Republican Party was the party that favored a strong central government. The Democratic Party was for state's rights. The national parties changed their stripes; my parents didn't. There was a lot of talk about political matters but not in a partisan context.

The question, however, was about the role that politics played in my *life as I was growing up. By my late teens, I had developed a strong interest in public affairs. Prior to Pearl Harbor, I was a fervent "America Firster," as the isolationists of that day were known, and I was an enthusiastic supporter of Wendell Wilkie's attempt to deny FDR a third term.*

WW: Did you have a family dinner during the week? Did you all sit down together?

JLB: We were a large family, right? There were three connected dining areas in our Sharon home. The layout was like the letter "T." A long room with two smaller tables intersected the main dining room, where the older children would eat with our parents. The younger children would eat at the other two tables.

WW: Did you graduate from one to the next?

JLB: Yes.

Five, and too young to sit at the big table.

WW: At your place, you were with the older children. Did your mother eat with you?

JLB: Yes.

WW: And did you talk about political events?

JLB: I don't recall political talk as such, although it was clear my father had zero sympathy for the New Deal. My principal memory is of stories my father would tell of his adventures in Mexico. He was a great storyteller.

WW: What other early memories do you have of being in Sharon?

JLB: Carpentry.

WW: Working on the house? That's interesting.

JLB: Our house kept needing expanding.

WW: As you had more children, you needed more rooms.

JLB: Exactly.

WW: Did you have your own room or did you share?

JLB: We all shared. I shared with my brother John.

WW: Do you remember what you cared about when you were little? What was important to you when you were a little kid in Sharon?

JLB: I would have odd pets—at one time or another, a crow, a cooper's hawk, a flying squirrel, a woodchuck. I would often go on long expeditions into the countryside alone or with my friend Deane Witt. My life was family centered. I have difficulty recapturing the details as I seem to have been born without an anecdotal memory. I'll meet an old friend and he'll say, "You remember when . . . ?" and I'll have no idea what he is talking about until he teases it back into my memory.

WW: Who were your friends; do you remember them?

JLB: Very, very few in number. It was a tiny community. My brothers and sisters were really my close friends. I had one very special buddy, Deane Witt, who was my pony pal. There was also Bill Coley, who lived up the hill, and two or three others. But these were all city people who would arrive the first week of June and then disappear after Labor Day.

WW: Where did you go to school?

JLB: The first three years after returning from Europe, my younger siblings and I, together with the children of two or three other year-round residents of Sharon, had the equivalent of home schooling—first at the home of the Congregational minister and then at our home. When I was 13, I went to Millbrook School, which is in New York State about 11 miles from Sharon.

WW: Is that co-ed? Or is it just boys?

JLB: It is co-ed now. Then it was a boarding school for boys. It had just been started. My father was able to cut a favorable deal with Mr. Pulling, the headmaster, because my father had four sons in inventory. The school had been started in 1931 or 1932, in the early days of the Depression. By the time I graduated, it had 60 students. It now has over 200. When my brother John first went there, the entire school had its meals in the headmaster's dining room.

WW: When did you see your family?

JLB: As a result of the deal cut by my father with Mr. Pulling, we were semi-boarders. At boarding schools in those days, Wednesday afternoons were free, as were the weekends after Saturday morning classes. We would come home Wednesday afternoon and return to school Thursday morning, and we would spend the weekends in Sharon.

WW: Do you have memories of Millbrook and what it was like to be there? Did you like it?

JLB: Yes, I did. The school had some marvelous teachers who knew how to make schoolwork interesting. It maintained high academic standards. I found the school particularly attractive because the year I arrived with a pair of armadillos my father had sent me from Texas, a new biology teacher, who had just graduated from Cornell, arrived with a sparrow hawk and a boa constrictor. We were instant soul mates. He established a zoo at Millbrook that is now nationally accredited and developed an advanced biology course that was more sophisticated than anything that was available to undergraduates when I entered Yale. So I was in my element there.

WW: How did your father decide to send you there? There were many choices in New England of where you might have gone.

JLB: He liked Mr. Pulling's approach to education and to the formation of a boy's character. Sharon is located within a very few miles of several first-rate boys' schools. Hotchkiss School is five miles away. Salisbury School is another five miles beyond that. Kent School is ten or 12 miles to our south. But this was a new venture, and my father felt that his own views on the education of his sons would get a fair hearing.

WW: Where did your sisters go?

JLB: They went to different places. All four of the boys went to Millbrook. Three of my sisters went to the Nightingale Banford School in New York City. Two others went to Ethel Walker in Simsbury, Connecticut, and my youngest sister went to the Sacred Heart Convent in Noroton, Connecticut.

WW: Anything else you remember about Millbrook and what it was like to be there?

JLB: It was small, rural.

WW: Other than the natural history and the study of birds, were there subjects that you liked?

JLB: History. I also liked math, geometry, algebra.

WW: Were there any teachers there that had a particular impact on your life, about whom you thought?

JLB: Several. Frank Trevor, who taught biology. Mr. Abbott, the Latin teacher — not because of the Latin, I assure you, because before every test I would have to re-memorize the same irregular verbs I had committed to memory three or four weeks earlier. But he ran the Glee Club, and in those days I was a soprano, and I enjoyed singing tremendously. He also taught a very sophisticated music course that was created by the Carnegie Foundation. It was absolutely first rate, and it has given me a lifetime of satisfaction because it caused me to love classical music. Mr. Tuttle, a businessman turned teacher, knew how to make mathematics fun. And then there was another wonderful man, Mr. Callard, who was the assistant headmaster. He was the person to whom I would turn if I had problems. He was outstanding.

Millbrook provided a first class education and was tailor-made for my own particular interests. I don't know of any other, at that time, that would have introduced me to bird banding or indulged my taste for odd pets. It is possible, however, that Millbrook's small size could have been a handicap when I moved from that sheltered environment to a major university. There are such things as social skills, and my universe of a tiny village and a tinier school was hardly conducive to their development. I was never antisocial; but I was painfully shy and, in my earlier years, I never quite knew how to handle myself when I found myself among relative strangers.

WW: Were your brothers there when you were there?

JLB: My brother John was. My brother Bill arrived the year after I graduated.

WW: Were you and John close during that period?

JLB: Yes.

WW: Anything in particular during that time that you were afraid or concerned about? Anything that as you think back on it now was worrisome to you during that period when you were in high school?

JLB: No. I do recall that there would be times when at home in Sharon I had the blues. I guess that term reflects my southern roots.

WW: Normal, teenage, adolescent stuff. Do you think of yourself, or as you think back on your childhood, as a child who was pretty happy?

JLB: Yes.

WW: Easy going—do you have a temper?

JLB: I'm told that I had a temper when I was one, two, and three years old.

WW: And not since.

JLB: Very placid.

WW: And were as a child?

JLB: I think so.

WW: Is there anything that you particularly loved that really made you happy?

JLB: Pets and birds and so on, my family, my mother's "Nancy" stories, from which we developed a special feeling for the American Revolution.

WW: Tell me about those.

JLB: Nancy was a girl who happened to be a confidante of George Washington. My mother would spin these stories right out of her head. I wish I had a recording of them. We learned a tremendous amount of history: the Battle of White Plains, General Bourgogne, the crossing of the Delaware. We developed a real reverence for what was going on in that struggle.

WW: And your mother knew that. It was really your mother who was communicating that, right?

JLB: Right.

WW: That's interesting. And did she learn that from reading? Was your mother a big reader?

JLB: She was a big reader, but I'm not sure she was reading about those sorts of things as an adult. I know she read a lot of novels. My father was also a very big reader and would be more likely to be reading things like history. But I have a feeling that in years past in the United States, the schools made sure that you had a thorough grounding in the history of this country.

WW: She just learned it in school.

JLB: When I was growing up we learned all about the American Revolution and the philosophical underpinnings of the American Republic. And George Washington was our hero. We celebrated his birthday with cherry pies, ice cream, and candy hatchets. It was a big occasion.

WW: And do your children?

JLB: No. Not as well as they should.

WW: Your mother wasn't around to tell them those stories. And what part did your father play in this? He wasn't home but he obviously played a major role in your life as you grew up. Did you spend time with him?

JLB: In that period I was very shy. My father I think tended to be shy with his children. Some of my brothers and sisters, however, had very close relationships with him. But although I was not especially close to my father, and although he was generally home only on weekends, he was a very large presence in my life. He was the pervasive authority figure, and it was obvious that he had us and our welfare constantly in mind. It was he who worried about our education; and he made sure we were exposed to just about every kind of activity just in case one of them would catch our fancy.

WW: And they all impacted on your siblings in very different ways. Other than going to Paris, did you travel much?

JLB: Well, not too much. During the three years we were in Europe, we spent several vacations in Switzerland, traveled around France, and ended up in England.

WW: Before you came back.

JLB: Yes, before we came back.

WW: What was your father doing, do you know?

JLB: Raising money. But we used to travel—when our grandmothers were still alive—we would take the train down to New Orleans and Texas. Then in 1934, after we returned, we took a trip to Wisconsin and the Chicago World's Fair. Then towards the latter part of the '30s, my parents, who never felt totally at home in the North, found a place in South Carolina called Camden where they began to take the family at Easter time—Easter break—and eventually bought a house there.

WW: You would go back and forth to the house in South Carolina. Did you go to summer camp?

JLB: No.

WW: Any book that you read as you were growing up that had a particular impact that you remember?

JLB: Serious books? Ernest Thompson Seton's *Wild Animals I Have Known* and his other books; Peattie's *An Almanac for Moderns*; Thoreau's *Walden*. I also read the Burgess books. [*These were tales told by Mother West Wind about Peter Rabbit, Jimmy the Skunk, Brer Fox and other denizens of the Green Meadow and the Great Forest.*] Did you read the Thornton Burgess books to your children?

WW: Absolutely. I read them all to my children. I loved the Thornton Burgess books.

JLB: There were some others.

WW: You read the Oz series? There is a whole series of them.

JLB: I confess to having read all of them.

WW: Did you like to read?

JLB: Very much. I like reading history.

WW: It's a quarter to four and I think this is a good place to break. You have a better memory than you thought.

JLB: You'll find out.

College, the Navy, Law School, Marriage and Children, Practicing Law, Oil Exploration, Becoming a Senator

WW: Today is September 7, 1995. I'm here with Judge Buckley for the second session of the Oral History Project. If you remember, last time we got you through high school and then we quit. I want to pick up today with college and military service and that general period of your life. You went to Yale. Had anybody in your family gone to Yale, any of your brothers or sisters before you?

JLB: In those days, no sisters could go.

WW: Oh that's right, of course. Had any of your brothers gone?

JLB: My oldest brother did. Subsequently, my two younger brothers went there.

WW: I see, but if I recall correctly from last time, your parents or grandparents or other relations had not gone. You did not come from a Yale family before that. Did many of the graduates of your high school go to Yale? Was there a relationship there?

JLB: None. The graduates of my school tended to go to Ivy League colleges;

but as the school was only nine years old when I graduated in 1940, there were no traditions of that kind. Only one of my classmates went to Yale.

WW: But since you were in Connecticut, it was not surprising that you chose Yale. Are there other reasons? Why do you think you ended up there?

JLB: I thought about Harvard. As a matter of fact, I visited Harvard, but Yale obviously had a great reputation, and my brother enjoyed it, and I spent one weekend there with him and liked his friends.

It was a reflection of the times, and of the reputation Millbrook had managed to establish in very short order, that we all took it for granted that we could enter the college of our choice.

WW: Did you overlap with your brother or had he graduated when you started?

JLB: We overlapped. He was two classes ahead of me. Are you an old "Eli"?

WW: No, but many people I know are. And I know there is intense loyalty to the college as well as to the university. Tell me about your college life; tell me what you were interested in academically, socially, what was your life like during that period?

JLB: Well, it was truncated, courtesy of the war; but it was enjoyable. I knew practically nobody in my class. I came from a very small town, went to a very small school. It took me a while to feel my way around. I had a tremendous interest in biology and subjects of that sort; but I was told by a Yale biology professor that the days of field work had gone, that from now on biology involved looking through microscopes, and that I didn't particularly like. Ecology had not been discovered yet.

WW: Environmental sciences were not taught.

JLB: Otherwise I would have undoubtedly gone in that direction. As it was, I majored in English and took history and other liberal arts courses as well.

WW: Were you interested in any particular sporting activity in that period?

JLB: No. My freshman year I did what was called heeling, i.e., competing for a position on the *Yale Daily News*. It was the toughest of the non-athletic extracurricular activities. The competition started the last week in October, and it continued until mid-February. Heelers would report for their assignments five days a week at one or two o'clock in the afternoon; and if they were required to do proofreading at the printer, they might not be through until two or three the next morning.

The Yale Daily News *held three competitions a year, the first being for Sophomores, and the next two for Freshmen. Heelers were required not only to do all the reporting, but to solicit ads and collect money due from defaulting tradesmen as well. They were awarded points based on performance, with special bonuses given for stories that they wrote on their own initiative. I did a good job on the editorial side but a very poor one when it came to selling advertising space and collecting money. On one occasion, the* News' *business manager, Ted White, took me aside to warn me that I couldn't expect to make the* News *unless I had earned some points on the business side. (Three years later, Ted would be in a plane shot down over the Pacific whose sole survivor was the pilot, George H. W. Bush.) Somehow, I managed to earn enough of them to be elected to the* News. *From a social perspective, it was the greatest thing that happened to me at Yale. When I arrived there, I knew only three members of my class, none of whom was close. The* News *competition was the Yale undergraduate world's nearest equivalent to a U.S. Marine Corps boot camp, and it created the same bonds among those who survived the ordeal. Its members called the* News *"the best fraternity on Fraternity Row," and with reason.*

WW: Sounds like law review.

JLB: I developed my closest friendships through my work on the *News*. Got my feet on the ground and enjoyed the work tremendously. So the *Yale Daily News* was very important to me.

WW: You came from a small town, you went to a very small school, and I suspect it was difficult to find a niche socially and otherwise. Would you say that the *Yale Daily News* was that niche?

JLB: It worked for me.

WW: Did you write for the paper all the way through?

JLB: Not so much writing—the heelers did most of the writing. Once you were elected to the *News* board, you spent most of your time editing the work of the heelers.

WW: Did you do this with your brother? Was he also doing it?

JLB: No.

My brother John encouraged me to heel the News, *but that was not an interest of his. My other two brothers, Bill and Reid, would later join the* News *and Bill would head it, but that was after I had graduated.*

WW: When you went to Yale, did you have a view about what you would do when you graduated?

JLB: No.

WW: Hadn't decided yet you were going to go to law school?

JLB: Not yet.

WW: Now this is a period right before the war?

JLB: Well, yes. The war was declared in December of my sophomore year. From then on, my immediate future was military. Thoughts as to what I would do after graduation were easily postponed. A lot of people in my class did that.

I learned of the attack on Pearl Harbor on the radio while driving back to Yale from Sharon, where I had spent the weekend. On my arrival, I rushed to the News to help put out the war issue. For whatever reason, Yale's president, Charles Seymour, had declined to issue a statement for the occasion. So three of the sopho-more editors, Stu Little, Seth Taft, and I, decided on a stratagem for extracting one from him. Seth found a drum somewhere and then the three of us went to the Old Campus (where Yale's freshmen are housed) and started marching through it, drum beating, while yelling, "To hell with Hirohito [the Japanese emperor]; on to Tokyo." We felt a little silly at first, but soon some freshmen began falling in line behind us and taking up the chant. Like the Pied Piper of Hamlin, we were soon leading a chain of students wherever we chose to go. After circling the campus, we moved through two of the residential colleges, then up Hillhouse Avenue to Presi-dent Seymour's house. By that time we had three or four hundred students in tow and Seymour had no choice but to come out and utter appropriately stirring words about country and duty, including the duty to study even harder to prepare our-selves for service to the nation. We then abandoned our chain to its own devices and rushed back to the News with our story.

It was an exhilarating experience, and we were too keyed up to consider going to bed. We decided, instead, to drive to Washington in the hope that Seth's uncle, Senator Robert A. Taft, might be able to get us into the Capitol to hear President Roosevelt ask Congress for a declaration of war. We drove all night (there were no superhighways in those days) and reached the city at around nine in the morning. We had breakfast at the home of Seth's grandmother, Mrs. William Howard Taft, and then went on to the senator's office to try our luck. Unfortunately, two other classmates had been there ahead of us, the senator's son, Lloyd, and his room-mate, Bob Sweet. Lloyd would be taking his mother's seat in the House gallery, and his roommate would be smuggled in in the guise of a page. Senator Taft suggested, however, that we accompany his wife to the Senate side where we could listen to the president's speech on her battery-operated radio, which was then some-

thing of a novelty. When Mrs. Taft arrived, the senator escorted us to the Capitol. On arriving there, Mrs. Taft led us to a room off the Senate floor. It was there that we heard Roosevelt request that Congress declare that we had been in a state of war since the prior day, the "day that will live in infamy." Following the conclusion of Roosevelt's speech, we moved to the Senate gallery where we saw the senators vote their approval of the declaration.

WW: So what was the impact of the war being declared? What did that mean for you and your military service?

JLB: The military services created a variety of programs that provided college students with alternatives to simply waiting to be called by the draft. I was then 18 and signed up with a naval officer training program that turned out to be the one that kept you in college the longest. It was called the V-12 program. But for the next year, life at Yale went on pretty much as usual, although on an accelerated basis. This meant that instead of having two semesters a year, we had three, with very brief vacations between each.

WW: Was that to accommodate military coming or leaving?

JLB: No, to rush us out faster.

WW: Oh, so you effectively could go through faster. I see.

JLB: It also meant that people graduating from high school in May or June of '42 would begin college in July. Beginning that summer, members of my class, the Class of 1944, began receiving letters from their draft boards or from one of the Army Air Force or Army programs they had enlisted in calling them to active duty, so our ranks began to thin out. Classmates who were in the ROTCs were allowed to stay through the first semester of senior year, which ended in June of 1943. Yale awarded degrees after seven semesters. After June, only about 110 of the original 860 or so members of my class remained at Yale. They were those who had signed up for medical or divinity schools, were disqualified for the draft for medical reasons, or were in the Navy or Marine V-12 programs. Those of us in those programs, however, were placed on active duty on July 1. As of that day, the whole atmosphere of the college was transformed. Although we continued with our academic programs virtually intact, we were in uniform, woke to the sounds of a recorded bugle, learned to march. Instead of living two to a three-room suite, there were four of us; instead of eating in dining rooms with linen and waitresses who would come around asking what choice of meals you wanted, we went through a chow line with our trays. These changes continued in effect after the war.

Wartime Yale. With classmates in front of the DKE fraternity house.

WW: And it never changed afterwards?

JLB: Before that we also had maid service in our rooms.

WW: That ended too?

JLB: That ended too.

WW: At Yale?

JLB: At Yale, yes.

WW: That's an interesting thing to think about.

JLB: We were required to take a "war course," which in my case was mechanical drawing, and to get some kind of physical exercise, but basically we followed our majors and got our degrees.

WW: Was there a lot of discussion about the world situation?

JLB: When I entered Yale, there was tremendous debate over America's role in what was still a European war—the interventionists versus the isolationists. I was in the latter camp and worked for the America First Committee, which brought speakers like Lindbergh and Senator Robert La Follette of Wisconsin to the campus.

WW: Did any of your brothers go into the service?

JLB: All of them did at one time or another.

WW: During this period, was anybody overseas?

JLB: My brother John was a senior when the war was declared. He graduated the June following Pearl Harbor and went right into the military. Believe it or not, he went into the horse cavalry.

WW: I don't even quite know what that means. What did he do?

JLB: Horses. Trained on horses, but that quickly disappeared. People don't realize how unprepared we were—the draft, I think, was inaugurated in 1940. First peacetime draft ever and people would drill with wooden mockups of guns and so on. If memory serves, Switzerland had a larger standing army than we did. So we had to build almost from scratch. As soon as tanks and things of that sort came along, the cavalry disappeared. In any event, my brother John, who was fluent in French, ended up in North Africa as a liaison officer with the French forces. He went overseas shortly after I graduated.

WW: What did you do after you graduated? You were then in the Naval Reserves.

JLB: I was sent to the Navy base in Norfolk, Virginia, to what they called a pre-midshipman school where we essentially marked time until openings developed at one of the several midshipmen schools around the country. I was in Norfolk for about four weeks, I guess, then shipped out to New York where I entered the midshipman school that had been established at Columbia University. That would have been in December of '43. I graduated from the school in April as a freshly minted ensign. I was then assigned to an LST, the acronym for Landing Ship Tank, which was the largest of the amphibious vessels. You've seen them in movies about D-Day, the very large ships that came up onto the beach and lowered a ramp to discharge vehicles. I was assigned to U.S.S. LST 1013, which was in the final stages of construction in Quincy, Massachusetts. I reported on board just before it was commissioned. I remained on board for the next two years and 13 days, and left it in Hong Kong with orders to return to New York for my discharge. During that period, I was off the ship just five nights.

WW: Two years on this craft. What was that like?

JLB: The first year and a half was pretty dull. There were three brief periods of intense interest when we were engaged in invasions, but in between them we would spend months on end transporting people and equipment over empty stretches of ocean.

In 1946, Thomas Heggen wrote a captivating (and mega-best-selling) novel, Mr. Roberts, *which chronicled the travails of a young naval officer assigned to the*

U.S.S. *Reluctant, a small Navy cargo ship consigned to the backwaters of the Pacific. The book's introduction contains the following paragraph which, I regret to say, stirs some not so "mystic chords of memory":*

What manner of ship is this? What does it do? What is its combat record? Well, those are fair questions, if difficult ones. The Reluctant, as was said, is a naval auxiliary. It operates in the back areas of the Pacific. In its holds it carries food and trucks and dungarees and toothpaste and toilet paper. For the most part it stays on its regular run, from Tedium to Apathy and back; about five days each way. It makes an occasional trip to Monotony, and once it made a run all the way to Ennui, a distance of two thousand nautical miles from Tedium. It performs its dreary and unthanked job, and performs it, if not inspiredly, then at least adequately.

The comparison is unfair. LST 1013 did participate in three adrenalin-generating landings. But I think this passage from Mr. Heggen's classic suggests something of what life was like during the very long stretches when we were engaged in more humdrum duties. It also poses the relevant questions: What manner of ship was our LST, and what did it do?

Unlike the Reluctant, our ship was designed to fill a specific military need: the delivery, often over great distances, of large numbers of men and quantities of equipment to hostile beachheads. LSTs were larger than destroyers — 328 feet long and 50 wide; but unlike destroyers, they carried only defensive weapons: eight 40-millimeter and twelve 20-millimeter antiaircraft guns. Because they had to be able to deliver men and materials to a beach, they had a very shallow draft — about three feet at the bow and eight at the stern when their ballast tanks were pumped out in preparation for going onto the beach, and only about five feet deeper at each end when the tanks were filled. As a result, they resembled floating shoe boxes with huge bow doors that would open to allow a ramp to be lowered so that tanks and other vehicles could roll out onto the beach. When not carrying supplies for a landing, an LST's cavernous "tank deck" could hold a great deal of cargo, and this capacity was put to full use during the periods between invasions either to resupply beachheads or to move supplies and personnel from remote bases constructed earlier in the war to newer, more advanced ones. At one time or another, we picked up cargos

---

in bases scattered from the southern Pacific islands of New Guinea, the Admiralties, and New Britain to remote atolls such as Kwajalein and Eniwetok and delivered them to new ones in the Philippines and then Okinawa.

While the war was on, we traveled in convoys protected by destroyers or destroyer escorts. Our cruising speed was around 11 knots; but when we were accompanied by merchant ships, which we often were when not headed for an invasion, we had to travel at the speed of the slowest of them, which might not be more than six or seven knots. Thus we might spend a week or more at sea before reaching a destination that was indistinguishable from the one we had left. Each of these bases had been built by the American military from scratch. They consisted of a patchwork of dusty dirt roads and Quonset huts, the ubiquitous steel structures found throughout the Pacific theater. There was nothing to suggest that the islands and atolls on which they were built had native populations. I recall seeing no more than a dozen natives in all our southern Pacific ports of call.

From my perspective, the one redeeming feature of these bases was their officers' clubs. At these, I would run into Yale friends with a frequency that astonished my shipmates who rarely met anyone from their own colleges. I have no explanation for this phenomenon other than a benign providence. These encounters were a delight, a chance to compare notes and catch up. Whether we met old friends or not, the clubs offered a welcome respite from life aboard ship. The enlisted men had no such facilities, but our ship would organize occasional beach parties where crew members could play softball and drink beer requisitioned from the base PX. Our officers scrupulously observed the Navy rule against drinking on board, the one exception I am aware of being the time a Catholic chaplain we were transporting felt a Christian obligation to share a bottle of altar wine. The enlisted men, on the other hand, showed an astonishing ingenuity in manufacturing the stuff from mixtures of canned fruit juices, raisins, and baker's yeast. Ferreting out caches of "jungle juice" was the main objective of periodic ship's inspections. On one occasion, we found that the water caskets on each of our life rafts had been converted into miniature breweries with God knows what consequences if we had ever had to abandon ship.

Because LSTs needed a large enough complement to man the battle stations on the rare occasions when they had to be manned, we had far more men aboard (nine officers and 105 enlisted men) than was required to actually run the ship. As *a result, most of us had acres of leisure time, the exceptions being the captain and the executive and engineering officers who had full-time responsibilities. The six of us who shared watch duties would stand a four hour watch each day and spend the remaining 20 eating, sleeping, reading, writing letters, playing cards, and (in most of our cases) attending to our minimal shipboard duties. In my case, they were those of the stores officer. I was responsible for the food and for ensuring that the ship never ran out of essential supplies. Fortunately, I had extremely competent petty officers in charge of these departments and I had little to do other than sign the papers they prepared so that when we reached a base, we could requisition the spare parts for our engines and guns, the food to refill our larders, and the varieties of clothing, toilet articles, tobacco, and what-nots that were dispensed by our ship's store. On shore I would be busy enough going from one supply depot to another to secure the goods listed on those papers.*

Life at sea had its delights. Dawns had a delicate beauty as the eastern horizon slowly brightened and the skies changed imperceptibly from gray to pink to blue, and the sunsets could be spectacular. I remember in particular the huge, turbulent clouds we encountered as we cruised up the west coast of Luzon on our resupply missions to Okinawa. As the sun moved towards the horizon, the immense clouds would be stained with a progression of colors beginning with a burnished gold and then moving to a range of deep pinks before becoming a blood red as the sun dropped out of sight. Then there were the flying fish. In certain seas, our blunt bow would flush coveys of them and send them skipping over the water before they dipped back below the surface a hundred yards away. The landfalls were always a particular delight. I never tired of watching a spot on the horizon slowly take on three-dimensional shape and then bustle with life as we reached our destination.

WW: There wasn't a lot of action. You weren't needed a lot.

JLB: True in a sense; but when we were needed, we were essential. We had a far larger crew than was needed to simply operate the vessel, so we didn't have the frequent watches that officers on smaller ships had. The extra manpower was only needed when we were at battle stations and had to man the antiaircraft and damage control stations. The officers had relatively comfortable quarters. My stateroom was able to sleep four people, but the other three berths were reserved for Army or Marine officers on the relatively rare occasions that we were moving troops. So we had more space than most people had in the Navy. But it was not glamorous duty.

Unloading supplies at Lingayen, Philippines, January 1945.

Life was vastly different when we were taking part in an invasion. We shared our cabins with seasoned Army or Marine officers who would give us first hand reports on much of the earlier fighting in the Pacific theater. There was also the building excitement as we came closer to our objectives and read the intelligence reports as to what we might expect. On one occasion, as we were approaching Okinawa, I had the eerie nighttime experience of having a low-flying Japanese observation plane fly up the length of our convoy. There was a full moon, and I could actually see the pilot as he passed our ship. Not a shot was fired.

On the day of an invasion, we would arrive at our designated offshore position in pre-dawn darkness. As the skies lightened, we could begin to make out the hundreds of ships that had been assembled for the assault: battleships, light and heavy cruisers, troop transports, supply ships, destroyers and destroyer escorts moving in and out among them, and scores of amphibious vessels of every size—LSTs, LSMs (Landing Ship, Medium), and LCIs (Landing Craft, Infantry) as well as a variety of smaller gunboats, minesweepers, and other craft. The invasion fleets ranged from over 700 vessels at Leyte to more than a thousand at Okinawa.

When the sun rose, the battleships and cruisers would begin a sustained bombardment of the beaches and whatever onshore defenses had survived the previous days' air attacks. We could hear the battleships' 16-inch shells rumbling overhead, sounding like muffled versions of New York City subway cars. From our position a couple of miles offshore, we could see the glow and hear the sounds of the exploding shells as a wall of dust and debris gradually rose to obscure the shoreline. It was truly awesome. When the capital ships ended their bombardment, the destroyers and other vessels would take over, firing from positions closer to shore as airplanes from escort carriers located somewhere over the horizon flew over the beaches to bomb and strafe whatever might have survived the big ships' pulverizing salvos. LCIs armed with banks of short range rockets would then move in to finish the job.

It was only after this sustained and massive softening up that amphibious vehicles and landing craft would begin delivering the first waves of troops to the beaches. No one who had witnessed this pummeling was surprised that the landings met with such little resistance. Because LSTs had earned the sobriquet of Large Slow Targets, we unloaded our troops into amphibious LCVPs (Landing Craft, Vehicles Personnel) and any amphibious vehicles we might be carrying, and these would then take them to the shore. Unless we were carrying priority items, we would not move onto the beaches to unload our cargoes until a day or two following the landings. We were lucky in this regard. At Leyte, while we were at anchor, several of the LSTs discharging priority cargoes were hit by mortar fire. At Lingayen, while we were unloading our cargo of ammunition, two LSTs anchored offshore had encounters with suicide swimmers.

On resupply trips to Okinawa following the initial invasion, we had endless calls to "General Quarters" when ships stationed in the radar picket lines to the north warned that kamikaze planes were headed our way. These were usually shot down long before they reached the harbor; but on occasion, one would come within sight before it was either blown apart by anti-aircraft fire or plowed into a ship. As our particular job during these alerts was to generate smoke to screen the anchorage, we generally heard more gunfire than we ever saw.

It was on one of these resupply missions that I had my first encounter with *bureaucratic idiocy. Our ship was on the beach unloading supplies when an Army Air Force lieutenant and college classmate, Bob Wickser, walked on board. He had spotted my LST and hoped I could help him find out if his brother Jack was in the neighborhood. Jack was an ensign serving on a destroyer escort and Bob thought he might be on the radar picket line duty, which was a notoriously dangerous place to be. We contacted a destroyer escort that was anchored nearby and asked whether anyone knew the whereabouts of Jack's ship. We learned that it had been sunk by a kamikaze two days earlier and that there had been some survivors, but no one aboard knew their identity. And so, Bob and I set off to find out whether Jack was dead or alive. We commandeered one of our small boats and spent the next two hours signaling or visiting hospital and command ships until we located one that had the information we were looking for. We were told, however, that we couldn't have it because whether Jack had survived was a military secret. As irrational as this was, we couldn't budge the high-ranking blockhead in charge, and a mere ensign was unable to go over his head. We already knew that his ship had been sunk; but somehow, for us to know whether one of its crewmen was alive might prolong the war. I received a letter from Bob a few weeks later advising me that Jack had survived and was on his way to a hospital in Hawaii at the time of our fruitless search.*

WW: Let's go back a bit. Where did you go after leaving the shipyard?

JLB: After we were commissioned, we sailed to New York City, where we spent three days picking up supplies. We left New York on June 6th on our way to Guantanamo Bay in Cuba. That's an easy date to remember because shortly after we set sail, we learned that the D-Day landings in Normandy had taken place. We spent two days in Cuba loading different kinds of equipment, headed through the Panama Canal, and, after a stopover in California for repairs, pushed on to Hawaii. When we reached Honolulu, we unloaded our cargo (mostly canned food and beer), loaded up with amphibious personnel carriers and other military equipment, and received orders to proceed to Manus, a base in the Admiralty Islands, which lie just north of eastern New Guinea. When we were en route to Manus, our captain opened sealed orders which informed us that we would be participating in the invasion of an island called Yap. Now, you do know about Yap.

WW: I don't know about Yap.

JLB: Well, Yap has the largest currency in the world; namely huge stone discs that can be six or seven feet in diameter. We never saw them because when we reached Manus, the high command decided to accelerate their grand plan and move directly to the Philippines.

WW: Is that where this island is?

JLB: No, Yap is in the mid-Pacific. Our new destination was the Philippines and so we ended up taking part in the invasion of Leyte, which was in October of 1944. After that we were engaged in several resupply missions, moving supplies from Manus and Hollandia, New Guinea, to Leyte. Our next invasion was in January 1945, when we landed at Lingayen on the Philippine island of Luzon. Then lots of traveling back and forth moving supplies to advance bases.

At the time of these invasions, I had no idea of the significant role the Philippines would later play in my life. I had, however, a tenuous connection with the country thanks to an old friend of my father, Captain Dame, who would occasionally visit us in Sharon. Captain Dame had served there during what we refer to as the Philippine Insurrection but which Filipinos more accurately call the Philippine-American War. His task had been to track down and capture the elusive General Emilio Aguinaldo who had declared the Philippines' independence from Spain in June 1898 and led the resulting fight against Spanish rule. That revolution was transformed into a prolonged struggle against American forces when, in December of that year, Spain ceded the Philippines, Guam, and Puerto Rico to the United States in the treaty that brought the Spanish-American War to a close. Captain Dame failed in his task, but he managed to "liberate" some of Aguinaldo's possessions, several of which he willed to my father. One of these, a beautifully embroidered Spanish artillery battalion banner on a corner of which a Philippine flag had been painted, graced a wall of my room at Yale during my sophomore and junior years. Twelve years later, I returned the banner to the Philippines.

WW: But you never got off the ship during this time?

JLB: We would go ashore for a few hours; but as I said before, I was only off the ship five nights.

In Manila in July 1945, a month before the war's end, on the first of what would be countless visits.

WW: I see. You would get off and then you would get back on.

JLB: There was almost nothing to see at Leyte and Lingayen, other than the destruction caused by naval bombardments. We were not in the streets of a London or Naples.

WW: No, you were in the Philippines.

JLB: We'd been out quite a while before we saw a town of any size and could get such delicacies as fresh eggs. But that was the following summer, a place called Iloilo on the Philippine island of Panay. Until very late in the war, we would shuttle between bases that had been built from scratch and consisted largely of Quonset huts and other prefabricated structures. Our last engagement was the invasion of Okinawa — on April Fool's Day, 1945 [*it was also Easter Sunday*]. We went all the way to Guadalcanal off the northeast coast of Australia and picked up over 600 Marines who were packed in like sardines during the 20 or so days before they landed in Okinawa. These three invasions were, next to Normandy, the largest in the war. But for LST's, among the least bloody.

The evening of our arrival in Guadalcanal, I visited the officer's club and learned that some Yale graduates were quartered at a nearby Marine camp and set out to find them. As bizarre as it sounds, as I approached the first group of tents, I heard the strains of the Yale football song, "Boola Boola," emanating from one of them. The singer was a classmate and good friend, Gene Constantin, who shared the tent with another, Bill Cahill. Within minutes three other Yale friends turned up and we shared a bottle of scotch one of them had been hoarding. It was a happy occasion. But within three months, two of them, Constantin and Ned Gaillard, would be killed, and a third, my brother John's classmate Frank Kemp, would be badly wounded in the fierce fighting that developed on Okinawa. This meeting took place within a few miles of where the first of my college classmates had lost his life in World War II. Russ Whittlesey had enlisted in the Marines a month after Pearl Harbor. Eight months later, he was killed in action on Guadalcanal.

WW: Did you have a sense at the time of how important these battles were?

JLB: Yes, because we were making giant strides towards Japan. No doubt about that. But I never felt personally threatened. I felt as if I had 50-yard line tickets at awesome military engagements with shells from the bombardment vessels roaring over our heads to the beaches while watching the infantry landing from small boats or amphibious vehicles.

WW: But you didn't physically feel that you were in danger? Was your sense of confidence because you were young and an officer in the Navy or because you were really not in danger?

JLB: You have a point there. I never felt in danger, but part of my job was to censor letters written by the enlisted men, many of whom just never got it through their heads that they couldn't say where they were or what they were engaged in. So many of those letters ended up looking like lacework as we cut out the verboten information with razor blades. I noticed that many of the married men were conscious of danger while young bachelors like me tended to feel that our manhood had not been tested.

LST 1013 crewmen receiving Purple Hearts.

WW: That's interesting.

JLB: We would hear some pretty grisly war stories from many of the Army and Marine personnel we would transport from time to time and feel terribly inadequate. We were, of course, exposed to danger even though there were far juicier targets than LSTs in the engagements in which we participated. In fact, ten members of our crew were awarded purple hearts for wounds inflicted off Okinawa by a 20-millimeter shell that had been shot by another LST at an American plane and exploded on our deck. These things happened.

WW: Doesn't make it any less dangerous, though. What did your mother think? You weren't feeling threatened, but what did she think about you being out there?

JLB: I never asked her. She was very reluctant to see any of us go overseas.

WW: I happen to think that is probably the hardest thing—mothers watching their sons feeling quite brave going off to these very serious battles. Do you think about that time—does it impact on your life now?

JLB: Not really, no.

From a personal, emotional point of view, it was an unsatisfactory war. I witnessed a fair amount of action, but never felt threatened. I heard the rumble of battleships' 16-inch shells passing overhead during pre-landing bombardments of invasion beaches, saw planes strafing beaches, kamikaze planes plowing into two cruisers and a half dozen more of them shot out of the skies over Okinawa, and we took on board the survivors of a destroyer escort that had been shepherding our convoy before it was sunk by a Japanese mini-submarine with a loss of 112 lives. But I never felt at risk. Because I had never been put to the test, I had decided that I would decline an offer of home leave if it meant that I would miss the invasion of the Japanese home islands which, according to the secret intelligence reports we were beginning to read, would have been far bloodier than anything we had previously experienced. I was not alone in wanting to be tested. It was because of the carnage those reports predicted that I have never had a problem with the decision to drop the Hiroshima bomb. It saved many hundreds of thousands of lives, Japanese as well as American. We heard about the bomb as we were cruising past the western coast of Luzon en route to Okinawa with air force reinforcements and military supplies. The night before our arrival, the Japanese had announced that they would be suing for peace and the ships in the anchorage celebrated the news by shooting signal flares and tracer shells into the air. It was a great show; but 20-millimeter shells returning to earth managed to kill a dozen soldiers, and a Japanese plane was able to take advantage of the confusion to sink a freighter while it was unloading its cargo. Within less than three weeks while anchored off Leyte, I would witness a later, glorious display of shipborne pyrotechnics in celebration of Japan's formal surrender in Tokyo Bay. This time there were no casualties.

VICTORY CELEBRATION

END OF JAPANESE WAR---Service Squadron Ten Anchorage, Leyte Gulf, Philippine Islands.

WW: Are there people that you met during that period that you stayed in touch with? Or is that a part of your life that was really over when the war ended?

JLB: I have kept in touch with one of my shipmates, but in a very desultory way. He ended up in California, so I have only been able to see him a couple of times over the past 40 years. I saw two or three others during the first few years after the war, but that's about it.

WW: This is the group you told me you spent every night with for two years. Have you ever had a reunion or ever met again with the people on the ship?

JLB: There is an organization called the U.S. LST Association that I came across a few years ago. I sent in my $15 in dues and receive its newsletters. I see that many LSTs do have reunions. A military organization is hierarchical. Our crew consisted of about 100 enlisted men and nine officers. If your universe is confined to nine persons, you may or may not find close buddies among them. And, of course, even close relationships tend to fade if you live too far apart ever to see one another.

WW: What did you do when you came back?

JLB: I applied for law school. I didn't go straight to law school because I didn't get back until May of '46 and there were too many other veterans waiting in line ahead of me. But let me backtrack and complete my description of my naval career. We were anchored off Leyte when the Japanese surrendered. After moving some Army Air Force personnel from the Philippines to Korea, we were assigned the duty of ferrying various groups of Asians from one place to another in the Far East—Japanese civilians and soldiers from various Chinese ports to Japan; Korean slave laborers from Japan to Korea; Chinese soldiers from Haiphong, in what was then French Indochina, to Manchuria—so I saw a fair amount of the Orient during my last six months or so aboard ship. Four of my five nights off the ship were spent in Peking.

WW: Was this after the war, during that period?

JLB: Yes.

If the normal overseas duty rotation policy had still been in effect, I could have expected to return on home leave by the end of December. Following Japan's surrender, however, our country embarked on a massive demobilization program that monopolized States-bound transportation. The armed services developed an elaborate point system that determined the order in which we would be returned home for discharge. Young single men were not on the fast track. As a result, I was treated to an extensive tour of the Chinese littoral that I would have enjoyed more if I hadn't been so anxious to return home. Given the passage of time, the following account is necessarily impressionistic.

Our first port of call on the Asian mainland was Inchon, Korea, where we were to pick up Japanese soldiers for return to Japan. It was there that I was introduced to the art of using chopsticks, in whose mastery I still take some pride. We were warned against eating raw vegetables, however, because the local farms relied on "night soil" (human excrement) for fertilizer. This was the source of my most vivid memory of the place: the overpowering stench accompanying the "honey wagons" that traveled narrow alleys collecting the stuff from open bins under the houses. Korea, in those days, was extremely poor. Ox- and donkey-drawn carts were a common form of transportation and the traditional style of clothing was still to be seen. The people were almost embarrassingly welcoming. On one occasion a little girl came up to me, unprompted, and gave me a little straw mat that I still have tucked away somewhere. It was a pleasure to be among them.

The same could not be said of our first encounters with the Japanese. We were puzzled and disgusted by what struck us as a suspect obsequiousness. The two or three Japanese naval vessels we passed had their guns pointed down, as required by the terms of surrender; but those terms did not require the sailors manning their rails to stand at attention and salute us. The soldiers and civilians we transported back to Japan would bow and scrape. But what most appalled (and amused) me was an experience I had in Sasebo, on the southern Japanese island of Kyushu, just two months after the surrender. Sasebo had been a major naval base and the city had been flattened by a succession of air raids. On stepping ashore, I was confronted by a large sign stuck in the rubble that read, "Sasebo Chamber of Commerce Welcomes U.S. Servicemen." This from a people whose military had literally fought to the death and engaged in wholesale atrocities against American prisoners even in the last days of the war. We wondered what had happened to their manhood, their self-respect. Then I read a fascinating study of Japanese culture that had been commissioned by the United States government. It was The Chrysanthemum and the Sword *by sociologist Ruth Benedict. In it, she described in detail the* rigid rules governing social relationships in which Japanese children were trained from their earliest days. These were totally foreign to the American experience, but the book satisfied me that the behavior that had so irritated us was both to be expected and totally sincere. The emperor had spoken. He had validated the American presence and, as a consequence, we were to be accorded the deference and courtesies to which those with lawful authority were entitled.

This does not suggest that I came to understand the Japanese. I didn't then, and never felt at ease with them in my later, admittedly limited, business dealings with them. Unlike the Chinese, with whom I have always felt at ease, I found something fundamentally different about the Japanese that I can't describe; and this feeling seems to be shared by most Americans of my generation. (A few years ago, I asked Mike Mansfield, who had been majority leader during my Senate years and had just completed a 12-year tour as U.S. ambassador to Japan, whether he had come to understand them. He answered with a smile and a characteristically terse "No.")

During those post-war months, I had the chance to visit a number of Chinese ports, to which I will apply the names by which they were then known among English-speaking people. The first of these was Tsingtao, which had been a German concessionary city. As was the case with almost every other city we visited in China, its architecture was wholly European. As might be expected from its German connection, Tsingtao boasted a first class brewery. I discovered this by happy accident. One afternoon, while on an errand, I saw a jeep coming my way in which there was a very familiar face. The jeep screeched to a stop, and out jumped Bill Cahill, whom I had last seen on Guadalcanal. I hopped into his car and was whisked off to the Marine Bachelor Officers Quarters, which happened to be located in what had been the headquarters of the Asahi Beer brewery. On my arrival, I found another old friend, Dick Williams. Once settled in, Bill asked if I would like a beer (I did). He then clapped his hands and, in a loud voice, yelled, "Number Two Boy, three beers," which Number Two Boy promptly brought. The joys of being an occupying power!

Now that any conceivable statute of limitations has expired, I can confess to my own abuse of that power. I noticed that Tsingtao boasted a small plantation of pine trees. It being mid-December, and acting in my capacity as LST 1013's stores officer, I assembled a work party, commandeered an Army truck, and liberated

*what would be our ship's first Christmas tree. (I had earlier demonstrated a simi-
lar solicitude for our crew's morale by resolving the then raging controversy over
the date on which Thanksgiving should be celebrated by ordering that turkey and
all the fixings be served on both "Franksgiving" (the third Thursday of November
which Franklin Roosevelt had ordained in order to extend the customary season
for Christmas sales) and the last Thursday of the month, when Thanksgiving had
traditionally been observed.*

 *A few weeks later, we were anchored in the Whangpoo River off Shanghai,
which was an impressive city swarming with people. On going ashore we would be
surrounded by rickshaw boys vying for the few pennies it would cost to take us to
wherever we wanted to go. It was there that I learned how good Chinese food could
be and how rapidly runaway inflation could destroy the value of money. Three of
my fellow officers and I became habitués of a superb restaurant, Sun Ya, where we
would invariably begin with mince meat and bean curd and then experiment with
three or four of the other offerings. During the four months in which we were in
and out of Shanghai, the value of the Chinese currency had so deteriorated that,
towards the end, the price of the bean curd course at Sun Ya exceeded that of the
entire meal when we first arrived, and packets of the money we had used to pay
rickshaw boys were being sold on the streets as souvenirs. On my last visit, I read
an article in an English language newspaper stating that as part of a campaign to
curb corruption, the Chiang Kai-shek government had granted the mayor of Shanghai a hundredfold increase in pay. On passing a store window that afternoon, I
discovered that the mayor's new monthly pay check would not have bought him a
pair of shoes.*

 *I have some special memories of Shanghai: of sampans coming alongside our
ship to peddle various goods (I continue to delight in a smiling soapstone Buddha
that cost me one dollar "gold," which is how the Chinese referred to U.S. currency,
a tribute to the fact that the dollar was then backed by gold); of a place name,
Bubbling Well Road, that continues to charm me; of the commercial energy manifest in its crowded streets and harbor; of China's overnight conversion from left-
side-of-the-road to right-side driving on New Year's Day, 1946; of chance encounters with old friends—with Dave Lindsay, who told me he had recently become
engaged and showed me the picture of his fiancée, with my brother John's closest
friend, Eddie Corning, who that morning had received a letter from John asking*

him to keep on eye out for LST 1013 and, on glancing out his porthole, saw our ship dropping anchor.

The one thing I could not find in Shanghai—or any of the other concessionary cities that Europeans had taken over in the 19th century—was an example of what might be described as Chinese architecture. That I found in glorious profusion during a four-day trip to Peking while our ship was being dry-docked in Shanghai. This was the first occasion we had had in almost two years to spend time away from the ship, so another officer and I took advantage of an Army program that offered brief tours of various parts of China. We were flown there in a military plane whose pilot startled peasants along the way with occasional hedgehopping to give us more intimate views of the February landscape.

On rickshaws with shipmate. Peking, January 1946.

We were met by an American missionary who had lived in China for more than 30 years and would be acting as our guide. Each day, we spent the morning visiting points of interest in the city or surrounding countryside and the afternoon at places where craftsmen were at work at such tasks as making cloisonné wares, or weaving fabrics, or carving ivory. Each evening we were treated to a new style of cooking, beginning with a superb Peking duck dinner (which began with nuts and ended with soup) and, on our last day, an all-mutton Mongolian meal. The sights

*we saw in the old imperial Forbidden City and Summer Palace were impressive;
but I have rarely seen anything to compare with the simplicity, elegance, and
beauty of the marble balustrades, plaza, and red temple that comprised Peking's
"Court of Heavenly Peace." Fortunately, in those days, the place was not defaced
with a giant portrait of Mao Tse Sung. During my stay, I had the chance to see
two human relics of the ancien regime: a benign-looking, wrinkle-faced eunuch (a
friend of our guide who had been in the service of the last empress of China) and
a women whose feet had been bound as an infant and who could walk only with
some difficulty. I also ran into an old friend from home, Hugh O'Neill, an Army
Chinese language specialist who was temporarily lodged in my hotel. One evening
after dinner, Hugh introduced me to hot rice wine. While we were reminiscing
about old times and exchanging such war stories as we had to tell, he would open
the door of his room from time to time and holler, "Room boy, another caddy of
wine." That was not a happy experience.*

*My favorite port of call was the Crown Colony of Hong Kong, which we
visited on three occasions. The harbor is nestled between the island of Hong Kong,
with its striking Victoria Peak, and the mainland city of Kowloon. At that time, it
still retained its colonial flavor. The great majority of the vessels in the harbor were
junks, including some large merchantmen armed with small brass cannons with
which to repel the pirates that still menaced shipping in those seas. In contrast
with today's jumble of huge high rise buildings that obliterate the visual impact of
Victoria Peak, the dominant structure on the Hong Kong side was the impressive
five or six storied Hongkong and Shanghai Banking Corporation building. It
faced the waterfront and was a few hundred yards from the white colonial-style
governor's mansion with its broad veranda and adjoining cricket field. I loved
walking through the streets of the commercial districts with their bustling crowds
and markets offering exotic foods and smells. I also enjoyed the first French
cooking I had tasted in a couple of years and an English high tea served to the
music of a genteel string orchestra at Kowloon's elegant Peninsula Hotel.*

*I was in Hong Kong when, in early May, I received not one, but two orders
home. The first was in response to a request for home leave that I had submitted
many months earlier; the other ordered me to report to the Navy district office in
New York City for my discharge. As the first entitled me to air transportation, I
used if to thumb a ride to Shanghai on a Navy amphibious plane. When I arrived*

there, however, I found that it would take weeks to find space on a plane to the United States, so I signed a paper waiving my privileges as an officer so that I could secure passage on a troop transport that took 16 days to reach San Francisco. I didn't mind being assigned to one of the four-decker bunks reserved for enlisted men or having to eat my meals standing up. I was headed home.

WW: And then you came back, and where did you go? Did you go back to Sharon?

JLB: Went back to Sharon.

WW: And then?

JLB: Sent applications to various law schools. Very, very crowded. Law schools, incidentally, were still operating on a war footing, with three semesters a year. They continued on this schedule for some time after the war was over. They had to absorb a three- to four-year backlog of men who, on leaving college, had gone off to war instead of law school. I was admitted to several law schools for the semester beginning in January. So what did I do during the fall? I returned to Yale as a special student. The GI Bill of Rights paid the way, and I was able to take five courses I had always wanted to take but could never fit into my schedule. It was a wonderful experience.

WW: That was a nice thing to be able to do.

JLB: It was lovely. Aside from the academic work, I was able to catch up with old friends I hadn't seen for three years and to help the *Yale Daily News* get started again.

WW: Not a lot of pressure—you had already graduated. This is not a bad way to spend a few months.

JLB: And then I started in law school at Columbia and later transferred to Yale.

WW: Why did you start at Columbia? Why didn't you go to Yale Law School?

JLB: Because I was not admitted there. I was admitted at Harvard, Columbia, and Virginia, but not Yale.

I have long wished I had had the prescience to save a copy of the Virginia Law School application form, which provided a classic example of the prejudices that influenced admissions decisions in those days. The form required me to attach my photograph, disclose my religion, state whether I had ever changed my name and, if I had, what my name had been before I changed it. It was widely known that many academic institutions maintained quotas for Catholics and Jews in those days, and blacks were only just beginning to gain access to the most prestigious universities. Virginia's application form at least had the virtue of wearing its institutional biases on its sleeve.

WW: But then Yale took you later—after a year. Did you spend the year at Columbia?

JLB: One semester.

WW: Just one semester?

JLB: Yale required a certain level of marks, and I got them.

WW: Then you went back to Yale?

JLB: Went back to Yale.

WW: And at this point did you have an idea what you wanted to do with your law degree?

JLB: I wanted to be a country lawyer.

WW: I suppose that's on your resumé somewhere.

JLB: But I didn't become one.

WW: I didn't see it anywhere in your resumé that you ever became a country lawyer.

JLB: That was my objective, and one of the reasons I went to law school was that it would have made it possible for me to earn a living in the country.

WW: I would say that many people who go to law school go with an idea that they will do something very different from what they end up doing. Were there particular teachers, law school professors, that were important to you during that period?

JLB: Not really. I must confess that when I asked a professor at Columbia for a recommendation to go to Yale, he called me a sap because, he said, at that time Columbia had by far the better teachers. Law schools go up and down, but at that particular time the professors at Columbia were tops in their fields.

WW: And who was it that told you that? Somebody I would know?

JLB: I don't think so. He taught a fascinating course called "The Development of Legal Institutions." It was a required course for first-year students. It taught them the origins of the common law and traced its development from the time of the Norman Conquest to the settlement of British America.

WW: That sounds like a course that would be offered at Yale.

JLB: But it wasn't. The luminaries at Yale were not, by and large, the ones who taught the bread and butter courses, and my interests were in bread and butter. There were a number of professors at Yale whom I liked but I wouldn't say that they molded me in any way. I was exposed to Eugene Rostow at that time and later got to know him well *(and much admired* *him). He taught me bad economics. (And 31 years later, he served as chairman of "Democrats for Buckley" during my failed campaign to be the junior senator from Connecticut.)*

WW: Would he agree with that?

JLB: He would agree it was economics that I would not subscribe to. It was pure Keynes.

WW: Did you have classmates who were particularly important to you then or now?

JLB: Yes. And several of them were individuals who were important to me as an undergraduate. In a very real sense, I was able to recapture some of the flavor of my undergraduate life.

WW: It was no longer military. Everybody wasn't walking around Yale in uniform. So it probably in some sense seemed like what college was supposed to be.

JLB: Right, except the dining rooms hadn't reverted.

WW: You never got the tablecloths back. Did you like your law school education? Did you like it while you were doing it?

JLB: I liked it; I wasn't excited by it, but I was learning a trade.

WW: You didn't meet with study groups and discuss the finer points of due process?

JLB: No.

WW: And at what point in your law school career did you decide that you were maybe not going to be a country lawyer?

JLB: I didn't make that decision until several years after I had graduated. From the beginning, I had decided that to succeed in the area where I wanted to be a country practitioner, it would be necessary for me first to work a few years with a top quality firm. I needed the legal background and preparation that would enable me to get the carriage trade when I moved to the country. I had a role model, a man who had been a partner in one of the very big New York firms for 10–15 years, and then moved up into the country. He was able to get the business of retired New Yorkers who would go to him for their wills and estate planning. That's what I more or less had in mind. So on leaving law school, I became an associate with Wiggin & Dana in New Haven, which was one of the top firms in Connecticut.

WW: Were you successful in law school? Did you do well?

JLB: By my way of thinking I was very successful. I ended up in the exact middle of a class to which I had not originally been admitted.

WW: And you thought that really showed them.

JLB: And I must confess I did not work as hard at Yale Law School as I had at Columbia.

WW: That was my next question. What were your study habits like? Were you one of those people who was always in the library or more like one who was generally on the soccer field? Where did you fall in that spectrum?

JLB: In the middle.

WW: As you think back on your law school education, do you think it was appropriate, useful, too academic, not academic enough? How do you think about your law school education?

JLB: I thought that Yale had too great a focus on the development of public policy. Its emphasis was not on training practitioners.

WW: That hasn't changed one bit at Yale as far as I know.

JLB: I have had some wonderful clerks out of Yale.

WW: We have wonderful Yale law students. I didn't mean to say otherwise. But they haven't learned a lot of bread and butter things in law school. I think that's characteristic of Yale. You weren't married during this period. I don't want to go out of order, but I can't remember exactly when you did meet your wife or when you got married. Was it shortly after law school?

JLB: No. I graduated from law school in '49, I was married in '53.

WW: How did you meet your wife?

JLB: There's a great argument about that.

WW: About the answer to this question?

JLB: Yes. The reason is that when I applied to Yale as an undergraduate, I said I wanted a roommate but I had nobody in mind. I received a postcard in the middle of the summer advising me that I would be rooming with somebody called Richard Cooley.

WW: Your future brother-in-law.

JLB: Right. Richard Cooley had three younger sisters. I am not aware of having met my wife during the two times I visited his home.

WW: But she has a different recollection.

JLB: I do recall meeting her younger sister. My wife was at a boarding school at the time. In any event, years go by and when it was suggested that I have a blind date with Ann Cooley, I figured this wouldn't entail a large risk. Ann and my sister Priscilla were both working in Washington for the CIA. I was working in New Haven. At the time I was in my late 20s and thought that I was doomed to perpetual bachelorhood, which I didn't want. Priscilla said that Ann was a splendid person and proposed bringing her to Sharon for a Memorial Day weekend, which is a long time. Having known her brother Dick, however, I figured it was a good risk.

Oral histories have their limitations, one of them being at least this subject's tendency to compress answers. I had actually met Ann a couple of years earlier while she was still in college in New York City, and I had had a date with her. But on her graduation, she returned to St. Louis where her family then lived. This was too long a commute from New Haven for me to pursue the relationship. (Ann had grown up in Rye, New York, from whence her father, Victor Cooley, commuted to his job as a vice president of the New York Telephone Company. Her family moved to St. Louis in 1946 when Mr. Cooley became president of the Southwest Telephone Company.) Later, when Ann had moved to Washington and my sister suggested that she bring her to Sharon, I knew (a) that this would involve no risk of spoiling a long holiday weekend and (b), that if it were to lead to that, a New Haven-Washington courtship was doable, even if daunting. Because I find it difficult to write about very personal matters, I will merely pass on a remark made about Ann by my brother John's wife, who had gone to boarding school with her and greatly admired her. At the time Ann moved back to St. Louis, thus ending any thought I might have had of a serious courtship, John's wife asked whether I was still seeing Ann. When I said I wasn't, she asked, "Is it because she's too perfect?" As I have explained, that was not the reason. But John's wife was essentially right in one respect. Ann is, well, almost perfect. The only flaw I have been able to detect in over 50 years of marriage is her refusal, as a matter of misguided principle, to cross either the Arctic or Antarctic Circle.

WW: Where did she go to college?

JLB: Manhattanville College, which was then in Manhattan. It's now in Purchase, New York.

WW: What was she doing for the CIA? Or can't you tell?

JLB: She never told me.

WW: That sounds like the CIA. You never know what they are doing.

JLB: I really don't know.

WW: How long after the Memorial Day weekend did you get married?

JLB: About a year.

WW: And then you were in Connecticut at that time and I take it she left the CIA?

JLB: She left the CIA, yes.

WW: Tell me a little bit about your children.

JLB: The oldest is Peter. We were married in '53 and he was born in '54. Therefore he is now 41. He has an MBA degree from Harvard and now works out of New York City for a San Francisco investment banking firm, lives in Connecticut, but seems to spend most of his time in an airplane. He was married three years ago—just before his 39th birthday. They now have a son. Number two child is called Jay, which is short for James. His middle names are those of my first boss, Frederick Wiggin, whom I greatly admired. Jay is married, has three children—two boys and a girl. He works for a computer software company and lives in Rhode Island. The next child is our only daughter, Priscilla, who has lived abroad for the last 14 years or so. She is married to a Frenchman who speaks no English; therefore the chances are she'll continue living in France, to our regret.

WW: Does she have children?

JLB: She has one child.

WW: Speaks only French?

JLB: She speaks to him only in English. He is now five-and-a-half and under-
stands English but he has trouble speaking it. And she also works for a
computer company. She is a, was a, freelance writer, but after her child
was born, she figured she needed a more predictable kind of work. She
translates computerese into understandable English and, I am told, is
very good at it.

With first-born child, Peter.

WW: She and her brothers have a lot to talk about when you have Christmas
together.

JLB: She got her job through Jay.

WW: That's one of the advantages of having a large family.

JLB: Next one in line is son Bill. He is one of the unmarried ones. Since he
was a boy, he has had an absolute passion for hunting and fishing. After

trying his hand in commercial real estate, he ended up working for a group of magazines in New York which included several hunting oriented magazines—one archery, one on white tail deer hunting, and so on. He subsequently moved to Bozeman, Montana, where he now works as a freelance hunting and fishing photographer and writer. A competitive field, but he has a freezer full of good meat.

WW: He probably doesn't need a lot to live on. And he is unmarried.

JLB: He is unmarried. The next child is David. David is the only lawyer. He went to Virginia Law School and, before that, Yale.

WW: Is he the only one who went to Yale?

JLB: Yes. After practicing for a few years with a firm in Los Angeles, he moved to Davis, Polk in New York City. He worked with their real estate group for about six years. He liked the work, but a point came when he got fed up with not knowing whether he could keep a dinner date that evening or have to cancel his weekend plans at the last minute. So he started shopping around and now works as a real estate lawyer for Host Marriott. This entailed a substantial reduction in pay, but he is happy as a lark.

WW: Does he live in New York?

JLB: No, he lives in Virginia and works at the Marriott headquarters in Bethesda, Maryland. He is engaged in the same kind of work as he was in New York but has a greater degree of responsibility. Likes the people he works with.

WW: I'm sure the stresses are so much different. Good. Is he married?

JLB: No. And then there is our youngest child, Andrew, who is married. He has one child, a daughter, who has the honor of being our oldest grandchild. His interest is photography. After a stint working for a weekly newspaper, he decided to go out on his own as a freelance photographer. He lives in York, Maine.

Shortly after we were married, Ann and I had the inevitable discussion about the size of the family we would like to have. Having known the joys of a very large one, I blurted out, "Surely, no fewer than six," to which Ann replied, with a certain panic in her voice, "Surely no more than six." So ours may be described as a planned family although they came along at a somewhat faster rate than either of us had anticipated. We are, however, utterly pleased by what we have produced. As my father once remarked to my mother, "Our blood lines clicked." Although differing widely in interests and temperament, they are each decent, caring, and bright individuals, and each is blessed with a glorious sense of humor. What more can anyone ask in the high risk business of merging DNAs?

Sharon, summer of 1969. Back row: JLB, Ann, Peter, Bill.
Front row: Andy, Priscilla, David, Jay.

WW: Do you get together as a family often?

JLB: Not often enough, but we have managed to get together virtually every Thanksgiving and Christmas. But now that families are being established, we are seeing competition from in-laws. So we count our blessings. Last Christmas we had everybody, but we don't expect that to continue.

WW: And when you have everybody, does everybody come here?

JLB: To Connecticut.

WW: Do you have a home in Connecticut?

JLB: We had a home until ten years ago, 11 years ago, but the house and the place where I grew up was rather large. After my mother could no longer use it, it was condominiumized. The main house was made into five units, two of which were purchased by two of my sisters. The place also had a large barn that was converted into three units. One of these was retained for members of the family, so between the surplus accommodations my sisters make available and this unit, we can all squeeze in.

WW: And do you still do that? When you go to Connecticut, is that where you go?

JLB: Yes.

WW: I remember last time you said that you had an enduring memory of construction on that house. How would you describe your role as a father as your children were growing up? Were you active in raising your children? You might compare it to the role that your father had in raising all of you.

JLB: Well, I think there is a fair degree of similarity between us. I think I told you that my father was in many ways an absentee father. He would be in New York during the week while we stayed in the country. My father's business involved Venezuela. From time to time he would have to take business trips to Venezuela which would last several weeks.

WW: Which was nowhere near Sharon.

JLB: Nowhere near Sharon. I ended up following a similar pattern except that when I was not away on business trips abroad, I would spend five nights a week in Sharon as opposed to his three. Our principal office was in New York City, but John and I also had a tiny office in Sharon that had a telephone tie-line to our New York switchboard. We would go into New York Tuesday mornings and return to the country Thursday evenings.

WW: That is in the model of your father. Did you ever take your children on trips when you were going?

JLB: Not as many as I wish we could have. We did have several trips. We went to California several times to visit Ann's parents and rented a house there. And one time I took a sabbatical and moved the whole family to Spain for five months. The group I worked with had this wonderful idea. Because we could pinch hit for one another, we would each take off for a period of six months with our families while we were still young enough to enjoy the experience. I was the second of the four of us actually to take off on a sabbatical when a series of corporate crises forced us to abandon the policy. As it was, I had to make two emergency trips from Madrid to the Philippines while we were in Spain.

WW: OK. Let's go back to your career now. After you graduated from law school you went to Wiggin & Dana, is that right?

JLB: Yes.

WW: Did you look at a lot of places? How did you pick Wiggin & Dana?

JLB: I looked at some firms in Hartford because the pattern that I wanted to duplicate was to gain big city experience to prepare me for a quality practice in a small community. My first thought was to work in Hartford.

I had a very good friend in New Haven, however—Lew Wiggin—who was the nephew of Frederick Wiggin of Wiggin & Dana. Lew, who was an orphan, lived with his Uncle Fritz and suggested that I discuss my plans with him. So I visited Uncle Fritz, whom I had known slightly through this connection, and he said, "Why don't you work for me?" So I did.

WW: Great way to get a job. So you went to work for Wiggin & Dana in New Haven. How large was it at the time?

JLB: As one of the largest law firms in Connecticut, it then had 10 partners and three associates.

WW: Were you the third?

JLB: Yes.

WW: How big is it now?

JLB: Fifty, 60 lawyers. I don't know.

WW: Is that all?

JLB: I don't know.

WW: And what did you do?

JLB: A little bit of everything, except criminal. I didn't do any trial work either, although I carried a partner's briefcase a couple of days and was assigned by the court to handle one divorce case. I represented some obstreperous Yale law students in a hearing before a city magistrate—not really a trial.

WW: But you didn't do a lot of litigation, you didn't find yourself in court. Is that what you wanted?

JLB: I was not drawn to litigation.

WW: How long were you at Wiggin & Dana?

JLB: Four years.

WW: What kind of views about law practice did you form during that period?

JLB: It seemed to me that a law practice would become truly rewarding once you had clients of your own where you could follow through with them and become part of their universe. The work of researching discrete issues and other tasks assigned by partners who had continuing relationships with clients did not excite me tremendously. But I could see how the practice could become more rewarding. Towards the end, I did begin to get my own clients. One in particular interested me—a fellow who dealt in rare books. He wanted to be incorporated, so I incorporated him; then he had a little zoning problem, and I had to look at that; and then there was something else. But by this time my father had become short-handed and sent my eldest brother John, who was working for him, as an emissary to woo me away; and because I was not totally excited about what I was doing, and even though it meant working in New York City, which I had hitherto gone to some lengths to avoid, and even though I had never considered a career in business, I found myself saying goodbye to Wiggin & Dana and going with my father's group. I began my new life doing primarily legal work with Dean Reasoner, a partner of the Washington, D.C., firm of Reasoner & Davis, who spent most of his time working for this group of companies and was in our New York office three days a week. So I started out working with these companies as an associate of Reasoner & Davis. For awhile we had a little apartment in Washington where we spent a few days a week, but I soon ended up spending all my time in New York.

WW: What is this group of companies?

JLB: The specific company I worked for was called The Catawba Corporation, which was family owned. Catawba in turn represented and worried about all of the non-technical aspects of a number of publicly held corporations engaged in petroleum exploration, mostly outside the United States. At the time I joined the group, there were four of them — all traded on the American Stock Exchange. By the time I left Catawba, in 1970, the group had grown to seven: Pantepec International (the lineal descendant of my father's original company), which held oil and gas interests in Venezuela and elsewhere; Pancoastal Petroleum, which also held concessions in Venezuela; Coastal Caribbean, which had oil and mineral exploration rights in Florida; Canada Southern Petroleum, with properties in western Canada; United Canso Oil and Gas, ditto; Magellan Petroleum, which held petroleum exploration rights in Australia; and San Jose Oil, with concessions in the Philippines

A word about the origins of these companies and their strategy for survival in the highly competitive and risky business of oil exploration. As mentioned earlier, on his expulsion from Mexico, my father decided he could make the best use of his Mexican experience by looking for oil in Venezuela. To that end, he moved to New York, secured the necessary seed money from a Wall Street firm, and organized a new company, Pantepec Oil Company of Venezuela.

Because he could not hope to compete against the major oil companies in areas where production had been established, my father sought concessions on reasonable terms in untested areas of Venezuela which appeared promising on the basis of regional geology. These would have to be extensive enough to permit the delineation of a significant number of drillable prospects. Once Pantepec's geologists had identified areas of particular interest, my father would be in a position to negotiate "farmout" agreements with major oil companies which would enable them to earn an interest in particular concessions by undertaking the heavy cost of drilling exploratory wells. After a number of failures and the passage of a dozen years of crises that would have daunted Pauline, oil was finally discovered on one of Pantepec's properties. To a significant degree, Pantepec (and the Buckley family) had been able to survive during the intervening years because its shares were actively traded on the old New York Curb Exchange, which later became the

American Stock Exchange. It was the only listed company exclusively engaged in looking for oil in Venezuela. Therefore, anyone wishing to bet on the likelihood of further discoveries there had no alternative but to become a Pantepec shareholder.

Following several additional discoveries, Pantepec's board decided to divide its properties between a dividend-paying Pantepec and a new company, Pancoastal Petroleum, which would hold the still untested Venezuelan concessions as well as newly acquired oil and gas rights over more than a million acres in Florida. As a result of subsequent corporate reorganizations, acquisitions, and distributions, by the early 1950s, my father was overseeing four independent companies with substantial production in Venezuela, marginal production in Ecuador, and extensive exploration rights in Florida and western Canada. The Catawba Corporation was then organized as a family owned vehicle for providing my father's knowhow and a variety of services to the public companies. Under its typical contract with the operating companies, Catawba would be reimbursed the cost of its services and earn a 1/64th overriding royalty on their exploratory properties. In time, Catawba would be providing services to oil companies operating in Venezuela, Ecuador, Florida, Canada, the Philippines, and Australia, and one engaged in hard-rock mineral exploration in the Canadian arctic.

As most of its clients had little or no income, one of Catawba's principal tasks was to keep them adequately financed. This was usually accomplished through the sale of shares using techniques developed by Catawba that kept financing costs to a minimum. Catawba also negotiated farmout agreements on their behalf and investigated new opportunities for expansion. And always, when entering a new petroleum frontier, these companies would follow the same basic pattern: the securing of exploration rights on reasonable terms over sufficiently large areas to make sure that the potential of the new hunting ground was adequately tested and that the company owning the rights could survive initial failures. These companies attracted wide investor interest. One year, for example, trading in the shares of Catawba's clients accounted for 5 percent of the total volume on the American Stock Exchange; and the quality of the prospects to which their 80,000 shareholders were exposed is illustrated by an article in the Oil and Gas Journal identifying the world's ten most carefully watched exploratory wells, of which three (in the Canadian arctic, central Australia, and off-shore South Africa) were testing properties held by client companies.

Catawba and its clients had to part ways in 1978 when the Securities and Exchange Commission ruled that because of the intimacy of the connection between Catawba and each of its clients, they would have to be treated as a single entity anytime any one of them wished to register its shares for sale. As most of the companies relied on regular access to equity markets for their survival, that would have imposed an intolerable burden on those that were not seeking new financing. As a consequence, their associations with Catawba came to an end. While it lasted, however, it was a class act.

WW: Which of your brothers were working for these businesses?

JLB: My brother John and my brother-in-law Benjamin Heath, who was married to my oldest sister, Aloïse.

WW: So this happened when you were a fourth-year associate. The fourth year is the usual time you go do something else.

JLB: Is it?

WW: Yes, because you have been practicing law, you think you ought to be on your own with your own clients. You are not, it's very frustrating, it's a hard period, so it's not surprising; and I wonder if, had it happened five years later, you would have gone. You probably would have become a partner at Wiggin & Dana.

JLB: Unless, of course, I had followed on my original course and hung out my shingle in Sharon.

WW: You were married when you did this?

JLB: I married during the transition. We were married on May 22, 1953, in St. Louis, Missouri. But I'd left Wiggin & Dana at the end of April and I reported for duty in my new job after my honeymoon.

WW: Where were you living? Did you stay in Connecticut?

JLB: We got an apartment in New York, and we had one in Washington and spent most weekends at my parents' home in Connecticut.

WW: Did Ann go back and forth with you?

JLB: Yes, she did. Then after a little over a year, after our first child was born, we bought a little cottage five miles from the village of Sharon and lived there weekends. Then after our third child was born, we built a house nearby. By then, Ann was spending most of her time in Connecticut.

WW: During this period in which you were working with your father's firm, I take it you are really not practicing law?

JLB: Basically working with lawyers. I understood the corporate problems and so, for example, I became engaged in negotiating concession contracts, checking prospectuses, and so on. The work I did required familiarity with the law and the ability to deal with lawyers as well as a thorough grasp of the corporate and operating requirements of Catawba's clients. I would find myself, for example, in Sicily working with an Italian lawyer to structure a corporate subsidiary in such a manner that it could both qualify to hold Sicilian concessions and enter into customary petroleum operating agreements that relied on trust concepts that were foreign to Italian law. I also worked with the Philippine Bureau of Mines in drafting a standard oil exploration concession form that would prove workable from the perspective of both parties. As I say, although I was concerned with legal problems and worked with lawyers, I no longer engaged in legal research or other work of that kind.

WW: It's more fun to be the client.

JLB: I negotiated a lot of contracts. I worked on SEC prospectuses. I helped write the Philippine geothermal energy law. But I did not practice law in any traditional sense.

WW: But it sounds like you were enjoying it.

JLB: Yes, I thoroughly enjoyed it. It was creative. I found that I had an entre-preneurial streak in me that I hadn't realized I had.

WW: Were you surprised that you actually ended up doing this?

JLB: Yes.

WW: While you were moving around the Pacific, I suppose one of the options must have been to go into your father's business.

JLB: I had never considered it.

WW: You'd never thought of it?

JLB: No.

WW: Why not?

JLB: Just never considered it. I didn't think I had any particular talent for business, and I wanted to work in the country.

WW: How long did you do it? How long were you involved with your father's businesses?

JLB: About 17 years.

WW: During this period, did your oldest brother continue and your brother-in-law?

JLB: Yes.

WW: And you must have traveled all over the place.

JLB: My work took me over a large part of the globe at one time or another.
        Because I was a lawyer as well as one of the Catawba principals, I was the
        one most likely to be dispatched to size up new opportunities; and be-
        cause of my particular responsibilities for our Philippine venture, during
        my last decade or so with the company I was traveling 50,000 miles a year
        and more. By the time I left Catawba in 1970, I had spent serious time in
        Canada, Israel, Libya, Italy, Nicaragua, Venezuela, Ecuador, the Philip-
        pines, South Africa, and Australia, and had visited a half dozen other
        countries as well in the line of duty. [*The latter included, in alphabetical
        order, Botswana, Greece, Guatemala, Indonesia, Malaysia, Malta, New
        Zealand, Sarawak, Sicily, Singapore, and Taiwan.*]

*Business travel to distant places is not as glamorous as it sounds. I spent endless
hours in look-alike hotel rooms or lawyers' offices awaiting calls to visit this minis-
try or that, or waiting for a cable or telephone call from Catawba in answer to some
urgent question that had to be answered before I could return to spend more hours
waiting for another appointment to meet with a particular official. It was usually
impossible to break free for serious sightseeing. In my 16 years in and out of the
Philippines, I was able to assume the role of tourist on fewer than a half dozen
occasions, but these were memorable. One that stands out in particular was Ann's
and my visit to the truly spectacular Igorot rice terraces in northern Luzon. They fill
an entire valley with the sound of water dripping from one layer of terraces cut into
the sides of steep mountains to the next. I will also confess that on three or four
occasions I took off on what can only be described as corporate junkets. The one
that remains in mind is a trip, in October 1964, to visit a well that one of Catawba's
clients, United Canso Oil & Gas, Ltd., was drilling on Bathurst Island, in the
Canadian Arctic, within a couple of hundred miles from where the Magnetic
North Pole was then located. It was the northernmost well yet drilled in the Western
Hemisphere. It was cold, bleak, windy, white, and I saw some muskox in the distance as we flew to the well site. It was there that I caught a seemingly incurable
fascination with polar regions. I have since visited them on more than a dozen
occasions, including two trips to Antarctica. I have helped capture muskox calves
on Ellesmere Island and Greenland; spent time with an Eskimo whaling party off
Point Hope; Alaska; hobnobbed with Antarctic penguins and elephant seals; ob-*

served walrus in Siberia's Chukchi Sea and Canada's Foxe Basin; watched migrating caribou in Alaska's Brooks Range; and fallen in love with polar bears. Even in the bleakest of arctic landscapes, I have marveled at the tenacity of its plant and animal life; but, in candor, I have never faced the rigors of an arctic winter.

Befriending an Adelie Penguin in Antarctica, 1972.

WW: Was it mostly oil or were there other businesses?

JLB: Almost exclusively oil and gas. Towards the end of my time with Catawba, I began to explore the possibilities of geothermal energy—the search for commercial sources of geothermal steam for the generation of electricity. We formed an informal partnership with a California corporation that had the technical expertise. I then spent time investigating the possibilities of securing geothermal exploration concessions in Nicaragua and the Philippines. I was also responsible for the organization of a mineral exploration venture in the Canadian arctic called Borealis Exploration Limited.

Because I was the only one in Catawba who knew anything about geothermal energy, nothing came of those initiatives when I left the company. Borealis, how-

ever discovered what appears to be North America's largest deposit of high grade magnetite iron ore on the Melville Peninsula, which lies north of Hudson Bay. Unfortunately, iron ore currently has a low value; and although these deposits are located close to salt water, that water is frozen solid for much of the year. In time, though, improvements in techniques for the onsite concentration of the ore and increases in world demand for iron will bring this resource to market. When that occurs, the royalty Catawba earned on the properties may educate a fourth or fifth generation of Buckleys.

WW: Well, up until this point we've talked about a lot of things you did in your life. None of them are political or associated with the political process directly. So either I've missed something or there's more to tell. So my next question is, sometime after this period you ran for the Senate and you became involved in politics. What happened; what have I missed? You said it all happened by accident.

It did. But before moving on to my entry into politics and the rest of my life, I want to add a word about our Philippine venture and the Philippines, which became very important to me.

Because ours was essentially the only group of independent oil companies with operations outside the United States, Catawba's New York office became a port of call for individuals who saw opportunities for oil exploration in areas where, for one reason or another, the major companies had yet to enter. Chester Baird was one of these. Chester had been a top Gulf Oil exploration geologist with long experience in Venezuela, North Africa, and Italy. Soon after his retirement, he came in contact with an American woman who was then living in Manila and was aware that the Philippine Congress had recently enacted a law permitting the issuance of petroleum exploration rights. The baroness (one of her several husbands had been a German baron) also claimed the ability to facilitate their issuance to qualified applicants. Chester persuaded us that the Philippines had excellent prospects for oil and gas and we found the law governing their exploration and production to be reasonable.

Accordingly, we dispatched Chester and a lawyer to Manila to establish an office, organize the Philippine corporation that would apply for exploration rights, and secure local legal representation. On their arrival, they discovered that the baroness had little influence to peddle (that was usually the case), but she did make two contributions to our new venture, one of them minor, the other of great importance to the enterprise and to me personally. The first was the suggestion that we name the new company after the Philippines' patron saint, San Jose; the second, that we retain Emmanuel Pelaez as its lawyer. Manny brought with him not only his own professional competence but also that of his partner, Rodeglio Jalondoni,

General Emilio Aguinaldo (flanked by his wife and mine) displays his finally recovered banner.

and of a young and very bright associate, Herminio Banico, who later became San Jose Oil Company's in-house counsel. All of them would become good personal friends. Manny was also a member of the Philippine Senate (and, in later years, Philippine vice president and ambassador to the United States) and, as such, could open important doors. But that was as far as he would go or, for that matter, as far as we would ever ask him to go. He was a man of total integrity and we, as a matter of policy, would not consider trying to buy results even though that was how too much of the business in that country was conducted. We were there for the longer haul and had our own corporate reputation to protect.

In 1956, when embarking on my first business trip to Manila, I decided that the old Spanish artillery company banner that had hung on the wall of my room at Yale should be returned to its proper home, and I brought it with me. I discovered, on my arrival, that it had a far greater historical significance than I could have imagined. The Philippine flag painted on the banner bore an inscription in Tagalog dedicating it to General Aguinaldo. It had been written by the man who had captured it, General Gregorio Del Pilar, who was himself a national hero. Within a week, the banner had won me a breakfast with President Ramon Magsaysay at Malacañan, the Philippine White House, as well as a visit to Cavite, some miles south of Manila, where I presented it to the then 87-year-old General Aguinaldo at the home where he had proclaimed his country's independence almost 60 years earlier. Not a bad beginning for a newcomer to the tangled world of Philippine business.

And it proved to be incredibly tangled. I was embarked on what would be a dozen-years of the greatest frustrations I have ever encountered, beginning with the job of negotiating the terms of the exploration contracts. The petroleum law was eminently reasonable, but the contract originally prepared by the Bureau of Mines contained arbitrary provisions that would have made it impossible to justify the huge expenditures of high risk money that petroleum exploration entails. It took endless months of waiting in anterooms, exchanging cables, and periodic 10,000 mile commutes between New York and Manila before an acceptable form of contract was agreed upon. That was just the beginning. I won't detail the other roadblocks, both legal and bureaucratic, that required me to fly to Manila two or three times a year for stays ranging from a week or two to one of three months. In the pre-jet age, it would take over 50 hours to fly from New York to Manila. There would be up to six hour lay-overs at San Francisco, Honolulu, and Midway Island; and on my arrival, I would have to cope with time changes of 11 or 12 hours, depending on whether we were on daylight savings time when I left.

From an operational point of view, we did a first class job, which made the constant bureaucratic delays all the more frustrating. It didn't take San Jose's geologists long to identify the areas we would like to explore. We then had to mark time for endless months while awaiting the final approval and signing of acceptable exploration contracts. The geologists then proceeded with the detailed geological mapping and magnetometer and seismic work that enabled us to delineate promising prospects in several areas of the Philippines. With this information in hand,

I was able to negotiate a farmout agreement with Union Oil that required that company to drill exploratory wells on those prospects in order to earn a 50 percent interest in the properties. Unfortunately, each of those wells was dry. So, once again, we managed to confirm that petroleum exploration is indeed a very risky business.

Yet despite these frustrations and our ultimate disappointment, I have the fondest feelings for the Philippines because of the caliber of the people I had the good fortune to meet and the lasting friendships I made there. Generalizations are

Reunion with Philippine friends Anselmo Trinidad, Emanuel and Edith Pelaez, Francisco and Nenita Ortigas, Herminio and Adela Banico, and Lourdes Jalandoni, in 1981.

suspect, I know, but I found a warmth, and hospitality, and genuine kindness among Filipinos that I have encountered nowhere else; and I felt a special affection for the friends I made there. Ann and I took a long, last trip to Manila in 1997 to say goodbye to them. It proved timely because within six years my closest friends there were all gone.

I view my Philippine experiences with both affection and sadness; sadness because a country with its human and natural resources, its political structure, and superior education should be among the most prosperous in the region. Instead, it has been ridden with an endemic corruption and "cronyism" that reached grotesque proportions during the years when Ferdinand Marcos was in power, and still persists. (During those years, the country's principal export was that of well trained engineers, accountants, doctors, lawyers, what have you, whose skills helped stoke the miracle economies of neighboring Southeast Asian states.) If two of my older friends were right, this sickness had its origins in the Japanese occupation. They told me that the pre-war civil service had been exemplary, but that after the Japanese took over, civil servants began to cheat as a matter of both patriotism and survival. My friends believed that the integrity of the civil service might have been restored if the United States had been less punctilious in honoring its promise to grant the Philippines its independence on July 4, 1946. Whether another three of four years of American stewardship would have done the trick, I don't know. What I do know is that these wonderful people deserve far better than the hand their governing elites have dealt them.

Now back to my venture into elective politics.

JLB: I've always been interested in political issues and at one time or another worked for various political committees, but I was never involved in traditional party work.

WW: But how did you end up as a candidate for the United States Senate?

JLB: You may have heard that I have an exotic brother.

WW: I've heard that.

JLB: In 1965, Bill was prevailed upon by the recently organized New York Conservative Party to run for mayor of New York City. That campaign has achieved folklore status because of Bill's answer to a question at the press conference announcing his candidacy. A reporter asked, "Do you expect to win"? Bill said "No." He was then asked what he would do if he did win. And his answer was, "Demand a recount." The Conservative Party was organized for the purpose of creating a counterforce, a counterbalance to New York's Liberal Party, which had proved enormously effective in influencing both of the major parties. Do you have any familiarity with New York politics?

WW: I do a little bit. I never lived there but New York was a very interesting political scene, which I was aware of at the time.

JLB: Let me give you the background. The Liberal Party was founded shortly after the war by the astute heads of two New York City garment workers' unions. They developed enough of a following to establish that a Liberal Party endorsement was worth a certain number of votes in any election. These endorsements normally went to Democratic Party candidates; but on occasion, the Liberal Party would endorse a particularly liberal Republican. New York elections are often decided by very narrow margins, so the perceived value of the Liberal endorsement had the effect of leveraging New York's Republican Party to the left, at least when it came to selecting candidates for statewide office and for races in New York City. In 1964, two very bright young New York City lawyers, one of them now a federal circuit judge with the Second Circuit, Dan Mahoney, founded the Conservative Party as a counterweight. To gain credibility, a leverage party must field its own candidate if it cannot in good conscience endorse the candidate of one of the major parties. This was the case in the 1965 mayoralty race. The Republican candidate was John Lindsay, a Yale classmate and friend of mine. He was not only a political liberal, he sought, and received, the Liberal Party's endorsement.

WW: That is what the Republicans in New York City were known for—they were Lindsay Republicans.

JLB: Right. So, Bill thought this might be interesting—(a) it would require him to focus on political issues in the urban arena as opposed to the national and international arenas that had been his principal concern, and (b) somebody had to run on the Conservative Party line. He referred to it as his jury duty.

WW: He thought it would be fun.

JLB: Right. Because it was conceded that there was no possibility that he would win, he was assured that he would not have to spend more than a day or two a week on his candidacy.

WW: Somebody lied.

JLB: Right, and so Bill said he would do it. I was then in California with Ann and our children visiting Ann's parents. I got a telephone call from Bill. He said, "I'm going to run for mayor of New York, and I want you to be my campaign manager." I said, "Bill, I don't know anything about campaign managing." Bill answered that that was not important. What he needed was someone to run interference for him, to protect him from all the amateur politicians in the Conservative Party who would be drowning him with advice. And I said, "Well, you know, Bill, I don't have the time." To which he replied, "It isn't going to take any time. A couple of mornings a week. I'll just be giving a few speeches; everybody knows I can't win." I confess I was a little intrigued, and with these assurances, I signed on.

WW: It wasn't the way it was portrayed.

JLB: It wasn't the way it was portrayed. So I became at least the titular campaign manager of a campaign that quickly caught a lot of people's imagination. John Lindsay, as splendid a figure as he cut, was very earnest on the campaign circuit; and his Democratic opponent, Abe Beame, was a typical product of the Democratic city machine. Bill brought a wit and irreverence to the enterprise that captivated the press corps. At the same time, he injected into the campaign a serious and penetrating critique of the liberal approaches to urban ills. Reporters would flock to Bill's press conferences at campaign headquarters for relief from the earnest seriousness of those given by the opposition.

WW: Just to be entertained.

JLB: To be entertained; plus the fact that some journalists, such as Murray Kempton, were intrigued by the unorthodox but serious ideas that Bill would float on different aspects of urban management. Time passed and Bill did not have to ask for a recount. Nevertheless, Bill did astonishingly well. John Lindsay won.

WW: Not to anybody's surprise.

JLB: Then, less than three years later, in February of '68, I found myself flat on my back in an American military hospital in Libya, having three days earlier ruptured a disc while tying my shoelaces preparatory to meeting some Libyan minister.

WW: That's painful.

It was indeed painful.

JLB: Fortunately, there was an American hospital there. It was there that I received a telephone call from Bill asking whether I would consider running for the Senate. I said, "What?" Bill explained that Senator Jacob Javits was running for reelection that fall, that obviously the Conservative Party couldn't endorse him, and that the party's chairman, Dan Mahoney, had asked him to call me to see if I might be interested. Apparently those Conservative Party stalwarts who had earlier consented to oblige by running for this or that office had finally said, "Enough." Having run out of names, someone said . . .

WW: There's another Buckley.

JLB: Exactly. I told Bill the idea was ridiculous.

WW: Why didn't Bill?

JLB: He had done his bit. He had done his jury duty. In any event, even though

I said the suggestion was ridiculous, I have had a practice of never saying no until I've thought something through. So I agreed to let Dan make his pitch in person after my return to the States. A week or so later, after I had returned home but still had to spend much of my time on my back, Dan called to see if he could come up to Sharon for a visit. I said fine. He was to join us for dinner, but that night was horrendous, with a bad fog. We waited and waited for Dan and finally ate dinner without him. We next heard from him at about 10:00 P.M. from a town about 20 miles north of us. Dan had assumed that Sharon was on the Connecticut shore to the east of his home instead of in the mountains about 80 miles to his north. Unfortunately, the fog was so dense by this time that it took him another hour to arrive at our house; so we put him to bed, and the next morning he made his pitch while I was flat on my back and defenseless. He pointed out the intellectual interest of being involved in a major political race and said that because I would have no chance whatever of winning, no one would expect me to spend much time campaigning. I told him that if I had a chance of winning, it would be irresponsible for me to run because of family and business obligations. As that wasn't in the cards, I said I would ponder the educational value of his proposal and then give him my answer.

WW: Was it a problem that you didn't happen to be a resident of New York?

JLB: One thing at a time.

WW: I'm sorry. I love this story.

JLB: Finally, I concluded that this would be an intriguing experience. I had never given a speech. I'd never been on television, let alone a televised debate. I had no idea whether I could handle this or not.

WW: You describe yourself as shy. Most people who describe themselves as shy don't then run for the Senate.

JLB: They've probably never been asked to. In any event, after a week or so talking it over with my wife and with my cohorts at Catawba, I told Dan that, if he hadn't come up with a better idea, I would give it a try. Ann gave me permission to undertake this mad venture and thought it might be fun; John and Ben who, along with me, were by that time in charge of Catawba, assured me that they could pinch-hit for me as required during the two months between Labor and Election Day that I would be a part-time campaigner. On the problem of New York and my residency: In 1968, the issue really didn't arise because everyone knew I couldn't possibly beat Javits. Furthermore, Bobby Kennedy had taken much of the edge off the carpetbagger issue in New York. He moved into the state as a total outsider in early 1964, bought himself an apartment, moved in his family, accepted the Democratic Party's nomination for the Senate, and won. In 1970, when I again ran for the Senate, this time with the hope of winning, the question of my residency was raised by some upstate New York newspapers that had opposed Kennedy on that basis. I was able to secure their endorsement, however, because unlike Kennedy, I had some genuine New York credentials. I had worked in New York, maintained an apartment there, and paid New York State and City income taxes over a period of 17 years. But I'm ahead of the game. We were talking about 1968.

WW: Your family thought you lived in New York. Your family would give you an affidavit. OK, I should know this and I am confused, but in 1968 Javits had that seat; it was the Javits seat, not the other seat, and you ran against Javits?

JLB: That's right. And the Democratic candidate was Paul O'Dwyer, the brother of the former mayor of New York City. A nice man.

WW: Who ran your campaign, your brother?

JLB: No. A fellow who was a full-time employee of the Conservative Party— its executive director, I believe. He was not very well organized. But I made the rounds and to everyone's surprise, most particularly mine, I came across well. I rattled off my first few speeches at 90 miles an hour. It took me a long while to sort of throttle back. I did a lot better in my televised appearances, answering questions on talk shows or participating in the three-way debates that were occasionally scheduled. I was able to reach large audiences through these freebies. My campaign was only able to raise about $180,000 or $200,000, so we couldn't buy TV coverage. On the other hand, a lot of volunteers flocked to the cause. They would set up store-front operations in various parts of the state, pass out literature, and so forth. I was the beneficiary of a great deal of grassroots activity. Also, because I was the candidate of an established party, I would get media coverage as I moved around the state. Turn up at the airport in one of New York's media centers, and you would be on the local television that night answering a lot of pertinent questions. I quickly found, however, that all this took a heroic amount of time and effort—not the few hours a week that Dan Mahoney had suggested. But to make a long story short, I did astonishingly well. I got approximately 1,200,000 votes, which was twice as many as any third-party candidate had ever received in New York. And so when it was all over, I felt that it had been a wonderful experience but that it was time to get back to work.

It was a shoestring campaign; but because I was accompanied by New York Times *and* New York *Daily News reporters and the local press wherever I went, what I had to say in the political hustings was well reported. I not only hammered away at the standard conservative themes but, on occasion, I added a couple of my own: namely, my concerns for both the environment and the problems that blacks continued to face.*

Rachel Carson's Silent Spring *had made me aware of the new and very real threats posed by the discharge into the environment of huge quantities of newly developed, biologically indigestible chemicals. These were imposing enormous costs on society that included, among others, the impairment of human health, destruction of fisheries, erosion of buildings, dramatic declines in bald eagle and other bird populations, and the fouling of recreational waters. This pollution had to be brought under control, and the cost of doing so placed on the shoulders of the polluters. I recognized that this would require creating a federal agency to set standards and ensure that they did because polluted air and water cross geographical boundaries. In searching for the appropriate venue in which to unveil these heretical thoughts, I noticed that I was scheduled to address a luncheon meeting of an organization whose title included the word "Conservation." And so I found myself delivering my first statement on the environment before what turned out to be an astonished group of hunters and fishermen. I received only a polite applause, but my remarks were reported in the* New York Times *and I continued to beat the environmental drum.*

In the summer of 1968, I became aware of a special burden borne by black Americans thanks to a lunch I had with Lawrence Chickering, a young Californian who was then working for National Review. *When the conversation turned to the subject of race, Lawry remarked that neither liberals nor conservatives understood that perhaps the greatest burden of being black in America was a pervasive feeling of powerlessness. It was this that made the Black Panther's "black power" battle cry so seductive. Although the civil rights revolution had eliminated legal discrimination based on race, most blacks in those days remained dependent on whites and white institutions; and when they tried to get ahead on their own, they faced a number of obstacles ranging from the absence of an entrepreneurial culture within the black community to the unavailability of credit. But perhaps the greatest obstacle, a psychological one, was the product of a white paternalism, as reflected in a host of well-meaning social programs and race-based preferences, that implied that blacks couldn't hack it on their own.*

I emerged from that lunch with the conviction that the best way to help blacks was to address the obstacles that held them back economically. That meant, among many other things, helping black entrepreneurs to find the training and capital required to launch viable businesses and black families to own their own homes. I believed that only when sufficient numbers of them had in fact hacked it on their own would blacks develop the sense of empowerment that would allow them to feel truly equal. I'll confess that when I touched on this theme on the campaign trail, I heard boos from rednecks in the back of the hall, and (I regret to say) the Conservative Party had its share of them. When elected to the Senate two years later, that was how I tried to help blacks become full participants in the American enterprise.

WW: When the campaign was over, you didn't say, "This was fun; I think I'll try this again"?

JLB: No. To the contrary, I told the press that it had been a great experience but never again. The New York *Daily News* ran the story under a headline that read, "First and Last Hurrah." Then, in the next couple of years, in 1969 and 1970, some very strange things started happening in the United States. I refer to the campus violence, the anti-war protests, the bombings and flag-burnings, the rejection of traditional standards that dominated the headlines during that period. At that time I was spending a considerable amount of time in places like Australia and the Philippines. What was going on in the States created headlines everywhere I went. I grew up thinking these sorts of things couldn't happen in the United States. We had too much sense. We had legal procedures, political procedures that allowed people who had grudges and problems to work them out within the system. I recall talking in Australia to a couple of Americans who had immigrated there because they felt the United States had had it. All of this aroused some Boy Scout impulses in me, especially as Charlie Goodell, whom Governor Rockefeller had appointed to serve out Bobby Kennedy's term, had begun to align himself with the anti-Vietnam forces and some of the (to my mind) ruinous social positions being advocated by campus radicals. So I returned from the Philippines with the thought that, based on my performance two years earlier and given Goodell's perceived shift from the conservative to the liberal wing of the Republican Party since moving from the House of Representatives to the Senate, it might not be implausible for me to win a primary contest for the Republican nomination. So, with great hesitation, I broached the subject with Ann, and she said OK based on the understanding that I would only undertake another race if I had a realistic chance of winning. So this was in earnest. I then met with Dan Mahoney and a couple of other people; and the first thing I learned was that because I had resumed my Connecticut voting residence in 1969, thereby forfeiting my New York registration, I could not challenge Goodell's nomination in a primary election unless I received the Republican Party's permission to do so. By virtue of that lack of foresight, I had to abandon the thought because Nelson Rockefeller controlled the Republican Party and he was not about to authorize a challenge to his nominee. So what I now had to find out was whether there was any possibility of winning as a third-party candidate. Incidentally, I am not sure I see the relevance of all of this to the legal background of a federal judge.

WW: Here's my view about that. I believe that the purpose of these interviews is much broader than that. You are a very unusual person. You've been in all three branches, and I want to talk at the end about comparing all of the experiences. So all of this is fascinating. And, in any event, you are not going to deprive me nor anybody else who listens to these tapes of the pleasure of hearing these stories. More to the point, who you are and who you are as a judge has been affected not only by your experiences at the Yale Law School, but I suspect much more by your experiences in the Senate. Have I persuaded you?

JLB: I yield. In any event, I decided that I wouldn't run unless somebody could assure me (a) that it was possible for a third-party candidate to win the election; (b) that I would be perceived at the outset as a credible candidate (credibility being essential if I were to secure the press coverage and financial support necessary for a successful campaign); and (c) that I could secure the initial financing required to establish the organizational base I would have to have in order to establish that credibility. So somebody suggested that I get hold of Clif White — F. Clifton White. Does that name mean anything to you?

WW: No.

JLB: He recently died — fascinating man. He made his national reputation by masterminding Barry Goldwater's nomination at the 1964 Republican National Convention. Absolute attention to detail. He was a native New Yorker and was very familiar with the structure and organization of the political machinery in New York, at the county level and so on. At one point he was the state Commissioner of Transportation. He paid enormous attention to detail, took every contingency into account in his planning. I spoke to Clif White and retained him to find the answers to the three questions. To find them, however, he would need to commission a poll, which would cost about $11,000. A family in New York City came up with enough money to pay for the poll and Clif's retainer. The poll satisfied him that there was enough public support for the positions that would distinguish me from the two major party candidates to make a victory in a three-way race possible. But no additional significant money was in sight. In the meantime, the date was rapidly approaching by which I would have to announce my candidacy in order to get on the ballot. Once I announced, I had another period in which I had to sign an affidavit that would commit me to remain a candidate. Clif was confident I would be viewed as a credible candidate provided I secured adequate financing, but I had to take a chance and commit to the race before there was any assurance that I would receive the funding required for a serious race. One critical need at the outset was a highly visible headquarters in New York City. That was really essential. The press had to have evidence that ours was a serious operation. We also had to have telephones. Because the campaign committees of several of the candidates for the 1968 Democratic presidential nomination had large debts outstanding, New York landlords were refusing to lease space, and Mother Bell declined to install telephones, unless all charges were paid in advance through election day. A friend of mine came to the rescue by lending the campaign sufficient securities to enable us to borrow $50,000 on the understanding that he would be repaid out of a portion of the first receipts from a fundraising mailing that that money would also finance. So that enabled us to lease the same space on Lexington Avenue that Bobby Kennedy had used in his presidential primary campaign two years earlier. We had the phones with which to make and receive calls, and we were off to the races.

But to remain in the race, it was necessary to have an effective organization and the money to keep it oiled and to spread the glad tidings of my candidacy. Clif White served as my campaign manager and quickly demonstrated his extraordi-

nary skills in building our organization and shaping its strategies. Clif enlisted David Jones as the campaign's executive director. Dave was an organizational genius who had worked closely with both the Young Americans for Freedom and Young Republicans organizations. As a result, he was able to recruit some stars of the nascent conservative movement to work for me. My research team, for example, consisted of Jackee Schafer (a future chairman of the Council on Environment Quality), Dan Oliver (a future chairman of the Federal Trade Commission), and Tony Dolan (a future presidential speechwriter).

An astonishing thing about my 1970 campaign was the number of volunteers I was able to attract, and they weren't limited to gray-haired reactionaries. The year had been marked by student protests and young Americans were supposed to be in revolt against everything I represented. That fall, under what was called the "Princeton Plan," colleges up and down the Eastern Seaboard gave their students several weeks off so that young idealists could become involved in politics in what was considered a critical year. To the astonishment of the press, more of them were licking stamps, stuffing envelopes, and manning telephones in the Buckley headquarters than in those of my two opponents combined. Nor were the volunteers limited to my New York City headquarters. As I moved around the state, I kept running into men and women who, on their own initiative and at their own expense, had rented storefronts from which to distribute my campaign literature and solicit votes.

I even had a volunteer from Hollywood, John Wayne, who sent me the raw tape of an endorsement. On viewing it, we saw a shot of Wayne in full cowboy regalia walking to a stool. He sat on it, and then turned to the camera and said: "If I lived in New York, you can bet your boots that I'd vote for Jim Buckley." That was it, and I'm told it proved effective. I celebrated its first showing by taking a group of Youths for Buckley volunteers to see the opening of a new Wayne film.

Even with the most enthusiastic volunteers, however, a campaign requires money, and mine needed a great deal of it when we started to run our television ads. In those days, campaign reformers hadn't placed the caps on individual contributions that have since made panhandling a major preoccupation of candidates who aren't wealthy enough to finance their own campaigns. As a result, I had very little to do with money-raising and never made a telephone call asking for a donation. That task was handled by yet another volunteer, a New York City *securities dealer and outdoorsman named Leon J. Weil, who did a most competent job in finding the money required to make mine an effective campaign. We were able to raise around $2,000,000—the amount that my Democratic opponent, Dick Ottinger, had spent in his primary campaign alone. (The disparity in the total amounts spent in our respective campaigns convinced me that money can't buy an election so long as opposing candidates have enough to get their messages heard. Anything beyond that is apt to be overkill.)*

WW: To a certain extent the rest is history. What do you remember most about that race? This is a very turbulent time in New York and everywhere across the United States. The war is raging.

JLB: And there are people who like seeing the flag burned.

WW: And there's a lot going on. You had been out of the country; and it was interesting, something that you said a little while ago, that a lot of your perception about what was going on was what you were reading in foreign newspapers. What did you find when you came back?

JLB: Well, you had this rampant lawlessness that was being condoned by college presidents and the editorial boards of papers like the *New York Times*. I thought there were serious social problems and the country as a whole was not yet ready to ditch Vietnam.

WW: How did you feel about that?

JLB: I thought that having gone in there, we should win it. I had no sympathy with the violence—the burning and bombing—that was associated with so much of the student protests. A lot of people agreed with me, because the money began coming in, and I was assured of enough to put up a decent race. I found that I was on the same wavelength with all kinds of people all over the state. I was well received, although there were some places, mostly campuses, where I was forbidden to go. I did go to some campuses—typically small Catholic colleges.

WW: It was a very angry time.

JLB: But it was hectic racing back and forth, which was planned to take advantage of the several distinct media markets that exist in New York. So long as you didn't overdo it, if you turned up in Utica, you would be met by the local press and broadcasting media, and you would be carried in the evening news programs and the next morning's papers. Ditto Buffalo, Albany, Syracuse, and so on. We had our debates. I worked with some wonderful people on my campaign and research staffs and had exceptional advance work. But it was not until early in October at a rally in Garden City, Long Island, that I suddenly realized that there was a real possibility that I might win. There was real enthusiasm.

I was asked a little earlier what I remembered most about my Senate race. No one thing stands out other than the roar in the Waldorf Astoria ballroom when I announced that I appeared to have won (TV networks would not concede the fact until the early hours of the following morning) and, with it, the awesome realization that I was being catapulted into an utterly new life. These, however, are some of the vignettes that linger with me.

The morning the newspapers carried the story of my candidacy, I received a call from Mickey Maye, the head of New York City's firemen's union asking for a meeting. He and an aide arrived at Catawba's office early that afternoon. As soon as we had shaken hands, Mickey announced that the union was going to endorse me. When the aide brought up the subject of legislation, Mickey shut him up. It was enough that I stood by our men in Vietnam and had called for enforcing the law against student vandals and arsonists. It was a great way to begin a campaign. Mickey's endorsement was followed by that of the city's powerful Policemen's Benevolent Association and other police organizations throughout the state. My "law and order" stand had struck an important chord among those charged with maintaining them. It also struck a chord among the leaders of the building trade unions who had organized a spectacular march up Broadway in protest against the flag-burning Vietnam protestors, and who gave me the substantial benefit of their benign neutrality.

I dreaded retail campaigning (e.g., being pushed into a supermarket on an early Saturday morning and being required to go up to housewives in curlers and say,"Hi, I'm Jim Buckley and I am running for the Senate") and suspect I wasn't very good at it. What I did enjoy and believe I did well in were televised debates and interviews. It was fun to be able to match wits, and these occasions enabled

Debating with encumbent Charlie Goodell
and Congressman Dick Ottinger.

me to present my views and the reasons for them on a wide range of issues. It was in the course of the debates that I came to know and grow fond of Charlie Goodell and to feel a bit sorry for Dick Ottinger. Dick had actually stated, at one campaign rally, that if I were elected, children would be bayoneted in the streets. I had fun teasing him about this in our TV appearances. Unlike the stilted, tightly controlled presidential debates of recent times, ours tended to be free wheeling. It was possible to give and take, and none of us abused the privilege. Dick was something of a Johnnie-one-note, that note being the condition of New York City's subways. Charlie and I didn't think this was a federal concern and would wink at one another every time Dick raised the subject.

And speaking of Charlie, I particularly remember the Archdiocese of New York's Al Smith Dinner, which is THE major event of any political season in New York City. It is a white tie affair that fills the Waldorf Astoria ballroom. The "head table" consists of tiers of daises at which just about every major office holder in New York is seated along with the candidates who hope to replace them. My seat was immediately above that of former Governor Thomas Dewey, who was seated next to Charlie. Halfway through the dinner, an aide came up to Charlie with a copy of an early edition of the New York Daily News. After a hurried, whispered conversation, the two of them left. Dewey then turned around and said to me, "Charlie keeps asking for advice, but he never takes it." What triggered Charlie's abrupt departure was a front page headline saying that the White House was tacitly supporting me. By then, Charlie was a distant third in the polls and, the next day, he made an emotional appearance on television in which he stated that he would not quit the race, as some had been urging him to do in the belief that he would merely split the liberal vote and allow me to sneak in.

I also recall the day I became the beneficiary of the legendary independence of the people of New York's sparsely settled "North Country." I was on my first campaign trip to the area when an excited campaign worker told me that the wife of popular Republican Congressman Bob McEwen was in the audience. She was; and before the meeting was over, she announced that I would be receiving the congressman's endorsement. This was an act of political courage because Governor Rockefeller had named Goodell to fill the vacancy created by Robert Kennedy's assassination, and the governor was known to use his considerable powers to keep Republican officeholders in line. Bob's early action made it easier for other prominent Republicans to follow suit. These endorsements were critically important because I couldn't expect to win unless sufficient numbers of Republicans came to think of me as one of their own. I was also endorsed by a respected Democratic congressman, Jim Delaney. This was also important because Jim's Queens County constituency contained large numbers of the socially conservative Democrats whom I would also have to reach.

And then there was my private plane . . . well, not mine, but one that was made available to the campaign by a friend of a friend anytime we could produce a pilot qualified to fly it. It was a converted World War II A-20 bomber, and it was flown by yet another volunteer, a Pan American Airways pilot who moonlit for us in between his round-trip flights to Europe. It was a great way to travel, and made it possible to reach corners of New York we might otherwise have missed.

Overlaying all of these memories is that of the aching tiredness that overtook me during the last few weeks before Election Day. A political campaign is a brutal psychic as well as physical experience. You are never alone, and there is almost always a reporter on hand to record the inevitable gaffes. In each of my Senate races, I developed a bad cold during the final two or three weeks that I could never take time off to nurse. The only humane thing about a political campaign is that it ends on a day certain.

But the last day of a campaign can be joyous, especially if the polls indicate, as they did in 1970, that you have a chance of winning. But win or lose, you know that the ordeal is about to be over. In 1970, it wasn't over until midnight. The last campaign event was a one hour radio debate which began at 11:00 P.M. I was tired, snuffling, happy, and munching on a late late sandwich as I watched Charlie and Dick begin the program (in the words of one reporter) "clawing at each other, each questioning the other's liberal credentials." And then to bed and a long, long sleep before getting up the next morning to cast my vote.

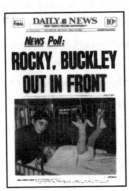

October 25

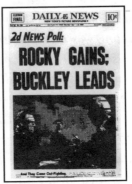

October 29

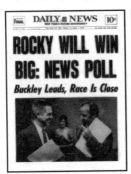

November 2

November 4

WW: What did your family think about this effort? Your wife and your children?

JLB: I did not involve them. The children did turn up at a county fair on Labor Day, when the campaign was officially launched; and Ann got dragged into a number of coffee klatches, but I didn't exploit them. They were still fairly young.

WW: I guess your oldest was probably just entering college?

JLB: He was 16 and still in high school.

WW: They were not in college yet so they were not caught up in the university scene.

JLB: Right. In any event, election day finally rolled around; and I won. It was really an experience, and the networks did not want to concede. I won with just 40 percent of the vote, and Goodell ended up in third place by a substantial margin. There is one point I would like to make about this election. The conventional wisdom is that I was able to win that race because Goodell and the Democratic candidate, Dick Ottinger, split the liberal vote. I don't think that is true. One of these days I am going to dig up an article in the now extinct *New York Mirror* that supports this view. The *Mirror* had an interview with Charlie a few days after the election. He was asked why he hadn't pulled out of the race when it became clear that he could not win it. A number of persons had urged him to withdraw. He told the reporter that that would not have changed the outcome because his polls showed that his major support was coming not from liberals, but from upstate Republicans, who are generally conservative. Had he pulled out, I would surely have received the majority of those votes. I'm told that I received 40 percent of the blue collar vote. I got a large proportion of the traditionally Democratic, socially conservative, ethnic vote in New York, people who didn't condone the burning of American flags.

I have done the digging. The article wasn't in the extinct Mirror, *but in the alive and lively* New York Post. *Here is the critical passage:*

> *Goodell said he had concluded from a number of polls that his departure from the race would have "guaranteed" victory for Conservative Senator-elect James L. Buckley rather than for Democratic Rep. Richard L. Ottinger.*
>
> *"We analyzed where Buckley's strength was," he said. "Our analysis was that a good portion of it was Republican. A good portion was upstate and suburban.*
>
> *"And if I had said, 'I'm withdrawing. Please don't vote for me. Vote for Ottinger,' that vote wasn't going to go to Ottinger. It was a Republican vote that would've gone to Buckley. My withdrawing at that stage would have guaranteed the election for Mr. Buckley."*

WW: It was really a transitional time in American politics.

JLB: Right.

Some campaign postscripts. Although the carpetbagger issue never emerged during the race, Dick Ottinger tried to keep it alive through radio ads consisting of a telephone operator saying, "Sorry, I can't find a James Buckley in Rochester. No James Buckley in Syracuse either . . . or in Manhattan . . .," and so on through a litany of New York cities. He behaved badly election night, telling his supporters: "None of us should forget that 62 percent of the voters of New York State today reaffirmed their desire for decent values in our society." (By the time all the votes had been counted, the ranks of humane New Yorkers had shrunk to 60 percent.) Two days later, having presumably exhausted New York State telephone books, he was able to track me down in Sharon to congratulate me on my victory. I've made fun of him in this chronicle, I know. Actually, he was a decent man but, for whatever reason, not up to a statewide campaign.

The New York Times *had a more difficult time recovering its civility. A week or so before election day, it had run an editorial asserting that if I were to win, there would be no way of stopping "the ruthless night riders of the radical right." The day after the election, it stated that although I was not an extremist, my victory "was built on a frank appeal to the frustrations and fears of New Yorkers unhappy about the disordered state of current society and yearning for pat solutions. His success will strengthen the forces intent on turning the Republican party in this state away from the imaginative policies initiated by Governor Rockefeller." The following morning, however, the* Times *adopted a more conciliatory tone. It acknowledged that my vote had "cut across normal party and*

Election night euphoria.

economic lines" and had reflected "the sincere concern many New Yorkers have over problems which are real, however inadequate the programs put forward by [any of the three parties] to deal with them." It then concluded: "His mandate is just as valid as the comparable one Mayor Lindsay received last year when he emerged victorious as the Liberal Party nominee in a race for reelection against two conservative rivals." It then expressed the hope that, "as a man of intelligence and capacity," I might "turn a negative vote into positive programs directed at reconciliation, not deeper animosities in urban society."

But the commentary that most delighted me was contained in a column by Robert Mayer that appeared two days after my election in the Long Island daily, Newsday. It was captioned "The Shame of New York." Herewith some of Mr. Mayer's turgid words:

> *It crept in during the night. It was hanging over the city when we awoke yesterday, gray and imponderable, like the fog. Morning became afternoon and still it would not go away, the shame, the burden, the thorny crown of collective guilt. We sat in darkened apartments, Dostoyevskyan, vaguely aware of gray light filtering in through windows, unable to stir outside, unwilling to face our neighbors, eyes cast down, unseeing. New York! New York had come to this.*
>
> *James Buckley had kept his first campaign promise. He had pledged that the world would not end the morning after he was elected, and it hadn't. The pushers were still out there near the schoolyards, shoving heroin into the hands of high school kids. The murderers and the rapists were still walking the streets. The public schools were still a scandal. The cost of living was still outrageous. None of the candidates, not Buckley, not Ottinger, not Goodell, could change that. But the Buckley victory had added something new, a heavy patina of shame that covered it all; the knowledge that New York had turned its back on the afflicted, had voted for bombs instead of bread. . . .*
>
> *If all of this sounds bitter, it is. It is difficult to be a gracious loser when you are branded before the nation, as all New Yorkers are today, with the letter C for Conservative on your forehead. But I suppose, in time, the shame will pass, and we shall learn to live with Buckley, just as, in time, we learned to live with Nixon. Already the lady of the house is planning to venture outside, as soon as she can find her dark glasses.*

I was told later that the Mayers not only ventured outside, they decided to leave New York altogether to find refuge in some less tainted state. The column is framed on a deep purple mat and hangs in a place of honor in my office.

In fairness to myself, I should note that I wasn't universally regarded as an ogre. The New York Daily News, for example, headlined a feature story about me with "Mr. Nice Goes to Washington." Given what Leo Durocher had to say about nice guys (they "finish last"), this may not have been a compliment. A New York magazine article titled "What Kind of Monster Is Jim Buckley?" contained the following backhanded kudos:

> *Ottinger doesn't deliver. He promised the people of New York a monster, and all he could produce was Jim Buckley. It was as if Dr. Frankenstein had attached all the electrodes, thrown the switch and come up with a Barbie doll. . . .*
>
> *The debate ended bloodlessly shortly after midnight, and the monster, naturally and easily, made the first move to shake hands with his opponents. Everyone shook hands. Goodell left the studio first, and then Ottinger—who didn't hear an aide whisper, "No, no, no"—shared an elevator with Buckley. As they reached the lobby, the aide sprang to hold the door open for Dick Ottinger. The monster held the door open for his aides.*
>
> *Sometimes, it's so hard to remember which side you're supposed to dislike. . . . As a monster, no matter what he says or how he votes in Washington, he's going to have trouble cracking the top five.*

Even though I failed the monster test, some New Yorkers refused to accept The People's verdict, or at least that of a plurality, and did what diehards do these days: they went to court. An ad hoc group that called itself the Committee for Fair Play for Voters filed a suit in federal district court challenging the constitutionality of my election on the theory that the Seventeenth Amendment to the Constitution, which provides for the direct election of senators, required that they be elected by an absolute majority of the votes cast. The court dismissed the suit on technical grounds on December 2, 1970. An appeal was taken and, with a speed that may qualify for the Guinness Book of Records, on December 11 the court of appeals declared that the amendment's requirement that senators be "elected by the people" was satisfied by a mere plurality. But the diehards hadn't given up. Another group, with the ingenuous name of "New Yorkers for a New York Senator," asked the Senate to deny me a seat on the ground that I was not a New Yorker, citing the fact that my wife and children lived in Connecticut, that I had been sighted attending Sunday Mass there, and that that was where I maintained my principal home. The Senate responded with a formal ruling holding that my physical presence in New York on election day satisfied the Constitution's condition that a senator, "when elected, be an Inhabitant of that State for which he shall be chosen."

These attempts to deny me a Senate seat resulted in the establishment of two legal precedents. Thus weeks before I was formally sworn in, I had the satisfaction of knowing that I was already making law.

WW: We have been at this about two hours, and your voice is probably going to give out. I propose that we quit and that we'll start next time and talk about the Senate and move on to your judicial career. Is that all right?

JLB: OK.

The Senate, the State Department, Radio Free Europe/Radio Liberty, Becoming a Judge

WW: Where we left off last time, if you will recall, is with your being elected to the Senate. I want to pick up from there and talk a little bit about your life in the Senate, what committees you were on, what your assignments were, what issues you focused on. Why don't we start by talking about your committee assignments.

But first, a word about the experience of being dropped into the middle of what was once known as the world's greatest deliberative body without an ounce of experience with either legislative work or the mechanics of government. Shortly after the election, that year's ten senators-elect were invited to Washington for briefings on the nuts and bolts of our new jobs. At the outset, we learned that senators are outrageously pampered. Need a haircut? There's a barber shop just down the hall from the Senate chamber that is maintained for the exclusive use of senators. There would be no charge for the cut, but we would be expected to tip the barber one dollar. (Thanks to public complaints, this perk has since been abolished.) Not feeling well this morning? Check in at the Office of the Attending Physician, a well-staffed clinic in the Capitol Building where, at no charge, members of Congress can receive competent medical care. Need a workout or a swim? These were available in the top floor of what was then the Old Senate Office Building. Need to take a trip? Your secretary will make the airline and hotel reservations and arrange to have you driven to the airport and picked up at your destination. Are you driving to the airport? Leave your car in the parking lot reserved, again at no charge, for members of Congress, the Supreme Court, and ambassadors. Flying overseas? A diplomatic passport will ease your passage through airport formalities. And so it went.

I also learned that I would rank 99 in the Senate pecking order. Adlai Stevenson III, who had been elected to fill a vacancy and had been sworn in soon after the

election, was at the top of the new class. I was also outranked by the seven senators-elect who had served in the House of Representatives. Under the rules, however, I outranked the remaining neophyte, Lawton Chiles, because New York had a larger population than his state, Florida. This seemed like a trivial matter at the time, but I would soon be introduced to the importance of seniority when it came to picking committees.

In the Senate, committee assignments are made by the Democratic and Republican caucuses, but I had been elected as the candidate of New York's Conservative Party in a contest in which I had unseated a Republican. When I applied for membership in the Republican caucus, my admission was strongly opposed by Senator Javits, whom I had run against two years earlier. After several days of media speculation and a certain amount of fingernail biting on my part, I was admitted by a vote of 41 to 3, but I was listed in the Congressional Directory *as "Conservative-Republican" in recognition of the party that had sent me to Washington. It was an accurate description of how I would be voting.*

Which brings me to the subject of party labels. Contrary to what most Americans believe, we do not have a single Democratic or Republican party in this country. Rather, we have 50 state parties that come together every four years to nominate a presidential candidate. The regional differences between them can be profound. Thus although I voted most often with Republicans from the Midwest and West, I voted with Southern Democrats more often than I did with Republicans from the Northeast. The southerners of those days believed in a strong defense and were still averse to concentrating power in Washington.

My most pressing task was to acquire a staff. I had to find over 40 individuals capable of handling a grab-bag of responsibilities ranging from the analysis of pending legislation, to helping constituents thread their way through bureaucratic mazes, to dealing with the thousands of letters and telegrams I would soon be receiving. Fortunately, David Jones, who had demonstrated both his political horse sense and organizational abilities during my campaign, agreed to serve as my administrative assistant. Dave immediately plunged into the job of recruiting a staff that proved second to none in brainpower.

But even the best of staffs is capable of a monumental gaffe. I shall never forget the panic I felt in the spring of 1976 while on a plane en route to a political dinner in upstate New York. As usual, my secretary had handed me a folder containing a briefing memorandum for the evening as well as a copy of the remarks I would be delivering. Because I had given the same talk a few weeks earlier, I stuffed the folder into my briefcase unexamined. It was only after I was airborne that I noticed that the folder was uncommonly thick. It was thick because, in addition to the usual materials, it contained a tape cassette and some sheet music. That's how I learned that, following the dinner, I was to serve as the narrator in a performance of Aaron Copland's "Lincoln Portrait" by the local high school's prize-winning band. I broke out in a sweat of arctic proportions. I had never heard the music, had no way of playing the tape, and it was far too late to back out. And so

I spent the 35 or 40 minutes that remained before we landed trying to learn my part ("Abe Lincoln said; this is what Abe Lincoln said. . . .").

I was met at the airport by both the band's conductor and the man who would be driving me to the dinner. The conductor only had time to tell me that he would nod in my direction each time I was to speak a line. That was it—the sum total of my preparation. The people at the reception preceding the dinner must have found me oddly distracted, and I couldn't have been much of a dinner companion as I poked at my food, dreading what lay ahead. But I gave my talk, and was driven off to the school.

I reached the auditorium in time to hear the number preceding the intermission. The band was absolutely first rate. I tried to find a corner where I could review the score one more time, but I kept being interrupted by well-wishers. And then the moment of truth arrived: the intermission was over, my constituents were back in their seats, and I walked onto the stage for my unrehearsed concert debut. The band played the opening bars, the conductor nodded in my direction, and I managed to deliver my opening line, and then the next and the next on time and in appropriately measured and audible tones. But the lights kept growing dimmer (for dramatic effect, apparently) until I could no longer read the text. So I had to interrupt the proceedings and suggest we start over again. That we did; and, miraculously, we proceeded to the end without a glitch. It was a moving piece of music, beautifully performed, and the audience gave us a standing ovation. My guardian angel had not deserted me.

It proved a wonderful experience, and the staffer who had committed me to the event was forgiven. I had only myself to blame, however, for another, more prolonged crisis. My mail room staff had to answer or at least acknowledge every one of the thousands of letters, postcards, and telegrams that flooded my office every week. This politically sensitive operation required that I approve the staff-drafted form letters dealing with the major issues of the day. Unfortunately, I once approved a rather pedantic discussion of the then very hot issue of Northern Ireland which gave a reasonably honest account of the nature of today's Irish Republican Army. It caused such an uproar in New York Irish circles that there was serious question as to whether it would be prudent for me to appear at the St. Patrick's Day parade that year. This required some urgent repair work among an important constituency which New York *magazine recorded in an article entitled*

"The Greening of a Senator." The reference was to green as in "shamrock," not as in "environment" where my credentials were secure.

I was able to attend the St. Patrick's Day parade, but it was a close call politically because I was viewed as an Irish-American by New York's important Irish community even though I am a product of the melting pot and have never thought of myself as other than "American." (A Polish intellectual I met in Warsaw made an interesting observation about our growing preoccupation with ethnicity. He said the trend worried him because the melting pot had produced an alloy, which is strong, while dividing our population into hyphenated groups threatened to convert our country into a mosaic, which is brittle.) Nevertheless, doubts about my Irish loyalties lingered on. As a result, four years later, when Ann and I were invited to attend a large dinner given by Queen Elizabeth II on the royal yacht Britannia, which was visiting New York in honor of the bicentennial of our declaration of independence from the British Crown, we had to sneak around a group

of pro-IRA protestors in order to board the ship unseen. Fortunately, my presence there was unreported, let alone the fact that the iron rules of protocol had seated Ann at Prince Philip's right, and me at the Queen's left. (I was outranked by U.N. Secretary General Waldheim, who sat at her right.)

Which brings me to my relations with the press. During my New York campaigns, and later while in office, I developed the highest respect for the "working press." The reporters who covered me asked searching questions, filed accurate reports, and were usually good company. Whatever problems I had were with their editors — a complaint that is common, I suspect, among elected officeholders. The substance could be edited out of the reporter's copy; the placement of a story could effectively bury it; and if no reporter was assigned to cover an event, the public would never know what was said or done there. I enjoyed good relations with the reporters and held weekly "press breakfasts" in my Senate office for the Washington representatives of the New York media. As a result, we came to know and trust one another.

At times, however, even the best of reporters can be, well, overreaching, and the New York Times' Martin Tolchin was among the very best. He had been assigned the task of covering the New York, Connecticut, and New Jersey congressional delegations, and he did a first rate job of it. One day, however, each member of those delegations received a letter from Marty in which he declared that the Watergate revelations had caused the American public great concern over the mixture of money and politics. Therefore, would we please send him a statement of our net worth as well as a copy of our most recent income tax return. This led to calls for emergency meetings of the three delegations to decide how to handle this hot potato. I declined to attend the New York meeting, but those who did decided to comply with the imperial demand. Instead, I wrote Marty that although I received on average more than 4,000 communications a week, my mail room had advised me that none had ever inquired about my personal finances, and that it was "presumptuous of the Times to see its own curiosity concerning private matters as synonymous with the public interest." I then noted that "it is a well-known, though regrettable, fact that the New York Times has a far greater influence over the public and financial affairs of this nation than do the New York, New Jersey and Connecticut Congressional delegations combined," and suggested that the Times could "demonstrate its good faith by publishing a statement of the net worth and copies of the latest income tax returns of" its publisher and senior editors. I issued a press release containing a copy of Marty's letter as well as my response.

Three days later, Nixon's congressional liaison officer, Tom Korlogos, handed me an envelope. It contained a copy of my press release to which was stapled a memorandum to the president that read, "We thought the enclosed press release from Senator Buckley's office might amuse you." At the top of it, Nixon had scribbled

"Dear Jim—Brilliant!" Although I understand that Marty felt hurt that I had made our letters public, we continued on good terms.
Now back to the question about my committee assignments.

JLB: Well, over a six-year period you wander from one to the other until you find your permanent legislative homes. And if you began, as I did, as number 99 on the Senate totem pole, you don't get the plums immediately. I did get one committee assignment I was anxious to have that, fortunately, was not high on most people's list. It was then called the Public Works Committee. What attracted me to it was that it had the primary jurisdiction over environmental issues, and I was very interested in that area. The environment was only just beginning to be a hot legislative field, but it was one that I had highlighted in both my campaigns. In fact, it was such a new area of public concern that one of the Conservative Party fathers wrote me a stern letter during the 1968 campaign scolding me for wasting time on such a non-issue. So I was able to get assigned to Public Works as one of my major committees. The way the Senate worked at that time, each senator was assigned to two major committees and one minor committee. My other major committee, which was not all that major, was Air and Space. My minor committee was the Committee for the District of Columbia. Within two years, I had moved from Air and Space to the Interior Committee and from D.C. to the Joint Atomic Energy Committee. Two years later, I moved from Interior to Commerce. Towards the end of my term I also joined the Budget Committee, which had been recently authorized and was not classified as a major committee. I remained on Public Works throughout my six years; and because it was so unglamourous, I ended up as its ranking minority member.

WW: Even though that involves the environment?

JLB: Yes.

WW: Well, things have changed.

JLB: Yes, things have changed, although the environment was becoming important in those days. Howard Baker outranked me on the committee, but when he became the Senate minority leader, he had to give up his position as the committee's ranking minority member. This explains my meteoric rise. I was very active in the first major revision of the Water Quality Act and in work on a number of new areas of environmental legislation. And because I was on the Interior Committee during our first energy crisis—the 1973 or 1974 Arab oil embargo—I worked on important legislation in that area as well. My key interest throughout my Senate career was in the development of intelligent environmental regulation, by which I meant regulation that balanced benefits against costs and that was not so rigid as to inhibit the development of new and more efficient technologies for controlling pollution. Federalism was always a preoccupation of mine and so I tried, whatever committee I was on, to draw lines as to what was an appropriate area for the exercise of federal as opposed to state and local responsibility. I'll give you two examples. I believed that, in most instances, the control of pollution requires national regulation for the simple reason that air and water move across state lines. But when we worked on legislation to control noise pollution, I took the position that we had to distinguish between noise generated from local or stationary sources, e.g. jackhammers, and that created by mobile sources like airplanes and trucks. I wanted to limit federal controls to sources that would cross state boundaries in the normal course. One of the proposals that the Commerce Committee held hearings on was no-fault insurance. I thought that no-fault was a great idea, but it seemed to me that the states were quite competent to decide for themselves whether mandating no-fault car insurance was in the best interest of their citizens. Moreover, experience had proven that no problems affecting interstate commerce had resulted from the fact that a car registered in a no-fault state was involved in an accident in a state that did not have no-fault. Anyway, that's the kind of line between appropriate and inappropriate federal action that I consciously drew when I was in the Senate.

In considering proposals for the expansion of federal authority, I applied the logic of the Constitution's division of governmental responsibilities between the federal and state governments. Because the Supreme Court had managed to erase just about every limitation on federal authority, there was little point in looking to the Court's decisions for coherent guidance. Nor was I tempted to because members of the legislative and executive branches have an independent obligation to apply the Constitution as they understand it. To me, at least, it was obvious from the nature

"Always smile when you meet the press." I tried.

of the powers conferred on Congress by the Constitution and from the later adoption of the Tenth Amendment reserving to the states and the people all powers not assigned by the Constitution to Congress, that the Founders intended to limit the new government's authority to areas that lay beyond the competence of state and local governments or required uniform rules. Those limitations, of course, had a more fundamental constitutional purpose. The Founders considered federalism, along with the separation of powers, to be essential safeguards of our liberties.

Although the Supreme Court has emasculated the Tenth Amendment, I believed (and continue to believe) that this division of labor is sound public policy. It permits a diversity of approaches to societal problems and, where feasible, it assigns rule-making responsibilities to the levels of government that are the closest to the people and most sensitive to their needs. As a consequence, when considering the merits of a particular bill, I would consciously apply the ancient "Rule of Subsidiarity" which holds that political authority should be assigned to the lowest level that is capable of exercising it. It was for this reason that I was comfortable with the role the federal government had assumed in protecting the environment. Air, water, and wildlife ignore political boundaries. Emissions from factories in Ohio can affect the health of New Yorkers; and New Jersey wetlands play a critical role in the life cycles of fish and other species that range up and down the Atlantic seaboard. I admit that it isn't always easy to decide where the line between federal and state responsibility should be drawn in today's complex world, but I found the rule a useful analytical tool and a wonderful antidote to the impulse to centralize power.

WW: What about the Clean Air Act and the Clean Water Act? Wasn't this legislation being enacted during this time?

JLB: They were passed shortly before my election. I think one of them — the Water Quality Act — was passed in 1968 or '69; the Clean Air Act was passed in 1970. The first work I participated in when I joined the Public Works Committee was a thorough revision of the Water Quality Act in light of the experience gained during its first three years. In my next to last year, we started work on doing the same thing for the Clean Air Act, but that was quite a different experience. I might as well go into that now. After I was elected to the Senate, somebody gave me a study of Congress that had just been published by the Bar Association of the City of New York. It concluded that the work load of the average congressional office had doubled every five years since 1935. In my own experience it may not have doubled, but it came close to doubling within my six years; and my favorite datum in support of that conclusion is that in January 1971, the Public Works Committee began a thorough review of the Water Quality Act. It held a series of hearings with witnesses from industry, environmental organizations, state governments, you name it. Amendments to the existing act were drafted, debated, revised in Committee mark-up sessions, adopted by the Senate, reconciled with the House version, and adopted in final form by Congress and signed into law by the end of the year. We started doing the same exercise with the Clean Air Act in 1975. By that time, however, so many committee and subcommittee meetings were being scheduled at identical times that often we couldn't proceed with any work because of the lack of a quorum. Moreover, even when we had a quorum, our meetings were constantly being interrupted by bells summoning senators to the floor for roll call votes. In any event, it took over a year and a half before the Senate finally enacted its version of the overdue revisions of the Act. But because the House hadn't been able to report out its version of the amendments, Congress was unable to enact any amendments before the 94th Congress became history. That meant that the process had to begin all over again in 1977.

WW: Now there is a famous piece of legislation that seems to impact everybody's life all the time which is known as the Buckley Amendment. That's in a different area. Tell me a little bit about the origins of the Buckley Amendment. [*The amendment's official title is the Education Rights and Privacy Act of 1974.*]

JLB: That amendment had its origins in an article that a member of my staff called to my attention. It was a report on a study by a foundation in New Jersey which dealt with damage that too often resulted from the refusal by schools to provide parents with information concerning their children. That information would contain test results, teacher's comments, and gossip that was often inaccurate or prejudicial and could have the most devastating effects on the children's futures. It could affect their course assignments, assumptions as to their ability to learn, and so forth. Because parents were denied access to this information, they had no opportunity to correct errors or to challenge decisions affecting their children. The foundation had developed draft legislation to address these problems and had circulated it for comment by various academic organizations. The article caught my interest because I had long been concerned by the failure of too many educational bureaucrats to recognize that parents had the primary responsibility for the welfare and education of their children. The purpose of my amendment was to strengthen the parental role by requiring schools that received federal funding to provide parents, on request, with all information relating to their children. I will confess, however, to an intellectual dilemma. I had long believed, and continue to believe, that the federal government had no business involving itself in public education, that this was an area that should have remained the exclusive concern of state and local governments. So, although I voted for the Buckley Amendment, I voted against the bill to which it had been appended.

This illustrates a dilemma I constantly faced. Much of the legislation that came before me dealt with matters that I believed were not the proper concern of the federal government. But because I knew they would become law, I expended considerable energy trying to improve bills I knew I would have to vote against.

WW: I don't even know what it was an amendment to. Was it one of the higher education acts?

JLB: I forget. Whatever the underlying bill, the amendment was accepted by the chairman of the sponsoring committee, Senator Claiborne Pell. As you no doubt know, it has proven controversial. About 99 percent of the complaints have been directed to the fact that the amendment gives parents, and students who have attained the age of 18, the right to see letters of recommendation that have been squirreled away in academic files. Frankly, it had never occurred to me that this would be a problem. I had naïvely assumed that any letter of recommendation I had ever written would have been thrown away after it had served its purpose. Nevertheless, there is a provision in the amendment that enables a student to waive his right of inspection which is routinely availed of by students who solicit such letters, so I have always felt that this particular complaint was something of a red herring.

WW: Of all the things that you did, the Buckley Amendment does stand out as a memorable piece of legislation.

That may well be the case, but I now regret having introduced it. Parents ought to have access to school records that may adversely affect their children, but it is not the constitutional business of Congress to guarantee it. Even though I voted against the bill to which the amendment was attached, the net effect of my initiative in this case was to expand the federal role in education and create another regulatory regime. I should have known better, but it illustrates how difficult it is for a member of Congress to resist the temptation to do good, especially when the Supreme Court has virtually obliterated the distinction between federal and state responsibilities. What I do not regret, however, is the focus my amendment placed on parental rights. I believe it was the first legislation to emphasize parents' prime responsibility for the education of their children, a concern that was at the heart of another of my legislative initiatives, the tuition tax credit. As such, it was a forerunner of a concern for "family values" that has become a central part of the Republican credo.

JLB: Incidentally, one of the things that has irritated me is the way that some colleges will play games with the amendment. I have learned that many of them will refuse to provide parents with the grades of children who are 18 and over and blame me for it. Yet the amendment specifically provides that the parents of dependent children, whatever their age, have the right to get their marks.

WW: Well, that I didn't know; but it is an important piece of legislation and it has had a real impact on higher education. Some staff person brought it to your attention?

JLB: Yes, and I was intrigued with the issue. Another child-related bill that caught my interest came up for a vote in the fall of my first year. It was described as a bill to extend the Head Start Program and "other matters." Among the other matters was one that was described in the committee report as "revolutionary." It would initiate a federal child development program of extraordinary scope that would apply to every child in America irrespective of economic need. It had an estimated cost of a billion dollars after five years, back when a billion dollars purchased quite a few things. [*I was mistaken. The program would have cost $2 billion the second year and ballooned thereafter.*] I was the only person in the Senate to vote against the bill. It was subsequently vetoed for the reasons I had given when I tried to have the child development program eliminated. I later persuaded Walter Mondale, who was chairman of the sponsoring committee, that a lot of problems hadn't been looked into; and at a hearing on a new bill, he invited a couple of the experts I had recommended to testify before the committee. As a result, Senator Mondale and I subsequently cosponsored some amendments to a traditional child care bill that incorporated certain safeguards that the experts had recommended.

The very liberal Fritz Mondale referred to this unlikely collaboration as "the Minnesota-New York axis." Needless to say, this was about the only area where we did collaborate; and, of course, I routinely voted against the bills to which our amendments were attached. The bills were adopted, but in this case, my amendments had the effect of mitigating the damage the bills might otherwise cause.

WW: What were the issues that you found in that bill?

JLB: Aside from the fact that it would inaugurate a huge new federal program that virtually no one had examined with any care, it was critically flawed in many of its details. It would have resulted, in effect, in the warehousing of children with little thought to the consequences for the children. A number of studies were available at the time that demonstrated that infants could suffer significant developmental problems if more than two or three of them were placed in the care of a single adult, especially if that adult was changed every few days. One of them observed that, in the Soviet Union, the people who ran similar programs would not allow their own children to be placed in them. French authorities were cognizant of the harm that could be done infants if entrusted to institutional care at too young an age. So in France, mothers were not required to return to work for umpteen months. These are just some of the problems I saw with a program that the sponsors themselves described as revolutionary.

WW: This was a federal child care program?

JLB: It was far, far more than that—they called it child development. It went beyond meeting the needs of mothers who have to work. The fact was, no one studied this part of the bill. They all thought of it as the extension of existing, apple pie programs.

The innocent sounding title of the legislation was "A Bill to Provide for the Continuation of Programs Authorized Under the Economic Opportunities Act of 1964 and Other Purposes." The assumption was that it did little more than provide for a modest extension of a group of established anti-poverty programs including the very popular Head Start Program. Yet, as described in the committee report, the "other purposes" included the establishment (for the benefit of all children—not just the indigent) of "comprehensive physical and mental health, social and cognitive developmental services; . . . specially designed programs (including after school, summer, weekend, and overnight programs); identification and treatment of physical, mental, and emotional problems . . . ; prenatal services . . . ; special activities for physically, mentally, and emotionally handicapped children and children with special learning disabilities; training in the fundamentals of child development for family members and prospective parents; use of child advocates to assist children and parents in securing full access to other services and other activities." The program's "tune-up" cost was set at $100 million for the first year, but was projected to increase to $2 billion the second year and continue to increase every year thereafter until it reached $20 billion in 1980.

WW: Because it was something for children and everyone thought it had to be passed?

JLB: It was labeled as a bill to extend Head Start and other matters. The child development program was buried under "other matters." A "little old lady in tennis shoes" brought it to the attention of one of my upstate New York offices during the summer recess. It had been reported out shortly before the Senate took its August break, and it was scheduled as the first order of business after the Senate returned.

WW: The problems? Do you know who that woman was? It wasn't the woman in the Senate who wears tennis shoes?

JLB: No.

WW: Are there other issues or other legislation that you think of now as being important in your senatorial career?

JLB: I think I told you at the outset that I have a bad memory for specifics. Most of a senator's legislative work is done in committee, and it involves shaping the bills that become law rather than initiating them. That work can be highly important but tends to be invisible. I believe I had a definite impact on the environmental bills I worked on. One consistent effort was to require regulations to balance costs against benefits. But my first accomplishment during my work on the revision to the Water Quality Act does come to mind because of its parochial interest for New Yorkers. As originally enacted, this legislation provided for 60 percent federal financing of water cleanup programs initiated by the states. The committee decided to increase the reimbursement to 80 percent. This would have rewarded those states that had dragged their heels in meeting the requirements of the act. I was able to persuade the committee to apply the increase retroactively by reimbursing the early bird states the difference between 60 percent and 80 percent of the cost of the completed programs. This resulted in a rebate to New York of $900 million. I can also claim credit for a few items outside the scope of my committee work. For example, I liberated America from the tyranny of the ignition interlock seat belt, that pesky device that made it impossible to start the engine unless seat belts were attached—and sometimes it wouldn't let you start your car even when they were. I introduced the Senate resolution that led to the reduction of U.S. payments to the UN from 30 percent of the total to 25 percent. I also initiated some legislative ideas that I wasn't around to see enacted. I am credited, for example, with introducing the concept of indexing the income tax. I also was the first to introduce some other concepts that have been seriously discussed, if not enacted, in recent years, e.g., tax credits for school tuition payments, the outlawing of preferences based on race or sex, and a constitutional amendment protecting the unborn.

As this off-the-cuff list suggests, I had my fingers in a number of legislative pies, probably too many of them; but the ability to introduce a new concept or reform by proposing a bill or an amendment accompanied by a floor speech and a press release can prove irresistible. I knew that nothing would come of most of my initiatives, but I was (and am) a strong believer in the value of the exercise. It takes time for new ideas to germinate, but if they have merit and are periodically watered, they can take root and, in time, become law.

This was the case with my proposal that the federal income tax tables be adjusted annually to reflect changes in the cost-of-living index. Economist Milton Friedman had suggested the idea to me. He pointed out that inflation had the effect of increasing the tax burden on lower income taxpayers by pushing them into higher tax brackets even though the purchasing power of their incomes hadn't changed. Thus wage earners and pensioners receiving cost-of-living wage increases found themselves sending a larger percentage of their income to Washington than Congress had intended at the time the tax tables had been adopted. I liked the idea, drafted a bill to index the tax tables, and circulated it to the members of the Senate along with an explanatory letter inviting co-sponsorships. I then introduced the bill and issued a press release explaining its purpose in the hope that it would generate a column or two explaining its inherent equity to a wider audience (it didn't). In accordance with Senate rules, the bill was referred to the Finance Committee, where it proceeded to gather dust.

I later introduced an indexing amendment to a tax bill. It was tabled without discussion. In 1976, however, I had better luck. My initiative had attracted the attention of Senate Minority Leader Bob Griffin and my reintroduction of the amendment resulted in a genuine debate. I stressed the fact that by failing to take inflation into account, the existing law imposed significant tax increases by stealth on Americans who could least afford them. Finance Committee Chairman Russell Long, an extremely intelligent and wily man, acknowledged the merit of my argument in a backhanded way, but he opposed my amendment for two reasons: because the revenue loss would be significant, the adoption of my amendment would require Congress to raise taxes explicitly, which would be in no one's interest politically; and because his committee hadn't held hearings on my proposal, he couldn't estimate how much revenue would be lost if it were adopted. Long, however, promised to hold hearings on indexation the following year. In due course, my concept became law, but I wasn't around to savor the victory.

I can't claim the same cause and effect relationship for another idea, but I was the first to call for tuition tax credits to cover a portion of the cost of private education. I have always favored giving parents vouchers that would allow them a wider choice of schooling for their children, but I saw no constitutional basis for a federal voucher system. Congress, however, is entirely free to decide what personal expenditures may be deducted from income in the computation of taxes or credited against taxes otherwise payable to the federal government.

I also tried to amend the Constitution. My purpose was to restore protection to unborn children by reversing the Supreme Court's appalling decisions in Roe v. Wade *and* Doe v. Bolton. *I use the word "appalling" advisedly. The Court's discovery* ex nihilo *of an unlimited right to abortion overturned the laws of 50 states and overrode a 2,000-year-old Judeo-Christian ethic in which the intrinsic worth and equal value of every human life was secured by law. As I was reasonably familiar with basic biological principles, I was also astonished by the Court's reference to "the difficult question of when life begins," an example of what the journal of the California Medical Association described as the attempt to "separate the idea of abortion from the idea of killing" through "a curious avoidance of the scientific fact, which everyone really knows, that human life begins at conception." It was in part for this reason that the key section of my Human Life Amendment was framed in biological terms: "With respect to the right to life, the word 'person,' as used in this Article and in the Fifth and Fourteenth Articles of Amendment to the Constitution of the United States, applies to all human beings, including their unborn offspring at every stage of their biological development, irrespective of age, health, function or condition or dependency."*

In other words, science rather than judicial whim, would determine what constituted a protected life. The last part of the amendment was crafted to cover the elderly as well as the unborn because dicta in the Wade *opinion appeared to condition the right to protection on whether one has the "capability of meaningful life" or is a "person in the whole sense," language that can be applied to the senile and incurably infirm as well as to the unborn. Anyone who believes this concern for the aged is overwrought need only look across the Atlantic to the open-handed practice of euthanasia in the Netherlands to see the consequences of substituting a utilitarian view of human life for the ancient Judeo-Christian belief in the equal value of all life.*

My amendment was referred to the Judiciary Committee's subcommittee on constitutional amendments. It lingered there for a couple of years before hearings were scheduled, and it was never reported out of committee. While waiting for the hearings, three of us—Senators Dewey Bartlett of Oklahoma, Jesse Helms of North Carolina, and I—took turns in introducing amendments to various bills whose purpose was to require senators to cast recorded votes on proposals that affirmed that unborn life has more than a casual value. One that I introduced, and which now adorns the statute books, forbids the execution of a woman while she is pregnant. Needless to say, it was adopted unanimously. Whether it has resulted in any statistical increase in death row pregnancies, I can't say.

It was during this prolonged involvement with the Human Life Amendment that I became aware of the enormous impact that Supreme Court decisions can have on cultural and moral perceptions. In the year preceding Roe v. Wade, *referenda were held in two states, one of them New Jersey, on proposals to liberalize existing abortion laws. Each of them was soundly defeated. Yet, in the post-*Wade *era, although polls continue to confirm that the vast majority of Americans strongly disapprove of the reasons most women give for having an abortion, a substantial majority no longer question a woman's right to have one. After all, while the thought of an abortion might be personally repugnant, how can one condemn the exercise of a constitutional right?*

WW: Did you live in Washington? Did your family move with you, or did they stay in Sharon?

JLB: Three children moved down. I came down alone in January of '71 and rented an apartment. My wife would commute back and forth. We bought a house that spring and, in the fall, my three youngest children came down with her, the oldest of them for just one year before going off to boarding school. My other children were already in boarding schools.

My wife and resident children went north during the summers, and I would join them on weekends.

WW: Did she like being a senator's wife?

JLB: Yes and no. It disrupted our normal family life, but the change from life in a small community to that of Washington officialdom did open up all kinds of interesting things to see and do that otherwise wouldn't have come her way. She does resent the fact that the only official trip I ever took her on was one to Puerto Rico. I had been appointed by Nixon as one of the U.S. representatives on a joint U.S.-Puerto Rican Commission to study the question of the latter's status, i.e, the choices between the existing commonwealth status, statehood, and independence.

WW: She keeps reading about all these great trips and wonders why you missed them all.

JLB: I went on a number of solo trips to investigate particular problems of international policy that interested me. None of these was financed by the taxpayers.

WW: Did she go with you?

JLB: No.

I never participated in any of the fabled congressional "junkets" on which a group of senators or congressmen travel abroad for a week or so with their wives and mix business with sightseeing and shopping. I had nothing against them because I saw the value of exposing members of Congress to the attitudes and cultures of people outside our borders. I was not convinced, however, that that was the most efficient way to ferret out information and exchange views with key individuals in countries that were important to the United States. As a result, on the three occasions that I went abroad to educate myself on specific issues, I asked the State Department to make the necessary appointments and then set off with a couple of members of my staff on a no-frills, all business tour. These trips were financed by a group called

"Friends of Jim Buckley" that my administrative assistant, Dave Jones, had created shortly after I took office as a source of funding for Senate-related expenditures such as these. Professional reformers would no doubt cite this as yet another example of how sinister special interests corrupt the legislative process. It happens, however, that I never knew the identity of those friends.

Which leads me to the prickly issue of campaign finance reform and my role as lead plaintiff in the controversial Supreme Court case of Buckley v. Valeo, *which has achieved "landmark" status and assured me a measure of immortality. In that case, my co-plaintiffs and I challenged the constitutionality of the Campaign Reform Act of 1974 which, among many other things, placed a $1,000 cap on individual contributions to a political campaign and set limits on the total amounts that could be spent in the course of a campaign for federal office.*

To understand the issues as we saw them, it is instructive to take a look at the Buckley *plaintiffs. We were political underdogs and outsiders who spanned the ideological spectrum. Although I was a United States senator at the time, I had squeaked into office four years earlier as the first third party candidate in 40 years to be elected to the Senate. My co-plaintiffs included former Senator Eugene McCarthy, who had bucked his party's establishment by running a sufficiently effective challenge to cause President Lyndon Johnson to withdraw his candidacy for reelection; the very conservative American Conservative Union and the equally liberal New York Civil Liberties Union; New York's Conservative Party and Stewart Mott, a wealthy sponsor of liberal causes who had contributed $220,000 to the McCarthy campaign. What we had in common was a concern that the restrictions imposed by the new law would squeeze independent voices out of the political process by making it even more difficult than it already was to raise effective challenges to the political status quo.*

We believed that these restrictions were fundamentally flawed both constitutionally and as a matter of public policy. The core value protected by the First Amendment is the freedom of political speech. It is incontrovertible that, in today's world, it takes money—and a great deal of it—for political speech to be heard. Therefore, we opposed the 1974 amendment's limits on contributions and spending as unlawful restrictions on political speech. We found the legislation equally objectionable on grounds of public policy because a healthy democracy should encourage competition in the political marketplace rather than increase the difficulties already faced by those challenging incumbents or the existing political establishment. Incumbents enjoy enormous advantages over challengers. These include name recognition, the use of the frank to communicate with voters, automatic access to the media, and the goodwill derived from handling constituent problems.

Given this fundamental political reality, a challenger who is not wealthy or a celebrity in his own right must be able to persuade both the media and a broad base of potential contributors that his candidacy is credible. This requires a substantial amount of seed money. As I testified in Buckley, I could not have won election in 1970 if the $1,000 limit on contributions had been in place. It was only after the media had taken my third party campaign seriously that I was able to reach out to a broad base of contributors.. Nor could Gene McCarthy have launched a serious challenge to a sitting president without the more than $1 million that was provided by fewer than a dozen early supporters.

We won a number of our arguments before the Supreme Court, but lost the critical one. The Court agreed with us that the restrictions placed on what could be spent in support of a congressional candidate were unconstitutional. It held, however, that the limitations placed on contributions by individuals was constitutional because of Congress's expressed concern for avoiding the appearance of improper influence in federal elections. But because an individual cannot corrupt himself, the Court overturned the limits that Congress had placed on what candidates can spend on their own campaigns. This, of course, explains the subsequent epidemic of super-rich candidates for federal office.

In the wake of this and a subsequent Supreme Court decision testing the constitutionality of an even more restrictive McCain-Feingold campaign finance law enacted in 2002, we are left with a package of federal campaign laws and regulations that have distorted virtually every aspect of the election process. The 1974 amendments were supposed to de-emphasize the role of money in federal elections. Instead, by severely limiting the size of individual contributions, today's law has made the search for money a candidate's central preoccupation. When I ran in 1970, I never made telephone calls requesting money, and I doubt that I attended as many as a dozen fund-raising functions. Passing the hat was the exclusive concern of my finance committee. Today, the need to scrounge for money has proven so burdensome that more than one senator has cited it as a principal reason for his decision to retire to private life.

Furthermore, the federal regulation of campaigns has virtually driven grass roots action from the political scene. The rules have become too complex, the costs of a misstep too great. In 1970, when on campaign tours around New York State, I would often run into groups that, on their own initiative, had rented storefronts from which to dispense my campaign literature, man the phones, and deploy volunteers. Today, anyone intrepid enough to engage in spontaneous grass roots action is well advised to enlist the counsel of an election lawyer and accountant; and even then, he must be prepared to prove his independence in court—as my brother Bill had to when, unbeknownst to me or my campaign, he placed an ad in a newspaper urging my election when I later ran for the Senate in Connecticut.

But perhaps the most disturbing consequence of these laws has been the way they have consolidated the political power of favored establishment forces. By compounding the difficulties faced by challengers, they have enlarged the advantages already enjoyed by incumbents. By restricting the political speech of outsiders, they have enhanced the power of the two major parties. By limiting individual contributions, they have enhanced the influence of trade associations, labor unions, and political action committees. And by placing restrictions on when so-called issue advocacy groups are allowed to broadcast their messages, they have increased still further the political power already exercised by the mass media.

The problem with these statutes is that they are driven by a faulty premise. While large contributions can corrupt, the likelihood that a candidate will be seduced by them is vastly overstated. The overwhelming majority of wealthy donors back candidates with whom they are in general agreement. Furthermore, they are far more tolerant of differences on this point or that than are the political action committees or single-issue organizations to which a candidate must otherwise turn for necessary financing. I received major, unsolicited help from two individuals in 1970. The first made a contribution of more than $200,000; the second provided a $100,000 line of credit against which my campaign drew $55,000. The understanding was that it would have to be repaid only if I won. During my six years in office, I never heard from the second benefactor. The first, however, did call my office on one occasion to ask if it would be possible for his wife and grandson to have lunch in the Senate dining room. I plead guilty to having obliged him.

It is true, of course, that a major financial contributor will have readier access to a candidate he has helped elect, and with access comes the opportunity to persuade. But corruption only occurs when a legislator casts a vote that violates his conviction in exchange for a contribution. The currency of political corruption these days is rarely cash: it is the promise of votes; and no matter how wealthy he might be, an individual contributor can only deliver a single vote.

This is not to deny the importance of the appearances of probity in a cynical age. A less damaging remedy is available, however, and that is full and immediate disclosure. The opposing campaign can be relied upon to publicize any gift that can give rise to an adverse inference. The public can make its own judgment as to whether it is apt to corrupt its recipient. What makes no sense to me is to retain a set of rules that make it impossible for a Stewart Mott to provide a Eugene McCarthy with the seed money essential to a credible challenge to a sitting president, or that make politics the playground of the super-rich who can finance their own campaigns.

Thus endeth the sermon for the day. Now back to my interrogator.

WW: And what about your children—did they enjoy being children of a senator?

JLB: I think they disliked it.

WW: Because they never saw you.

JLB: I hope that was one part of it, but I suspect that the major reason was that being the child of a public official, especially one elected on something called the Conservative Party line, made them rather conspicuous at their respective schools. A couple of them told me, after I was dis-elected, that one or more teachers had given them a hard time or made fun of them in class over stands I had taken.

WW: How did your children handle that? That was very difficult.

JLB: They seem to have survived.

WW: And they didn't tell you at the time?

JLB: No, but I wish they had because it was outrageous.

WW: Just out of curiosity, where are your children on the political spectrum?

JLB: I've never quizzed them, but I suspect that they are conservative.

WW: Well, you haven't quizzed them, but generally in talking to your children you must talk politics somewhat and sort of know where they are.

JLB: I can say that there are no crashing liberals among them, although they don't by any means share all of my positions. They even campaigned for my reelection. On their own. I didn't ask them to do it.

It wasn't until late in the campaign that I learned how much time Peter and Priscilla had been devoting to it and what effective surrogate speakers they had proven to be. It was a tremendous boost to my morale at a time I needed one.

WW: They were no doubt very proud that their father was in the Senate; more so than you probably realized. What would you say was your greatest accomplishment in the Senate? What are you the most proud of?

JLB: I worked consistently and a little bit creatively to require environmental regulators to take costs as well as benefits into consideration. I also kept emphasizing the need for flexibility and the role of economic incentives if we were to achieve the most efficient results. One of the things that I succeeded in having included in the Senate revision of the Clean Air Act, in 1976, was a test of the effectiveness of using so-called pollution taxes to achieve the maximum feasible results. One of the problems with the one-standard-fits-all approach of existing environmental regulations was that they failed to recognize that the cost of controlling a particular pollutant could vary enormously, depending on the nature of the polluter. Thus, standards would be set that could readily have been bettered by some industries because the imposition of more stringent standards would have put others out of business. Also, because existing regulations tended to require the utilization of the best available technology, there was a disincentive to the development of new technologies that would clean out more of a particular pollutant lest this require the developer to spend still more on pollution controls. The new bill would place controls for the first time on the emission of nitrous oxide from stationary sources. I was persuaded that this would be the ideal opportunity to discover whether we could achieve the targeted reductions more efficiently by taxing the emission of nitrous oxide rather than by imposing rigid, uniform regulations on the emitters. This would create an incentive for the emitters of these gases to devise the most efficient ways to reduce the release of nitrous oxide from their particular plants. Because it would be far less costly for some of them to do the job, some industries would end up eliminating far larger percentages than others; but on average, the target goals would be met. And if they weren't, an increase in the tax would increase the incentives to find new and better ways to reduce the emissions. Unfortunately, although the bill incorporating that test was adopted by the Senate, I was not on hand to make sure it was incorporated in the new bill that was enacted by a new Congress the following year.

One of the hazards of an oral history is that the answer to a question can veer off course, and when the answer is very long, as in this case, the responder will have forgotten its genesis. What I was asked was, "What was your greatest accomplishment in the Senate? What are you most proud of?" My answer did describe a small but significant accomplishment in an area that was important to me, but it can hardly be described as a great one. The problem, of course, is that very junior members of a minority party have few opportunities to do more than achieve largely invisible though often significant improvements in the legislation that comes before their committees.

To return to the question that triggered these meanderings, I suspect that my most consequential achievement may have been to derail the legislative sleeper, the child development program I described earlier, that would have launched a new mega-billion dollar program that no one but the sponsoring Senate committee had focused on. I qualify this statement with a "may" because I can't prove the cause and effect although I believe my lonely opposition to the bill caught the White House's attention and led to the Nixon veto. Although subsequent legislation provided federal financing for child care programs, none reinstated the original bill's breathtakingly preemptive and comprehensive child development provisions. I will take this occasion, however, to describe certain areas on which I focused and then address the second part of the question, "What are you most proud of?" If my recollections of those days appear uncharacteristically sharp, it is because I have a book in hand that I wrote in 1975 (If Men Were Angels: A View from the Senate) and have, in fact, incorporated snippets from it into this narrative.

An area of primary concern was, of course, the environment. I have already discussed the principles I sought to advance while working on pollution control and other environment bills. What I have not mentioned is the satisfaction I felt in my work as a member of the Public Works Committee and its environmental sub-committee. The Committee's chairman, Jennings Randolph, prided himself on the absence of the partisanship I found on other committees, and I had the full support of its excellent staff from the moment I reported for duty. Nevertheless, I was regarded as an oddity—a staunch conservative who took environmental problems seriously. Such an oddity, in fact, that columnist Jack Anderson accused me of having selected the committee in order to protect my family's oil interests. He later recanted when he learned that I had voted to halt the construction of the Alaskan pipeline until certain environmental problems had been resolved.

Because my concern for the environment was genuine, I was invited to address such groups as the Audubon Society and The Nature Conservancy. But because I recognized that there were economic tradeoffs that had to be taken into account in drafting legislation, I began to earn the confidence of conservative senators who tended to hold all "tree huggers" suspect. In my last two years, when an environmental bill came up for a vote, some would regularly ask me whether it was sound; and if I said yes, they would vote for it. What I have yet to understand is why conservatives find it so hard to appreciate that uncontrolled pollution had cost the economy tens of billions of dollars a year before the landmark bills of the late '60s and early '70s began to bring it under control. As for the protection of critical ecosystems and the species that depend on them, one would think that conservatives in particular would understand Edmund Burke's caution that "temporary possessors and life-rentors should not think it among their rights to . . . commit waste on the inheritance [and] leave to those who come after them a ruin instead of a habitation." As I reminded National Review *readers in a 1978 defense of the*

Endangered Species Act, a Wood Thrush's haunting song may have no monetary value, but it enriches countless lives. One problem, of course, is that too much of current environmental regulation is needlessly rigid, and too many environmentalists are unreasonable in their demands.

I was also an active participant in debates on defense and foreign policy. It would have been impossible to avoid those concerning Vietnam, given the passions sparked by that war. A bomb had exploded in a Senate hallway shortly be-

Visiting the troops, 1972.

fore I took office, and hordes of anti-war protestors prowled the corridors of the Senate office buildings. But I soon found myself drawn into a far wider range of issues, all of them interconnected. These included the implications of the Nixon Doctrine, the arcana of strategic arms and their control, and the merits of Nixon's policy of détente with the Soviet Union.

In a November 1969 address from the Oval Office, Nixon stated that his policy towards Asia (which came to be known as the "Nixon Doctrine") was based on three principles: the United States would honor its treaty obligations; it would provide "a shield if a nuclear power threatens the freedom" of a nation with whom we were allied or whose survival was considered vital to our security; and "in cases involving other types of aggression, we shall furnish military and economic assistance when requested in accordance with our treaty commitments. But we shall look to the nation directly threatened to assume the primary responsibility of providing the manpower for its defense." The last principle provided the framework for Nixon's plan for extricating America from the Vietnam morass while giving the South Vietnamese a fair opportunity to protect their own freedom.

When I entered the Senate, the administration was in the process of "Vietnamizing" the war through an accelerated program for the training and upgrading of South Vietnam's military forces so they could assume the brunt of the fighting and allow a gradual American withdrawal. The ultimate success of Vietnamization depended on our continuing to supply those forces with the quantity and quality of military equipment required to match the weapons with which the Soviet block and China were supplying the North Vietnamese. And therein lay the rub. Under our system, a president has the authority to design foreign policy, but Congress can deny him the money with which to carry it out. During my first year, Congress routinely appropriated the money required to meet our obligations in Vietnam, but it was beginning to become balky.

The year 1972 saw a gradual increase in anti-war sentiment in Congress. Every morning, Senate Majority Leader Mike Mansfield opened the session with an update on American casualties, and Republican Senator George Aiken threw in the towel with the suggestion that the United States declare victory and bring its forces home. But the required money continued to be voted, although by dwindling margins. In the meantime, Nixon pursued increasingly desperate efforts to find a diplomatic solution. These culminated in the lopsided Paris Accords signed in January 1973 by the United States, South Vietnam, North Vietnam, and the Vietcong, which had been elevated to the status of the "Provisional Revolutionary Government of the Republic of South Viet-Nam." The accords were lopsided because although they required the United States to withdraw all of its troops, military advisors, armaments, and war material from South Vietnam and to dismantle its military bases there, no such obligations were imposed on the North Vietnamese, who continued to maintain their "Who, me?" posture to the end. And so, the infrastructure they had built and their considerable caches of weapons remained undisturbed. North Vietnam was, by inference, required to observe and maintain the cease-fire scheduled to begin on January 27, 1973, but no one familiar with the communist modus operandi really expected it or the Vietcong to honor it once the

American military had pulled up stakes and returned home. Quite predictably, the fighting soon resumed.

The Nixon Doctrine was now being put to the test. The South Vietnamese were on their own and, contrary to what most Americans believed, they acquitted themselves honorably under increasingly difficult circumstances. In the two years between the time the Paris Accords' cease-fire was supposed to take effect and North Vietnam launched its final offensive in January 1975, the South Vietnamese forces had lost more than 59,000 killed out of a population less than one-tenth the size of ours. Although the accords allowed the South Vietnamese "to make periodic replacement of armaments, munitions and war material which have been destroyed, damaged, worn out or used up after the cease-fire," Congress was increasingly reluctant to provide the needed replacements, let alone increase their quality to match that of the new arms provided the North by its allies. In August 1974, the Senate cut $1.5 billion from an urgent Ford administration Vietnam funding request by a stunning vote of 86 to 5. I was one of the five. The end now became inevitable—and shameful.

I recall the night a few months later when the Senate finally pulled the plug on its hapless ally. During the consideration of yet another emergency funding request, I was invited by CBS television to step outside the Senate chamber for an impromptu hallway debate with Senators George McGovern and Frank Church. My opponents maintained that sending any further military aid was a waste of money because the South Vietnamese were incapable of defending themselves, citing recent stories of troops abandoning tanks and guns in panicked retreats. Yes they had, I replied, but they had done so only because they had run out of the ammunition with which to hold their ground and the gasoline required to operate their tanks and withdraw their artillery. That night, the Senate cut off all further military supplies.

In March 1975, I was visited by a Vietnamese senator I had met in Saigon three years earlier. She was engaged in a desperate attempt to persuade Congress to honor the Paris Accords and resume the shipment of essential materiel. On entering my office, she placed a calling card on my desk which read, "Madame Nguyen Van Tho, Senateur, République du Vietnam." I told her that I believed in her cause, but that it was hopeless. She then picked up the card, wrote "Ex" before the word "Senateur," and said: "I now realize I am a refugee." I was overcome by a *deep sense of shame—not for myself, but for my country.*

Saigon fell the following month. We had been tested, and found wanting. I was among those who believed the war could have been won. I also believed that we had an obligation to live up to our implicit commitments under both the Nixon Doctrine and the Paris Accords and that our failure to do so would have serious consequences. I may have been wrong about our ability to win the war, but I was certainly right as to the consequences of abandoning the South Vietnamese. Our

A White House reception for congressional
supporters of Nixon's Vietnam policies.

failure of nerve encouraged the Soviets to embark on a series of initiatives that, within a half dozen years, had set up friendly regimes in Angola, Mozambique, South Yemen, Ethiopia, and Afghanistan, and established beachheads in our own hemisphere, in Nicaragua and El Salvador. A traumatized Congress's only response, on my watch, was to pass the Clark Amendment, which forbade the president from taking any action to resist the Soviet penetration of Angola.

Vietnam, however, was not the only defense policy issue on the table when I entered the Senate. The other concerned the highly complex question of what constituted "strategic sufficiency"—the mix and quality of nuclear arms required to protect the United States and its allies. Thanks to the encyclopedic knowledge of my in-house expert, Bill Schneider, I was able to take an active part in debating the merits of the two nuclear arms agreements that the Nixon administration had negotiated with the Soviet Union as well as those of the prevailing strategic doctrine of "mutual assured destruction" or "MAD," to use the acronym employed by its critics. That doctrine held that we could best deter a nuclear war by ensuring that the initiation of a nuclear attack would be an act of national suicide; hence it was essential that we and the Soviets remain able to absorb a first strike with enough retaliatory weapons surviving to inflict unacceptable damage on the aggressor. The doctrine required, in other words, that the civilian populations of each country be held hostage to ensure their own government's good behavior. It also assumed that the Soviets had the same strategic objectives, which they didn't.

As critically important and divisive as these issues were at the time, they are now very ancient history. So I will spare the reader a learned discussion of intercontinental ballistic missile throw-weights, multiple independently targetable warheads, and the Soviet drive to achieve a counter-force capability (the ability to knock out our nuclear strike forces while sparing our cities) that would have confirmed that the MAD doctrine was indeed mad. Instead I will merely note that while I voted in favor of the Strategic Arms Limitation Treaty, which froze the parties' nuclear missiles at their current levels for a period of five years, I was one of two senators to oppose ratification of the Anti-Ballistic Missile Treaty, which would prevent the deployment of a defense against nuclear weapons.

I opposed the ABM Treaty for two reasons. First and foremost, I questioned the morality of denying ourselves whatever means we might be able to develop to protect our people, it having been my understanding that that was the first obligation of any government. Second, there was the substantial problem of verifying Soviet compliance with its terms. Our satellites had uncanny capabilities, but at the time they didn't have the ability to penetrate the cloud cover that often blanketed large areas of the USSR. I voted to ratify the SALT agreement, however, because it was of a limited duration and it didn't prevent us from developing a counter-force capability of our own.

The strategic arms debates were played out against the background of the Nixon administration's policy of détente with the Soviet Union. The policy's objective of defusing tensions with the Soviets was laudable enough, but I had *problems with it. We were granting the Soviets important concessions in exchange for paper promises that were never kept, and the "peace in our times" rhetoric issuing from the White House encouraged Congress to make damaging cuts in defense spending while encouraging the public to underestimate the threats that the Soviets continued to pose. Furthermore, Nixon's reliance on balance-of-power diplomacy stripped the policy of the moral compass that might ensure its long-term support by the American people.*

Nixon was particularly anxious to oblige the Soviets on the matter of trade. To that end, in 1972, he and Brezhnev signed an agreement providing for the elimination of a number of barriers to Soviet-American trade. This was of particular importance to the Soviets because their economy was in shambles and they were anxious to gain access to our industrial technology and know-how. The agreement, however, ran into a buzz saw in the form of an amendment introduced by Senator Henry "Scoop" Jackson of Washington that would deny the Soviets "most favored nation" treatment and other advantages until they had lifted the obstacles they had placed on emigration from their country. I was an enthusiastic supporter of the Jackson Amendment, not because I thought that it would induce the Kremlin to allow its citizens to leave in any appreciable numbers (I didn't), but because it would kill an ill-advised bill that would provide a significant boost to the Soviet's economy without any tangible benefits for the United States.

What followed was a classic standoff between the White House and Congress. Nixon declared that any trade bill that was conditioned on Soviet behavior was unacceptable, and the Senate declined to enact one without the Jackson Amendment. There followed two years of negotiations between Jackson and Nixon's secretary of state, Henry Kissinger. Finally, they came to an understanding in an exchange of letters that was released in October 1974. In his letter, Kissinger advised Jackson that he had been assured that if the trade bill were enacted, the Soviets would stop harassing applicants for exit permits and lift the barriers to emigration. Based on that assurance, Jackson agreed to modify his amendment so as to permit the extension of credits and other advantages to the Soviets subject to termination within 18 months if the president could not certify that harassment had ceased and the doors to emigration opened.

The following month, I spent a week in the Soviet Union with my arms/foreign policy expert Bill Schneider and press secretary Len Saffir to see how the intended beneficiaries of the Jackson Amendment viewed the prospects of the Jackson-Kissinger compromise. Because those were largely Russian Jews who wished to emigrate to Israel, I met with Malcolm Hoenlein of the Conference on Soviet Jewry before departing for Moscow. He told me that if I was interested in meeting "refuseniks," as Jews who had been denied exit visas to Israel were called, I should go to the plaza outside the main synagogue in Moscow at noontime on the Jewish Sabbath when worshipers would be taking a breather between services. He gave me the names and telephone numbers of two or three prominent refuseniks he recommended that I meet. I asked whether my doing so would expose them to harassment by the government. I was assured that it would not. To the contrary, he told me that if I published the names of those with whom I met, I would provide them with immunity from retaliation because that would convert them into tests of the Kremlin's bona fides. This proved to be true. Within the next six months, several of the men and women I had in met in Moscow wrote to me that, following my departure, they had been issued exit visas with astonishing speed.

We arrived in Moscow on a Saturday morning and were met at the airport by a member of the American Embassy staff. As he was driving us to our hotel, he told me that the embassy had not yet been able to schedule any of the meetings with Soviet officials that I had requested, but that it had arranged for me to visit a still functioning monastery some miles out of town that afternoon. As he was talking, it occurred to me that we had arrived on the Jewish Sabbath and I asked to be dropped off at the synagogue. (Because Pravda, the official Communist Party newspaper, had labeled me the week before as one of the foremost enemies of détente, I suspect that the embassy found the Soviet officialdom especially uncooperative and me, a sticky diplomatic wicket.)

When we reached the synagogue, we found a number of people walking around in the plaza, apparently killing time. Len passed out cards identifying himself as the press secretary of a United States senator, and pointed me out. Within minutes, one person and then another and another walked up and either slipped me a note or asked, in very broken English, whether it would be possible for us to meet at a later date. Then an Associated Press reporter, who had been telephoned by someone in the plaza, turned up with notebook in hand and offered to act as my interpreter. So the story of my impromptu meeting with Soviet Jews was carried in American newspapers the following day, and added to official displeasure over my visit.

During the next few days, a number of men and women visited me in my hotel room. Because of the likelihood that it was bugged, whenever they had something of importance to say, they would write it out on a sheet of paper and hand it to me. What emerged was a pervasive worry over how the Jackson compromise would work in practice. Even though only three weeks had elapsed since the release of the Jackson-Kissinger letters, harassment had already been intensified. Telephones had been disconnected, work permits revoked, and individuals arrested for questioning on the most spurious grounds. What the dissidents feared was that the Soviets would bring such pressures to bear on those applying for exit permits that the supply of candidates for emigration would dry up before the Jackson Amendment's 18-month probation period had expired. The Soviets would claim compliance with its terms, however, by allowing token emigration while intensifying their internal suppression. In the meantime, they would be enjoying all the advantages they sought under the trade bill. It was clear that day-by-day monitoring of Soviet performance would be essential if the compromise Amendment became law.

Fortunately, the Soviets hadn't yet disconnected the phone of Alexander Goldfarb, one of the refuseniks whom Mr. Hoenlein had suggested I contact because he provided me with the highlight of my trip—an introduction to Dr. Andrei Sakharov, the brilliant Russian physicist who had developed the Soviet hydrogen bomb and then given up every privilege that had earned him by becoming the most persistent critic of his country's systematic violations of human rights. Only pressures from the West had kept the Kremlin from silencing him. He was, however, under the equivalent of house arrest when I met him and his wife, Elena Bonner, in their small Moscow apartment. I spend about two hours with him on the first afternoon and another two the following morning. Despite the hesitant Russian of my AP reporter/interpreter, we managed to cover subjects ranging from freedom of information and emigration to disarmament, amnesty for political prisoners, and the perils of détente. Unlike the visitors to my hotel room, he ignored the microphones in his walls. "I have nothing to hide," he told me. (In the preface to a slender volume, My Country and the World, *that he wrote the following year, Sakharov stated that I was "the first American statesman who considered it feasible to meet" with him and that our meeting was "very important" to him, as it certainly was to me. Two years later, when I was in Israel, a sun-*

burned Goldfarb told me that he owed his exit visa to the newspaper reports of our Moscow encounter.)

I was coming to the end of my stay, and I had yet to see a Soviet official. The Soviets, however, were anxious to have me visit their Institute for United States and Canadian Studies where they could place this obnoxious specimen of Americana under their institutional microscope, as was their practice with visiting Americans of any prominence. Accordingly, two days before I was to leave Moscow, while I was on an overnight visit to Leningrad, I issued a press statement, at Len Saffir's suggestion, in which I expressed my regret that I hadn't been granted an interview with any of the people I had wanted to see and stated that if they were too busy to see me, I was certainly too busy to visit the Institute the following day. Because we were advised that the consulate's electric typewriters might be bugged, my statement was typed in a safe room in the attic. Within two hours, I was invited to meet the Soviet Union's head jailer, Minister of the Interior Nikolai Shchelokov, whose portfolio included emigration as well as the complex of slave labor camps that Aleksandr Solzhenitsyn described in The Gulag Archipelago.

The next morning, when ushered into the minister's office, I told him that I had sought the interview for several reasons, most of them dealing with such things as a constituent's request that certain Lithuanians be allowed to leave the USSR so that they might join relatives in New York, a plea for clemency for a couple of political prisoners who were reported to be near death, and American concerns over reported increases in religious persecution. The minister said he would look into the Lithuanian matter, assured me that imprisoned criminals received the very best of medical care, and dismissed the charge of religious persecutions as "more dead cats" because, he assured me, the Soviet Constitution guaranteed freedom of worship. I then brought up the subject of the Jackson Amendment. In response to the standard Soviet complaint that emigration was a purely internal matter of no legitimate interest to outsiders, I said that the minister would surely agree that whom we chose to trade with was also an internal matter. When I suggested that his government was harassing applicants for exit visas, he looked me in the eye and said that I must have been talking to malcontents because (a) Soviet law guaranteed the right of emigration and (b) anyone seeking to emigrate was free to do so unless he happened to be in possession of state secrets, in which case a five-year quarantine period must first elapse. He then asked me to assure members of the Senate that "Soviet leaders are as good as their words."

Now it happens that, at the time, I was in possession of a petition containing the signatures of over 6,000 heads of ethnic German households that Sakharov had asked me two days earlier to deliver to a representative of the West German government. For years, these "Volga Germans" had been seeking permission to emigrate to Germany without success, and were now seeking help from their ancient fatherland. As most of those listed were farmers and miners living in the Soviet Central Asian Republic of Kazakhstan where they had been moved by Stalin following the Nazi invasion, it was not likely that they were in possession of state secrets. Furthermore, within the last few days I had spoken with dozens of Jews who had described in detail the harassment to which they had been subjected after applying for permission to go to Israel. It was a fascinating experience to talk with a man who knows that you know that what he is telling you is not the truth. It was also an instructive exposure to the mentality of our partners in détente.

The following morning, before going to the airport, I had a final taste of the Soviet system. I had been anxious to meet a particularly prominent dissident, Evgeny Agursky, who had co-authored From Under the Rubble with Solzhenitsyn. He suggested that we take a ten-minute walk in the street behind my hotel so that we might speak freely without being overheard by the ubiquitous microphones. After a few minutes, I noticed that we were being followed—at walking speed—by a black sedan. It was easy to understand why that afternoon, when the wheels of the plane taking us away from the Soviet Union lifted off the tarmac, the passengers burst out with spontaneous cheers. My staffer, Bill Schneider, muttered that the only way he would want to see Moscow again was through the bomb sight of an American bomber.

A few weeks later, when the revised Jackson Amendment was finally being debated, I raised the problem of verification, and Jackson agreed to have his Senate Permanent Subcommittee on Investigations monitor, on a day-by-day basis, the experience of individuals seeking to leave the Soviet Union after enactment of the trade bill. This would be done by maintaining contact with dissident groups in Moscow who would provide Congress with reasonably accurate estimates of the numbers seeking to emigrate and the treatment accorded them. When I expressed concern that the Soviets might nevertheless end up enjoying the benefits of preferential treatment for 18 months without in any way *relaxing their emigration policies, Jackson stated that he had received assurances from President Ford that any benefits extended would be terminated immediately on evidence of bad faith—the kind that the senator's subcommittee would be in a position to provide.*

The response to the adoption of the Jackson Amendment was immediate. The Soviet news agency Tass denied the existence of any understanding on the matter of emigration; and a few weeks later, in the midst of rumblings about the precarious state of détente, Moscow repudiated the Nixon-Brezhnev trade agreement on the not unreasonable basis that it had been scuttled by Congress. It appeared that however much they wanted the benefits of freer trade with the United States, the Soviets feared even more the brain drain that would occur if they met the amendment's conditions.

The fate of the U.S.-Soviet trade bill highlighted the inherent problem with policies, like détente, that have no clear moral anchor and are not based on readily understood imperatives of national interest. For better or worse, Americans tend to see things in terms of black and white. We need to know who the good guys are, and who the bad. The historical record of Soviet international trouble-making in the years immediately following World War II made it easy to decide that Communists were very, very bad; and a foreign policy rooted in an unwavering opposition to the spread of Communism was the key to our success in forging the NATO alliance and in containing the Soviets during the decades immediately following the end of World War II. That policy had the continuing support of Congress and the American people because it was based on a consistent (and realistic) view of the Soviet Union as a malevolent threat. When Nixon toasted the Soviet leadership in the Kremlin, the moral underpinnings of our policy towards the Soviets began to disintegrate and the public was left in confusion. Détente ultimately failed because it required a reliance on pragmatism and maneuver that Congress was unable or unwilling to accommodate and a moral ambiguity that is alien to the American psyche.

I would revisit the question of trade with the Soviet Union seven years later when I was in the State Department, where the central issues were again political rather than economic. In the meantime, however, I had to wrestle with economic problems here at home. One of my early surprises was how unaware some of my new colleagues were of how the market place works. I recall being in the Senate *chamber early my first year where four or five senators were decrying the "export of American jobs." This was a reference to the increasing numbers of American manufacturers who established subsidiaries in low-wage countries in Southeast Asia where parts manufactured in the United States could be assembled into finished products for sale in international markets. The senators were supporting a bill that would penalize companies so engaged. What puzzled me was their apparent assumption that an act of Congress could cause Filipinos to pay $50 for an all-American-manufactured-and-assembled transistor radio rather than the $25 it would cost them to buy a Japanese product of equal quality. It seemed self-evident that if the bill were enacted into law (fortunately, it wasn't), its only effect would be to ensure that no American-designed radios would be sold abroad and that the American workers producing the parts exported to the foreign subsidiaries would lose their jobs.*

I was so intrigued by this display of economic innocence that on returning to my office, I examined the biographies of senators in the Congressional Directory *to see how many of them had ever been exposed to the productive side of our economy. I found that of the 95 senators who had described their work before entering public office, only 18 had had any extensive experience in business or agriculture. Sixty-three of them were lawyers, and two-thirds of these had moved into one governmental position or another within a half-dozen years of receiving their law degrees. Five others were academics. I believe this explains why members of the Senate so often fail to appreciate the economic consequences of governmental actions.*

This applies with particular force to price controls, whose highly predictable effect is to create shortages. This has been the experience of humankind since the first recorded attempt to fix prices almost 4,000 years ago in the reign of the Babylonian monarch, Hammurabi. His decrees didn't curb inflation, but they did cause items of commerce to disappear from the marketplace. The Roman Emperor Diocletian had no better luck in the third century A.D. even though his price edicts were enforced by the death penalty. If an article of trade can't be sold at a profit, it will not be produced, and no government can control the cost of every item that goes into the production of at least some goods.

And so it proved with the wage and price controls that Richard Nixon imposed in the summer of 1971, the first in our peace-time history. I believe that Nixon knew better, but he had been mouse-trapped by Congress which, the year before and over his objection, had responded to a jump of inflation to more than 6 percent by granting him the standby authority to impose them. Although inflation had begun to recede in 1971, the president yielded to political pressures to "do something" and used his standby power to freeze wages and prices. The controls reduced inflation in the shorter term; but by late 1973, the rate had reached 8 percent and was heading up, and shortages of key commodities began to crop up here and there around the country. So, in the fall of 1973, I introduced legislation to bring the controls to an end. It had eight cosponsors and 26 senators voted for termination. Others expressed sympathy but said they wanted to wait for a more "appropriate" time when conditions were less unsettled, ignoring the fact that the controls were responsible for the unsettling. Rather than acknowledge that it had made a mistake in authorizing them, Congress simply allowed them to expire the following April. In the meantime, a number of plants had had to shut down, and a lot of people had lost their jobs.

The price of one commodity, natural gas, remained regulated thanks to a Supreme Court decision some years earlier that held that the Federal Power Commission's price-setting authority extended beyond interstate pipelines, which are natural monopolies, to the wells that fed them, which are not. The result was that a newly discovered natural gas field that could not be economically developed at the price set by the FPC was never produced unless there was a market for the gas within the state in which the field was located. Thus gas-producing states like Texas and Louisiana had ample supplies at the higher prices their consumers were happy to pay while the interstate pipelines began to exhaust the fields to which they were connected. By the early 1970s, serious shortages of natural gas were developing in various parts of the country, especially the Northeast.

Given my own experience in oil and gas exploration, I wasn't bashful about pointing out the economic consequences of the current arrangement, and joined a group of oil state senators in urging the decontrol of natural gas. When a reporter suggested that I was acting from a certain self-interest, I pointed out that none of my oil and gas income came from the United States and that gas shortages in this country could only enhance the value of my Canadian royalties; and so, undeterred by the press, I kept plugging away on the theme that the deregulation of natural gas was the surest way to provide my constituents with ample domestic supplies at reasonable prices, a position that was vindicated when the controls were finally lifted.

In describing my work in the Senate, I suppose I should also mention my Don Quixote-like assault on the venerable institution of pork barrel politics. I refer to the appalling practice of larding appropriations bills with projects that add billions of dollars to the federal deficit but serve no national purpose other than assuring their congressional sponsors' reelection. In 1975, I was provoked by a particularly porcine bill to see if I could shame at least some senators into exercising a degree of restraint in their raids on the federal treasury. I drafted twenty or so amendments to strike specific projects that met my definition of "pork;" namely, any localized public works expenditure that did not fall within the scope of existing national legislation. Thus a provision in the bill authorizing construction of a dam in a particular township in Tennessee that was authorized by a law controlling flooding in the Tennessee River watershed would pass muster whereas a dam whose purpose was to create a lake for the delight of the local citizenry would not. My purpose in offering a series of amendments rather than a single one to delete all the offending extravagances was to hammer home what the exercise was all about by requiring senators to vote on each of them. I also hoped that the exercise might generate some media stories on the cost of pork.

And so, one afternoon, I called up my amendments one at a time, and a senator from the state in which the offending project would be built took to the floor to defend the virtues of a proposed town library, or athletic facility, or what have you in the most moving, even poetic terms, and my amendment would be rejected. Well, not all of them. Being a man of honor, I had to include two New York proposals that met my definition of pork. These went undefended, and my amendments striking them were adopted. Fortunately, New York Congresswoman Bella Abzug was on the relevant House committee and saw to it that the items were restored. In saying "fortunately," I don't mean to suggest that New York pork is any more defensible than that for any other state. Rather, because New York taxpayers would be paying for a disproportionate share of the projects I failed to kill, there was a certain elemental justice in the fact that, in these instances, the rest of the country would be contributing to the construction of facilities that would benefit New Yorkers alone.

These samplings should suffice to illustrate how this senator tried to have an impact on public policy in areas lying outside his committee responsibilities. So I return to my interrogator's second question: "What are you most proud of?" Some friends have suggested that I ought to be most proud of my call for Nixon's resignation on March 19, 1974, six months before the impeachment proceedings in the House of Representatives forced him to resign. But I'm not. I feel enormously sad about that whole affair. As I told the press at the time, my call for his resignation was not based on any conclusions as to his personal conduct in connection with the Watergate fiasco. Rather, it was based on a judgment that Nixon had lost the capacity to govern and that his continuation in office in the face of the increasingly damaging Senate Watergate investigations would undermine his authority abroad, jeopardize the domestic programs he had been reelected to pursue, and his continuance in office would be a disaster for Republicans in the fall elections—as it proved to be.

A few weeks earlier, I was in one of three groups of Republican senators invited (in alphabetical order) to the White House for a "hair down" discussion of the growing crisis. When it came my turn to speak, I summoned the courage to tell the president that, rightly or wrongly, he had lost his credibility and that he now had the burden of establishing his innocence of the charges being brought against him. I said that the only way he could do so was to turn over every scrap of information remotely related to Watergate to someone of Senator John Stennis's integrity so that he in turn could make available to the Watergate investigating committee all information relevant to the accusations being leveled against him. The president nodded from time to time while I was speaking, thanked me for my comments, and moved on to the next senator. I left doubting that he had any understanding of what I was trying to say; and in the weeks ahead, I reached the conclusion that someone needed to engage in some shock therapy and that I was that person because a call for Nixon's resignation had to come from a conservative considered to be solidly in the Nixon camp, as I had been. He had to be disabused of any thought that if it came to an impeachment, he could count on the unquestioned support of a block of Senate loyalists.

And so, after consultations with close friends and advisors, I called a press conference in the Senate Caucus Room and proposed that the president resign "as an extraordinary act of statesmanship and courage." Within minutes, my switchboard was swamped, and telegrams and letters began to pore in—over 25,000 of them within the next couple of days, most of them violently objecting to my position. There was an office pool to determine whether I would be compared most frequently with Benedict Arnold, Brutus, or Judas Iscariot. It didn't help when, a few hours after my press conference, while walking from my office to the Capitol, Senator Ted Kennedy (with whom I disagreed on almost every issue) crossed the street to congratulate me or when, on reaching the Senate floor, I heard Senator Carl Curtis (a close Senate friend and ally) winding up a talk denouncing me. I had managed to please people who would never vote with or for me and to dismay tens of thousands of those who had elected me to office. Needless to say, the president didn't follow my advice to resign while he could still do so with some dignity.

It was a bruising experience, but it did have its consolations. One year later, Congressman William Cohen of Maine called my office to say that a constituent wanted to present me with an award. A few minutes later, he walked in with a young man who was the son of the proprietor of a popular Bangor, Maine, restaurant called "Momma Carparelli." He was carrying a yard-high, three-tiered trophy

Presentation of Mamma Carperelli Award.

that bore the inscription, "James L. Buckley, New York/Mamma Carparelli Award for Most Honest and Frank in National Politics/Selected by the People of Maine." The people in question were the 3,384 readers of Maine newspapers who had responded to a poll conducted by the restaurant. This was, evidently, their assessment of my call for Nixon's resignation. Unfortunately, those enlightened citizens were not able to vote in New York in 1976. The trophy, however, is a marvelous piece of American kitsch and is proudly displayed in my office.

So, how do I answer that second question, "What are you most proud of?" I'm uncomfortable with the word "proud," so let me rephrase the question: " What aspect of your Senate career do you least regret?" The answer is, my willingness to take unpopular positions that I believed to be right. The temptation to go with the crowd is great, but my understanding of my job was that I had to use my best judgment in assessing the merits of a particular bill and cast my vote accordingly. I believed this to be true even when voting against a measure I knew was bound to win by a significant margin. I thought it important for the public to be able to measure the true strength of the opposing position as this might encourage a reconsideration of the merits. Unfortunately, in too many cases, lopsided votes were cast in support of measures that might actually be opposed by as many as 35 or 40 senators.

For better or worse, the Senate ethos encouraged votes based on purely political considerations. I recall a meeting of newly-elected Republican senators that had been called by John Tower in his capacity as chairman of the Senate Republican Campaign Committee. He told us that our most importance task over the next six years was to ensure our own reelection. Beginning in late 1975, when I would ask Clif Hansen of Wyoming, a close friend whose judgment I trusted, how I should vote on an obscure matter that fell within the jurisdiction of his Finance Committee, he would often say, "This bill is no good, Jim; but you're from New York and are coming up for election next year, so you should vote 'Aye.'" I was unable to follow his prudential advice, and so often found myself casting rather lonely votes. I can't claim total purity, however. I remember in particular one occasion when a politically appealing "motherhood" bill had come up for a vote which, on complicated analysis, was very bad policy. Faced with the inability to explain its flaws to constituents in less then a dozen pages of finely honed logic, I voted "Aye." A few minutes later, Jim McClure of Idaho, a political soul mate whose seat was in the row ahead of mine, also voted for the bill. After doing so, he turned to me and said, "I feel unclean." And so did I. Such are the pressures of elective office.

One question my astute interrogator failed to ask was, "What aspect of your Senate life did you find most depressing?" The answer is, my periodic exposure to the less edifying sides of human nature. The federal government is in position to grant a vast range of privileges and immunities, and members of Congress have to deal with an endless line of often well-heeled mendicants seeking special advantages. People in desperate circumstances will tend to equate the national interest with their own. This I understood and was happy to see if I could be of any principled help to them, as I tried to be to New York's besieged dairy farmers. What I found dispiriting was the myopic self-interest and hypocrisy exhibited by so many of the other special pleaders who knocked on my door, such as the high ranking delegation from Columbia University that sought my help in keeping the Labor Department from applying affirmative action quotas to faculty hiring while insisting that I not publicize the fact because of its support for such quotas when applied to other employers. And there were the endless requests for protection from competition by corporate beneficiaries of an economic system that is based on the same.

I have been described as "pro business," which is wrong. What I am is passionately "pro" the competitive free enterprise system that has provided us with such an extraordinarily productive economy. I have little sympathy with businessmen who seek special favors or who are the victims of their own mismanagement. In 1974 or '75, I was among the minority who opposed a federal bailout of a bankrupt Lockheed Corporation because the market place's weeding out of business failures is precisely what rewards efficiency and keeps the economy strong. What particularly depressed me was the failure of corporate leaders to come to the defense of the economic system that had so benefitted them. While they were quick to protest any legislation that might adversely affect their particular industry, they remained silent when another was threatened by legislation that could establish the most devastating precedents. A case in point was the failure of any of the heads of non-petroleum corporations to protest when, in response to the price increases and shortages that resulted from the 1972–74 Arab oil embargo, the chairman of the Senate Interior Committee seriously considered a proposal that would have placed a government representative on the board of every major oil company. I urged the executives attending a business conference, many of them Fortune 500 CEOs, to take a stand against so revolutionary an intrusion into corporate governance, but to no avail. I was not surprised because I had long since learned that "corporate statesmanship" is an oxymoron.

WW: Is there anything you can identify that you regret about your Senate career or any major disappointments that as you think back on you would rather have turned out differently?

JLB: Well, the election.

WW: I haven't gotten to that yet. That's next.

JLB: Other than that, I am sure that there are but I would have to really sit down and think about it. I am having the same trouble with my mind as you are having with this machine.

On reflection, my major disappointment was with the Senate as it exists today. For anyone interested in questions of public policy, I can think of no experience more glorious than to have been a United States senator back in the days when Congress pretty much limited itself to the responsibilities specifically assigned to it by the Constitution. But those days are gone. As I mentioned earlier, a 1970 study of Congress concluded that its workload had doubled every five years since 1935. Given the fact that, in simpler times, Congress worked at a leisurely pace and was in session for only six or seven months a year, its members could no doubt take the initial increases in stride simply by devoting more hours per day and more months per year to their work. Over time, however, the available hours and months were exhausted, and the increasing demands could only be accommodated at the sacrifice of quality. Another consequence of this doubling and redoubling has been the conversion of what had once been citizen-legislators, who would return to their home communities and their normal lives during half the year, into Washington-based careerists with a diminished taste for taking political risks in the line of duty.

The Senate I knew, however, did retain one characteristic of its glory days, and that was a palpable civility. I was struck by it on entering the Senate; and it went far deeper than such statements, on the Senate floor, as "Unfortunately, the honorable Senior Senator from North Carolina, whom I greatly admire, has misstated every fact" as a substitute for a more direct "Senator So-and-so has lied to us." There were occasional lapses, of course, but this civility permeated every relationship on and off the floor and created an atmosphere that made it easier to conduct business on highly emotional issues in a reasonably civilized way. I am told that this too has been in retreat under the unrelenting pressures encountered today.

WW: Let's talk about the campaign in 1976. Am I right that you campaigned against [*Daniel Patrick*] Moynihan?

JLB: Yes.

Given what I have just said about life in the Senate, it is fair to ask why I sought another term instead of just packing up and moving on to other more constructive pursuits. I had seeded some ground that I thought I could cultivate and harvest in the course of another term, and I wanted the chance to do so.

WW: Tell me about that campaign. What were the major issues? What were the politics? What happened?

JLB: I think I should say something as a prelude to all of this because it is very relevant to how the campaign turned out. You may or may not recall that in 1975 New York City experienced a huge financial crisis, faced bankruptcy, and actually became bankrupt, although no one used that word.

WW: That's when the *New York Post* had the headline that said "Governor to New York City: Drop Dead."

JLB: Actually, it was the *Daily News*, and the headline was "Ford to City: Drop Dead." The instant appeal from people in New York City and New York State was for federal guarantees of New York City borrowing, and I flatly opposed that. As a result, during the campaign leaflets were handed out that reprinted that headline with an added line reading, "and Buckley was the pallbearer."

If Gerald Ford had listened to my advice, that headline would never have been written and he might have won the election. A few days before it came out, I had a meeting with the president at which I expressed my concern over his use of New York City's financial crisis as the whipping boy in a series of speeches about civic irresponsibility that he had been delivering around the country in the preceding weeks. His tone was harsh, and his poll ratings began to plummet in the city's normally Republican suburbs. I told him that while his refusal to have the federal government guarantee New York's bonds was sound policy, he was coming across as holding all New Yorkers responsible for the mess rather than the City Hall

With Cardinal Cooke, welcoming Cardinal Wojtyla of Krakow to New York in 1976. (Three years later, he would be Pope John Paul II.)

incompetents who had created it, and they resented it. I urged him to express his sympathy for the city's residents as victims of wretched political mismanagement, explain that New York State had both the responsibility and the capacity to straighten out the city's affairs, and assure New Yorkers that his administration would work with state officials in any appropriate way to ease the pain. Ford told me he hadn't realized he had made so bad an impression on New Yorkers, asked an aide to take note of what I had been saying, and sent me on my way. Two days later, when the White House announced that the president would be making an important statement about New York City, I turned on my office TV set, and waited in confidence for some sympathetic words. Instead, his tone was harsher than ever and the resulting Daily News *headline could only be described as fair comment. Yet despite this, Ford came close to carrying New York, and that would have given him the election. Now back to my well-advertised opposition to federal guarantees of the city's debt.*

WW: Now there's a campaign issue. You knew you were handing him a campaign issue.

JLB: Yes, but I didn't know how I could be credible in the future if I didn't apply the same standards to my state that I would apply to anybody else's. A very important point of principle was involved. New York City's problems were the direct result of gross mismanagement. City employees were paid substantially more than those of any other major city; they could retire earlier with larger pensions, and so on. How a city is managed is the direct responsibility of its citizens and of the state in which it is located, not the federal government. While it is reasonable to call on the citizens of all the states to help victims of a natural disaster that strikes one part of the country this year and another the next, I could (and can) see no reason why they should be called upon to bail out the victims of a man-made municipal disaster. I worked with the Ford administration on an alternative approach to New York's problems that did provide New York with some significant help. Even well-run municipalities will do periodic short-term financing to maintain their cash flow—that is to say, to fill the gap between the periodic collection of taxes and the need to pay bills on a weekly or monthly basis. New York City, however, was no longer able to borrow. So the plan I worked on with the Treasury Department involved helping the city with its cash flow by accelerating certain federal payments that would fall due later in the year. This approach enabled the city to pay its operating costs and maintain its essential services, but it didn't involve additional subsidies from the federal government. In the meantime New York State passed legislation that created a board with the power to manage the city's affairs. The New York State legislature went a step further: it suspended payment on one series of New York City obligations, which is basically what happens when you go into bankruptcy. The suspension of debt payments was subsequently found to be unconstitutional by New York State's highest court. That, however, was well after the election. In the meantime I had to face Moynihan. He had been a very effective ambassador to the UN and was particularly effective in defending Israel against Third World attempts to paint it as a pariah state. He stood out as a lonely champion of fair play, and it made him an enormously popular public figure in New York. On one television program, which I happened to see, he was asked if he had any thought of running for the Senate; and he said "no," that it would be dishonorable of him to use his position at the UN to do that.

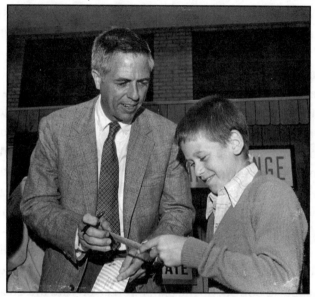

Hustling votes at the New York State Fair, 1976.

WW: You picked that up in your campaign literature?

JLB: No, nor did he flash the letter I sent him saying, "I'm much relieved, because if you did I would probably have to step down." But anyway, he was my opponent—by a very, very narrow margin. He won the Democratic primary against Congresswoman Bella Abzug by less than 1 percent. It would have been a different story had she been the candidate. So all of this was undoubtedly destined by someone way up there.

WW: Well, it's all politics. You never know.

JLB: My position on New York City was enormously harmful to me. Whereas, in my first election, I had substantial pluralities in the bedroom counties around New York City—Nassau, Suffolk, and Westchester. I lost them in 1976; but I did have a very healthy majority—about 63 percent or 64 percent of the vote—upstate. Also, of course, it didn't help to have Moynihan as my opponent. He was generally viewed as a conservative Democrat, which cut into my earlier blue collar vote; and because of his eloquent defense of Israel in the United Nations, he had an absolutely solid hold on the Jewish vote. In fact, two of New York's most prominent Jewish Republicans told me, at a strategy meeting in my New York City office before the Democratic primaries, that if Moynihan won the nomination, they would be unable to help me because they had to protect their own positions within the Jewish community. There was, however, one thing that did please me about the 1976 election. Right after my 1970 election as the Conservative Party's candidate, which caused the press such horror, I was asked what I would like to accomplish in the Senate. I said that one of the things I hoped to accomplish was to demonstrate that conservatives do care. I very consciously worked at this during my six years in office, and I assigned a woman in my New York City office the task of showing blacks how they could take advantage of programs that would help them in all kinds of areas based on their own abilities and merit—the establishment of small enterprises, home ownership, you name it. We showed them how to do such things as get access to credit and training. [*I also introduced legislation designed to help blacks establish businesses and own their homes.*] That was very much appreciated. I received several awards from black organizations, something that neither the *New York Times* nor the television stations ever reported. During the 1976 campaign, I marched across 125th Street in Harlem in the company of Floyd Patterson, the black heavyweight boxing champion, and the president of the Malcolm X Democratic Club of Harlem. This was a pro-Buckley demonstration that went unreported by the broadcast media. I'm told that I received about 20 percent of the black vote as opposed to the 6 or 7 percent who voted for Gerald Ford. Anyway, I was very pleased with this.

I suspect that one reason I received so large a percentage was that Pat Moynihan was in disfavor with much of the black leadership because of his advice to Nixon, some years earlier, that he treat them with "benign neglect." That advice was probably sound in its particular context, but it was bound to be misunderstood. The fact remained that I had earned the trust of a number of black leaders because I neither ignored nor pandered to them. Rather, I had demonstrated that I understood the problems faced by too many blacks and had done my best to help them work their way up the economic ladder. To put it another way, I had demonstrated that I really did care.

WW: So Moynihan won for whatever reasons and then you did run again. Didn't you run later against Senator Dodd?

JLB: Yes.

WW: Was that two years later?

JLB: Four years.

WW: How did you decide to run against Dodd and what about that campaign?

JLB: I felt that I had earned a position in the Senate that would enable me to achieve some of my goals in a second term. But I had privately decided that I would not serve more than two terms. I felt that, in twelve years, I should be able to contribute whatever I had to contribute in the framing of public policy. Moreover, for the reasons I have mentioned earlier, it was getting harder and harder to be a serious legislator. The Senate could no longer claim to be a truly deliberative body because it was trying to juggle a host of problems and complaints that previously would have been handled by county seats or state houses—or resolved without government intervention of any kind.

If I had been returned to the Senate, I would have added several items to my legislative agenda. One that had reached the top of my list was the desirability of term limitations on all federal elective offices.

My epiphany on that subject occurred in November 1970. Nixon had invited me to meet with him shortly after my election. When I was ushered into the Oval Office, Nixon was standing behind his desk. He was completing a meeting with George Shultz (then director of the Office of Management and Budget) and John Erlichman, who was the president's domestic affairs advisor. As I entered, I heard Nixon say, ". . . but Milton Friedman doesn't understand that an election will be coming up." It seemed clear that the three men had been discussing Friedman's advice on a particular economic matter, that they agreed with that advice, but that the president was reluctant to act on it because of its possible impact on his 1972 reelection campaign. That persuaded me that the presidency should be limited to a single six-year term. I felt (and continue to feel) that six years is long enough to give a president a fair opportunity to deliver on his campaign promises, but not so long as to enable him to inflict irreparable harm on the Republic should he prove to be a disaster.

In time, I came to realize that the temptation to avoid any position that might jeopardize reelection applied with equal force to members of Congress. By the time I left the Senate, I had blocked out a constitutional amendment that would have limited a president to a single six-year term and members of the Senate and House to 12 years in each of those bodies—with, of course, appropriate grandfathering provisions to encourage disinterested votes on the part of those who would have to approve it. Although this would allow one reelection campaign in the case of senators and five for members of the House and therefore permit a member of the House who made it to the Senate to spend up to 24 years on Capitol Hill, my amendment would make it impossible for most of them to make careers of legislative service.

If I had had the opportunity to introduce my amendment, I would not have expected senators to stand in line for the privilege of cosponsoring it. It would have been my hope, however, that its introduction would catch the media's attention and start a national debate on the subject. New ideas take time to take root. In this case (as events in 1994 would prove), the soil was apparently more receptive than I had realized. I refer to the provision for term limitations in House Speaker Newt Gingrich's "Contract with America." The idea caught the public's fancy and helped elect, that year, the first Republican majority in the House of Representatives since 1954.

Another project that would have been high on my second term agenda was the organization of a sustained assault on congressional pork. It was my plan to enlist two or three other senators in a systematic crusade to focus public outrage on a practice that was bad enough in my time and has since escalated to scandalous proportions. (In 2005, for example, the highway appropriations bill enacted by Congress and signed by the president contained 6,371 items of purely local interest that would add over $24 billion to the ballooning federal deficit.) The only way to curb the practice would be to put the spotlight on the worst offenders and shame them into acting as national legislators rather than as county officials hustling votes. We wouldn't have been popular; but over time, I believe we could have made a difference. Of course, it might have required the enactment of term limitations to find enough colleagues willing to take the heat and to relinquish this means of currying favor with local constituencies.

I now return to the second part of the question I had been asked: "what about [the Dodd] campaign?" Needless to say, I lost—and it wasn't even close. Chris had two significant advantages that I wasn't able to overcome. The first was Connecticut's liberal coloration; the second, his last name. Before announcing my decision to seek election to the Senate in Connecticut, I called on Lowell Weicker as a matter of courtesy to inform him of the fact. He was not pleased. He told me that, while I had been a good senator, my political views wouldn't fly in today's Connecticut, and he was proven right. Unfortunately, one campaign season was insufficient to breathe enlightenment into the state's citizenry and, I must admit, Chris was a more effective campaigner.

Chris Dodd's second advantage derived from the fact that he was the son of former Senator Thomas Dodd, a man I and a large part of the state much admired even though his career had a sad and, I believe, unjust ending. I had met Tom Dodd at a retreat house near Hartford a year or two before he was elected to the

Senate and followed his career with special interest. He had a first class record in the areas of defense and foreign policy which, alas, his son did not emulate; and on the domestic front, he was far better than most northeastern Democrats. So Chris had the advantages of a well-known and respected name, a pleasing public presence, and political views that were more in tune with those of the electorate than mine. On election night, when I made my concession speech (at an insultingly early hour), I said that while obviously disappointed at the outcome, I took pleasure in the joy that the Dodd family must be feeling that evening, and I meant it. I also offered Chris a bound volume of my position papers for his guidance once he took his Senate seat. But as his subsequent voting record has demonstrated, he failed to accept my offer.

WW: Do you think it's worse now than it was when you were in the Senate?

JLB: Yes. I'm told so.

WW: People of course are leaving the Senate that you might not otherwise expect to leave.

During my last two or three years, more than one senior senator remarked to me that "the Senate isn't fun anymore," or words to that effect. They had seen some substantial changes in the institution, and they didn't like them.

JLB: There are only so many hours in a day; and if your job is to give careful thought to national needs and national strategies for achieving those needs, you have to have uninterrupted time. You need time to study.

WW: And there's no time to do that in the Senate; that's what everybody says.

JLB: It used to be a reflective place where people could examine and discuss matters in depth; and when the scope of federal authority was understood to be limited to the areas enumerated in the Constitution, senators were able to be truly deliberative and to complete their work in five or six months and then go home.

WW: Did you find that it changed over the six years you were there?

JLB: Yes. At the beginning of every morning my secretary would hand me an index card with my schedule for the day, including my committee and subcommittee assignments, hearings, and so on. When I first arrived, I sometimes found that I had two committee meetings scheduled for the same time. During my last year, it was not uncommon for me to have three committees or subcommittees meeting at the same time. Yet a senator's primary institutional responsibility was to master all of his own committees' work. As a practical matter, this was no longer possible.

To give some idea of how congested a senator's day could be, I reproduce the schedule my secretary handed me on my arrival at my office on Tuesday, April 6, 1976:

> *9:00 a.m. — Press breakfast [a weekly coffee and doughnut meeting with New York reporters]*
> *9:15 a.m. — Public Works Committee on National Public Works Program*
> *9:30 a.m. — Consumer Subcommittee of Commerce on Price Disclosure*
> *10:00 a.m. — Subcommittee on Water Resources*
> *10:00 a.m. — Joint Committee on Atomic Energy on nuclear fuel assurance*
> *12:30-2:00 p.m. — stop by luncheon hosted by Congressman Ham Fish for Hudson Valley labor leaders*
> *12:30 p.m. — Republican Policy Committee lunch*
> *2:00 p.m. — Joint Committee on Atomic Energy on Clinch River Breeder Reactor Program*
> *4:00 p.m. — Meeting with Chairman of Board of Pfizer Pharmaceutical and Vice President on tax reform*
> *4:30 p.m. — Republican Steering Committee [the name adopted by a group of conservative senators who met periodically to plan and coordinate legislative initiatives]*

On that day, I was unable to attend most of my committee meetings, and I had no time to read mail, study pending legislation, review staff memos, or work off my list of telephone calls before heading off for home with a very full briefcase. April

6, 1976, was a particularly bad day; but, as I said, during my last years, it was not unusual to find two or three committee meetings scheduled for the same time. I can only believe that the situation has continued to deteriorate.

During my six years in office, I witnessed both a significant increase in the already frenetic pace of the Senate as well as an equally significant decline in its ability to get very much done that could honestly be labeled "thoughtful." This is not a reflection on the quality of its members, who were generally an able lot. The fact remains that senators' days have become so fractured by competing claims on finite time that they, as well as their colleagues in the House, have too often found themselves incapable of handling even such fundamental obligations as the timely enactment of the appropriations required for the orderly functioning of the government.

WW: You think it's going to get any better? Is there any way to make it any better?

JLB: I have my own thoughts on the matter. They boil down to the need to rediscover federalism and decide that the federal government should not become involved in areas that state governments are capable of handling—whether or not one approves of the manner in which they do so. This was the division of governmental labor that was originally written into the Constitution. Modern developments may require some rethinking as to where the line is to be drawn, but the principle remains sound. Anyway, that is my solution.

There are ways, no doubt, to increase the efficiency of the institution and carve out a little more time for reflection. But any such improvements would be marginal at best. Having since served in the other two branches of the federal government, I believe more than ever that there is only one road to true reform, and that is to rediscover and reapply the principle of federalism and, in that way, reduce the scope of federal responsibilities to manageable size. I don't suggest that it is either possible or even desirable to replicate the division between state and federal authority that once obtained in this country. Too much water is over the dam, too many fundamental changes have occurred in American life. What I do hope is that we can rediscover the wisdom of the original constitutional design and that we then determine, in the light of today's conditions, which level of government should be doing what.

There will always be an argument as to where the line is to be drawn. But I think it less important where it is drawn than that one be drawn that leaves no question as to the outer limits of federal authority. Of course, having done so, all parties—especially the courts—would have to take a blood oath to abide by the new dispensation. This means that if the more enlightened folk who gravitate to Washington don't like the way the citizens of Arizona, or Delaware, or Michigan choose to manage their own affairs, they will have to suppress the impulse to impose enlightenment on them. But perhaps in the fullness of time, Washington could learn to set aside the arrogance that assumes that the citizens of the several states can't be trusted to govern themselves.

I recognize that my modest proposal would require an uncommon substitution of philosophy for politics; but ours, after all, is a system uniquely based on a philosophical conception of the nature of Man and of the limits of human institutions. Those limits are being tested; and perhaps it is not altogether romantic to hope that necessity, if not philosophy, will lead us to rediscover the merits of the Constitution's original design. If so, the Senate may once again achieve its former greatness.

WW: Do you think a lot of it is just increased demand from the public? The expectations of the citizenry are greater now than they used to be? People expect their senators to be able to do more?

JLB: Yes, that is true today; but I would blame this on the encroachment by Washington on what used to be understood to be the exclusive jurisdiction of state and local governments. Until the Johnson Great Society programs came on stream, most Americans were never affected by legislation coming out of Washington, except the income tax. But now you have a federal finger in just about every pie. Now, if people want relief or if they want help, they have been conditioned to turn to friendly representatives in Washington. I happened to be in the office of Senator Robert A. Taft on the morning of December 8, 1941, waiting to be escorted to the

Capitol with his nephew and another Yale friend. We couldn't get into the House of Representatives to hear Roosevelt ask for the Declaration of War, but Mrs. Taft invited us to hear it on her portable radio in a room off the Senate floor. In any event, while waiting until it was time to leave, we volunteered to sort his mail, which filled about a third of a standard mail bag; and Taft was a very important senator in those days. Thirty years later, I found myself serving in the Senate with his son, Robert Jr. I asked him how many bags of mail he received on the average morning. He told me four or five. That difference is a measure of the increased impact of federal laws on the average citizen over the intervening years.

In 1941, when my friends and I visited Senator Taft's office, the United States Code on his shelf consisted of three volumes (exclusive of tables and index) containing 4,499 pages of federal statutes, including all of those enacted in the haydays of the New Deal. Thirty years later, when his son and I reported for senatorial duty, the code contained 12,582 pages of statutes; and by the end of my six-year term, the number had increased to 17,330. To illustrate the explosive growth of the regulatory state, the 1964 edition of the Code, which came out the year after Lyndon Johnson took office, contained 519 pages dealing with programs under Title 42, "The Public Health and Welfare," which has become a dumping ground for new laws expanding the federal government's regulatory authority. Thanks in substantial part to five years of Johnson's Great Society legislation, by 1970, the laws falling within Title 42 covered 1,202 pages. By 2000, the year in which I hung up my judicial robe, the United States Code had exploded to 26 volumes of statutory law, five of which contained 6,265 pages devoted exclusively to Title 42 programs—a number that is almost 50 percent greater than that of the entire body of federal legislation when I visited Washington in 1941. But nowadays, statutory law is just the tip of the federal iceberg. By the year 2000, federal bureaus, agencies, and departments had generated enough fine print regulations to fill 19 feet of shelf space. These are often arbitrary, but they have the force of law. It is small wonder that bewildered citizens generate such a flood of congressional mail.

WW: Is it just that people are writing their senators? Aren't they also expecting more out of state government? Everybody is expecting more from government.

JLB: Oh sure. Everybody is expecting more from government. We've moved into the age of the welfare state; but still, in the past they would not have turned to Washington the way they do today.

WW: After you left the Senate what did you do? It looks like you did a number of things, including going to the State Department. But before you went to the State Department, did you work at Donaldson, Lufkin & Jenrette?

JLB: Yes.

WW: As a consultant of some kind?

JLB: I was there for about a year working on spot assignments and continued to serve on their board of directors for a couple of years thereafter.

WW: Were you doing international work?

JLB: I did one international project, yes. I went over to Saudi Arabia to help raise money for a venture capital program that had been pioneered by a subsidiary of DLJ. It was beautifully conceived and was supervised by a wonderful team. But after that, there were some dramatic developments in our family business that took me away. I worked as a consultant for a couple of years to see if we could develop a new line of business. And then I became involved in my Senate campaign in Connecticut.

WW: Who was running the family business while you were in the Senate?

JLB: My brother John and Ben Heath.

WW: When last we talked about it, the company was involved with oil ventures.

JLB: Catawba provided a variety of services to seven companies that were publicly owned. They were engaged in oil and gas exploration ventures in different areas outside the United States with the exception of Florida and had altogether about 80,000 shareholders.

WW: And did it move into a different business?

JLB: Its old business had disappeared. The SEC decided that because the public companies all had what was deemed to be a management contract with Catawba, they would all have to be treated as affiliated. This in turn would have raised financing and other problems for Catawba's clients. Therefore, the contracts were terminated and virtually all of Catawba's executives went to work for the various client companies. This left Catawba with some capital and a history in the oil exploration business, but with only a couple of employees with any experience in it. Then the question was whether it was possible to develop a new business. We decided to enter the oil tax shelter business; but it turned out that our timing couldn't have been worse. After a great deal of work investigating various drilling deals that we could then market, oil and gas prices started tumbling, and the interest in petroleum-related tax shelters simply dried up. So we finally decided to liquidate the company. In the meantime, I continued to work on several projects, served on a couple of corporate boards, and did radio commentaries for the Westinghouse Group and as the house conservative on the Public Broadcasting System's "All Things Considered." This takes me to 1980 and my campaign as the Connecticut Republican Party's candidate for election to the Senate. I again failed to get elected; but a man I much admired became president of the United States, and I decided to see if there might be an interesting position for me in the Reagan administration.

During my six years representing New York in the Senate, I never had a private meal with its governor, Nelson Rockefeller. During those same years, I twice dined with the Reagans in their Sacramento, California home and saw him on a number of occasions in Washington and New York. Reagan and I marched to the same political drummer; Rockefeller and I did not. Soon after Reagan's election, I contacted the people in charge of recruiting his presidential team. In doing so, I expressed my preference for a position that was involved in the formulation of policy and cautioned the recruiters that management was not my strong suit; it was and is, in fact, a very weak one. In early December, I received a call from Reagan's choice for Secretary of Defense, Cap Weinberger, who offered me the position of Secretary of the Air Force. I thanked him, said that I was concerned about the administrative responsibilities that came with that job, and told him I would give his offer careful consideration and get back to him. A few hours later, Secretary of State-designate Al Haig called to offer me the position of Under Secretary of State for Security Assistance, which was principally concerned with the provision of military and economic assistance to nations important to our national security. I told him it sounded interesting, and after making a few telephone calls to get a better picture of what it would entail, I accepted. It was with some regret that I turned down the Pentagon job because I had come to know Weinberger rather well during my Senate days and was very fond of him, but I never regretted my decision.

WW: And that's when you went to the State Department.

JLB: That's right.

WW: What did you do while you were at the State Department?

JLB: I was Under Secretary of State for Security Assistance. Security Assistance involved a variety of military and economic programs designed to help and strengthen countries in which we had a security interest. The latter are not to be confused with our A.I.D. [*Agency for International Development*] programs, which sought to help the needy irrespective of how they fit into the security equation. The countries that were the beneficiaries of the economic programs I administered included such strategically located ones as Malaysia, Thailand, the Philippines, Israel, and Egypt. The military programs involved both the gift of military hardware and the sale of such equipment and the provision of military training on a discounted basis. Those programs accounted for the major part of the State Department budget and required a fair amount of traveling on my part. One of my major assignments was to reestablish a cooperative security relationship with Pakistan in response to the Soviet invasion of Afghanistan. I also headed a task group consisting of under secretaries of state, defense, and commerce and a representative of the National Security Council in a failed attempt to persuade our NATO allies that their extension of credits to the Soviets at sweetheart, below-market rates made little sense. An important part of my job was to persuade Congress of the merits of the administration's initiatives— including such touchy ones as the need to provide Saudi Arabia with AWACS aircraft in the face of fierce opposition from Jewish groups. It was an interesting couple of years.

My full title was Under Secretary for Security Assistance, Science and Technology. Most of my responsibilities fell under "Security Assistance," but "Science" provided me a welcomed but limited opportunity to be involved in environmental concerns. I was the fifth-ranking officer in the department, was formally responsible for the lion's share of its budget, and had direct command authority over a staff consisting of a very able and experienced foreign service officer, Dick Aherne, three recently fledged ones, and two secretaries. At a later date, when numbers had to be crunched and a budget negotiated among competing supplicants, I was able to secure the services of a bright young man, John Wolf, who understood both figures and the art of intra-departmental diplomacy; and on the rare occasions when I had to attend to a matter that fell under the rubric of Science and Technology, I was able to secure the assistance of Bill Salmon, who knew his way around such occult subjects as the international allocation of the radio spectrum. That was it. To secure the information, analyses, and research I needed to do my job, I had to turn, hat in hand, to the heads of an autonomous fiefdom within the department, such as the director of the Bureau for Politico-Military Affairs or the assistant secretaries in charge of the relevant regional bureaus, and ask for it. Each of these satraps would oblige in short order and with unfailing competence, but I could never shake the impression that I was getting the requested information as a favor rather than as a matter of right. It was an odd system organizationally, but it worked.

My first task after settling in concerned the Reagan administration's policy regarding military assistance, which represented a sharp reversal from that in effect under President Jimmy Carter. The Carter administration appeared to regard the sale or transfer of arms to countries with whom we shared a common security interest as somehow unclean, or even morally reprehensible, and it adopted policies towards military aid to friends and allies that substituted a provincial theology for a healthy sense of self-preservation. Although our most critical allies continued to be provided with necessary arms, however grudgingly, the effect of the Carter policy was to erode our ability to work with a number of nations in defending common interests and deterring threats by the Soviet Union and its surrogates. And those threats were growing. Since our debacle in Vietnam, the Soviets had established bases in South Yemen and Ethiopia, encouraged insurgencies in southern Africa and Central America, and invaded Afghanistan.

I unveiled the Reagan arms transfer policy in a speech delivered in May 1981 at a Williamsburg, Virginia meeting of the Aerospace Industries Association. I noted that the current administration proposed to ensure that nations with whom we shared common security concerns had the kinds of military equipment required to enable them to protect their own independence and contribute to regional stability. Needless to say, given its audience, it was a smashing success. It is one thing, of course, to proclaim a new policy and quite another to implement it. Congress was still suffering from its post-Vietnam traumas and was wary of any new commitments of military hardware; and weaker allies that were under pressure either to join the "Nonaligned Movement" led by nations like India or change sides had to be satisfied that the United States could be trusted over the longer run. As a consequence, I spent much time during the ensuing months defending the new policy before congressional committees and making courtesy calls on often skeptical nations in Southeast Asia and the Near East to allay understandable fears about our reliability.

A major Reagan administration objective was to restore a security relationship with Pakistan and provide it with the weapons required to meet the new threat posed by the Soviet invasion of Afghanistan. President Carter had suspended both economic and military assistance in early 1979 in response to intelligence reports that the Pakistanis were pursuing a covert program to enrich uranium. Pakistan responded by joining the Nonaligned Movement. Then came the Soviets' Christmas Eve invasion of Afghanistan, which converted Pakistan *overnight into a front line state in the Cold War. Carter then directed his people to work on a new package of military and economic assistance. What they came up with was an offer of $400 million in economic and military aid over a two year period, which Pakistan's president, General Mohammed Zia ul-Haq, dismissed as "Peanuts!" Further discussions led nowhere; and by mid-summer, it appeared that Zia had concluded that his best recourse was to await the outcome of our 1980 presidential election.*

On taking office, the Reagan administration developed a program that would provide Pakistan with a credible deterrent to either a Soviet incursion or a Soviet attempt to dismember the country by exploiting tribal rivalries. It consisted of a comprehensive $3.2 billion five-year package of economic assistance and sales of military equipment including 40 F-16 jet fighters. It was my job to present it to General Zia and seek his agreement. And so, in June 1981, I headed for Pakistan's capitol, Islamabad. My party and I were met at the airport by our ambassador, Arthur Hummel, and we drove off to our hotel. As we were approaching it, I saw a large whitewashed wall on which was written, in huge letters, "BUCKLEY YANKEE GO HOME." I was flattered by the attention, but the authorities must have considered the sign impolitic as it was painted over by the next morning.

The following day, Ambassador Hummel and I went to Zia's residence to present the American proposal. After the usual pleasantries, Zia noted that Pakistanis had become highly skeptical about the reliability of American promises and that his government had gone to some trouble to consolidate his country's status as a nonaligned nation abroad and to sell its virtues at home. I replied that Pakistan now had the best of all reasons for trusting us. As a result of the Soviet occupation of Afghanistan, we had a most compelling interest in Pakistan's ability to protect its independence and prevent the establishment of a Soviet base on the Arabian Sea. Pakistan, of course, had even stronger reasons for wanting to enhance its ability to deter incursions from Afghanistan. After discussing some of the details of our offer, Zia thanked me for my presentation, acknowledged that the United States was offering more than peanuts, and told me he would give our proposal very serious thought.

As we left Zia's residence, Ambassador Hummel turned to me and said, "You done good." I have often thought of the trepidations that career diplomats must feel when they stand by silently while delicate and important negotiations are conducted by high level political appointees whose competence had yet to be tested. It was reassuring to know that I had passed the Hummel test.

Two days later, I received a call advising me that Zia wished to see me. He met me with a smile, told me that he had discussed our proposal with his key advisors and that he was inclined to accept it. He would not be able to do so, however, until after he had prepared his country for what would be viewed as a dramatic change of course. He then said something that I found both curious and instructive: "Because I am a dictator, I have to make sure the people are with me when I make a decision of this importance." I had always assumed that dictators neither described themselves as such nor paid that much attention to what the people might want. His remark suggested that he was a cautious man. It may also be the case that he was using the word "dictator" in the old Roman sense of one who, like Cincinnatus, is entrusted with plenary power in order to deal with a crisis. What Zia proposed to do was conduct the Pakistani equivalent of town meetings in various parts of the country where the alternatives facing Pakistan could be examined and the reasons favoring a change of course discussed.

Whatever his concerns over Pakistani public opinion, it seemed clear that Zia himself was delighted by our offer. He provided a government plane to fly us to

Karachi, where we would have to spend seven or eight hours before catching a very early morning flight back to the United States. On our arrival in Karachi, while the other members of my party were taken to a standard issue guest house, I was whisked off to one reserved for only the most exalted of VIPs. By then, it was nine in the evening and we would be leaving for the airport in another few hours. I was ushered into an elegant apartment where I found plates of fruits and cheeses awaiting me as well as a man who was to serve as my personal valet, a service for which I had had no previous experience. I also found a large wooden crate containing a marble

With General Mohammed Zia ul-Hag.

table that, I was told, General Zia had ordered to be presented to me just hours before. I was dog tired, but had to address the logistics of getting this gift to Washington before I could turn in; but before I could do that, I had to persuade my valet that I really didn't need his help in order to undress. (For the benefit of grandchildren who might wonder what happened to that table, it was turned over to the U.S. government, as must all gifts over a nominal value that are received by officers of the United States from a foreign government.)

In due course, the town hall meetings were held and, on September 14, 1981, we were able to announce the outlines of the new relationship. Pakistan and the Reagan administration may have been delighted, but certain members of

Congress, particularly Senator John Glenn, were far less so. The sticking point was Pakistan's clandestine efforts to develop a nuclear weapons capability. I use the word "capability" because I am persuaded that Zia did not intend to build a bomb; rather, he wanted the ability to produce a weapon in short order in the event India tested one, and India had already exploded an underground nuclear device. As I pointed out in hearings in both the Senate and the House, the with-holding of American economic and military assistance, as mandated by a provi-sion of the Foreign Assistance Act, had not kept the Pakistanis from proceeding with their nuclear program. On the other hand, the establishment of a close secu-rity relationship with that country would give us a better chance of dissuading them from actually building a weapon. In the meantime, a Pakistan strong enough to discourage a Soviet thrust to the Arabian Sea was clearly in our interest. So we sought, and secured, congressional approval of our package as well as a waiver of the provision prohibiting economic and military assistance to that country.

This was hard going, but not nearly as hard as persuading Congress on the merits of selling Saudi Arabia five Airborne Warning and Control System aircraft. These served as aerial platforms for super-sophisticated radar systems capable of tracking large numbers of planes. They had formidable capabilities, and the Saudis had a clear need for them. Two well-armed Soviet proxies, Ethiopia and South Yemen, now straddled the approaches to the Red Sea, aircraft based in Afghanistan could easily reach the oil facilities bordering on the Persian Gulf, and during the Iraq-Iran war, Iran had sent combat aircraft across the Gulf to demonstrate its ability to threaten targets in the oil-producing states bordering it. And Saudi targets were extraordinarily vulnerable. Because they were located on a flat landscape, ground-based radar could give less than five minutes' warning of an attack by low flying aircraft. An AWACS flying at an altitude of 30,000 feet would provide Saudi fighters ample time to scramble and meet attacking planes.

The problem was in satisfying nervous senators and congressmen that the AWACS would pose no threat to Israel. In my visits to congressional offices, I made three points: first, the Saudis had a legitimate need for them; if we failed to provide them for purely political reasons, we would seriously undermine our ability to deal effectively with the Saudis and the neighboring states on whose oil the West depended. Second, the Saudis had agreed to a series of operational safeguards that would ensure that the AWACS would be used for defensive purposes only. And third, the Israelis had the unchallengeable capability of destroying any AWACS foolhardy enough to come within operational range of their country. The Jewish lobbies, however, kept turning up the heat. On the day the issue came to a vote in the Senate, I stood by in a room off the Senate floor in case any last-minute proselytizing was required, and the vice president was on hand to cast the deciding vote in the event of a tie. It wasn't until the end of the roll call that I knew we had won, albeit by the razor thin margin of 52 to 48. I was particularly impressed by the political courage exhibited by Senator Bill Cohen's "Aye" vote because, as a Jew, he was under extraordinary pressure to vote against the AWACS sale.

I learned from these experiences the exquisite difficulties the United States faces in areas, like the Middle East, where countries with whom we need to maintain security relationships can be at one another's throats; and so we have to calibrate our assistance in such a manner that one partner will not feel threatened by the weapons we provide another. Saudi Arabia needed the AWACS for its own protection, and we had a large self-interest in its having them. But the safeguards we had to negotiate in order to satisfy the critics, and the questions raised in Congress over Saudi Arabia's reliability and motives, proved so humiliating that the Saudis subsequently turned to other sources for substantial portions of their arms purchases, sources that were far less scrupulous about upsetting regional balances than we had been.

Another one of my jobs was to explain the administration's positions on such hot potato issues as our assistance to the rebels who were trying to oust a Communist-supported government in Nicaragua and to the beleaguered government in El Salvador which was trying to avoid being ousted by Communist-supplied guerrillas. I use the terms "Communist-supported" and "Communist-supplied" advisedly as there was ample evidence that, in each case, the bad guys were receiving large quantities of military equipment produced in Soviet East European satellites and shipped to Central America through Cuba. My description of the El Salvadoran government as "beleaguered" is equally well-advised. During a brief visit there in early 1982, I heard gunfire every night from my bedroom in the American ambassador's residence. During the day, when the ambassador and I were making our calls, we drove in a heavily armored military vehicle preceded and followed by jeeps filled with soldiers who, at each stop, would jump out, machine guns in hand, to make sure the coast was clear before the ambassador and I were allowed to leave our car.

Unfortunately, elements of the Salvadoran military were capable of some ugly actions. These included the assassination of an archbishop and the murder of a group of American nuns, which generated a lot of understandable hostility in the United States towards the administration's Central American policies. The killing of the nuns led to the most charming reason I ever heard on my congressional rounds for why a particular legislator would not back the administration's position. The legendary and enormously engaging Speaker of the House, Tip O'Neill, told me he couldn't support the president's policy in El Salvador because his favorite aunt was a nun, and she would never forgive him if he did. I admired both the sentiment and his candor.

My role as a proselytizer was not limited to Capitol Hill. From time to time, an issue involving security matters would arise that had to be addressed in the public arena, and I would be deployed to do the addressing, usually at meetings that commanded significant media attention. One of them was the call by a number of prestigious groups, including the United States Conference of Catholic Bishops, for an immediate, unilateral halt to the testing, production, and deployment of nuclear missiles by the United States. The advocates of the "nuclear freeze" reasoned that as each side had enough atomic weapons to destroy the world ten times over, a further build-up of our doomsday forces could serve no rational purpose and would merely provoke the Kremlin into building still more weapons of its own. They also argued that a unilateral freeze would induce the Soviets to follow suit and encourage them to negotiate mutual reductions in existing nuclear forces. This was in response to Reagan's decision to launch a crash program to upgrade our strategic capabilities. My job was to show why this was the saner course, and the one more likely to lead to negotiated arms reductions.

As I explained to a key audience at the Chicago Economic Club and tried to before a blue ribbon group at San Francisco's Commonwealth Club of California, among the many problems with the arguments of the nuclear freezers was that while American nuclear inventories had remained largely unchanged over the past dozen years, the Soviets were continuing to deploy new weapons at an unprecedented rate. Within the previous ten years, they had built three new classes of intercontinental missiles, added 60 nuclear submarines to their fleet to our one, *deployed over 250 modern bombers (which they were continuing to produce at the rate of two a month), and installed a massive air defense system. Thanks to this build-up, the Soviets had acquired the ability to destroy virtually all of our land-based missiles and command, control, and communications systems in an initial strike while their own hardened installations remained relatively immune to a U.S. counterattack. They had also constructed formidable anti-aircraft barriers to bombers not destroyed on the ground and they were hard at work on breakthroughs in antisubmarine warfare technology. Furthermore, although we had been exercising unilateral restraint, the Soviets had declined Jimmy Carter's invitation to discuss a cut-back in our respective inventories. I suggested that the surest way to halt Soviet adventurism and bring the Kremlin to the bargaining table was to restore the credibility of our deterrence.*

My remarks in Chicago were well received and well reported. It was hard to tell, however, whether they were received at all in San Francisco. I was reminded yet again of the impossibility of communicating serious thoughts about serious matters late in the evening following a long dinner that has been preceded by an even longer cocktail "hour." The conversations at the back of the room never stopped and I tried, without much success, to cut my somber dissertation in half. I'm not sure anyone was listening; and under the circumstances, I couldn't blame them if they weren't. What I can affirm is that I had very little success when, in private meetings with two princes of the Catholic Church, I tried to explain why their valid moral objectives required not a freeze, but a vigorous modernization of our nuclear arsenal.

I have an enormous respect for members of the Catholic hierarchy. They have a duty to call attention to our moral responsibilities as individuals and as a society. There is nothing in their training, however, that provides them with special insights on how moral imperatives can best be achieved in the untidy world we live in. Those decisions are best made by moral men and women who have both the responsibility to make them and an understanding of how the world actually works. Fortunately, such a man was in charge of our country at that time, and history has vindicated Ronald Reagan's judgment that a resolute restoration of American power was the surest way to defuse the threat of nuclear war that had hung over us since the end of World War II.

Reagan's strategy for winning the Cold War went far beyond the restoration of an effective nuclear deterrence. He moved from the three decade-old policy of containment to an aggressive one designed, among many other things, to exploit the severe weaknesses he and his advisors had detected in the Soviet economy. Accordingly, he set out to choke off its access to the hard currency and technology it needed to modernize its industrial base, produce still more sophisticated weapons, and meet such basic needs as the importation of wheat. Part of my job was to try to persuade our European allies that it was in no one's interest (other than Moscow's) to permit the transfer of Western know-how, whether industrial or military, to the Soviet Union or to facilitate its trade with the West.

My first venture in Eurosuasion took me to a January 1982 meeting of the Coordinating Committee for Multilateral Export Controls in Paris in the company of the estimable Under Secretary of Defense for International Affairs, Fred Iklé. CoCom was a voluntary association consisting of the NATO nations, minus Iceland, plus Australia and Japan; its purpose was to maintain lists of items whose export was to be restricted for security reasons. Fred's and my mission was to secure agreement to the addition of a host of newly developed technologies to the CoCom list of embargoed goods and to persuade our allies to exercise restraint in building plants within the Soviet bloc that would teach the Soviets new industrial skills. Although the Europeans were impressed by a CIA demonstration of some of the malevolent uses to which Moscow had been putting advanced Western technologies, we met with only partial success. Their compulsion to trade reminded me of Lenin's prediction that when just two capitalists remained on earth, one of them would sell the rope with which to hang the other.

My next exposure to the European mindset came in March when I led a bevy of high level American officials on a six-day tour of five capitals—Bonn, London, Paris, Rome, and Brussels. What came to be called the "Buckley Group" included Fred Iklé as well as Under Secretary of Commerce for International Trade Lionel Olmer, Assistant Secretary of the Treasury for International Affairs Marc Leland, and National Security Council Director of International Economic Affairs Norman Bailey—all under the care of a highly competent and enthusiastic NSC staffer, Bill Martin, whom I would later swear in as deputy secretary of energy. Our job was to point out the folly of strengthening the economy, and therefore the military capabilities, of a country against whose potential aggressions we had built a military alliance that was costing all of us billions of dollars a year. Yet our European allies were providing credits at bargain basement rates in order to facilitate sales of often strategically sensitive equipment to the Soviet Union. Of particular concern was the help they were providing for the construction of a pipeline that would bring Siberian natural gas to Western Europe. Not only would this become a hard currency-earning bonanza for the Soviets, it would give them an enormous leverage over our NATO allies once they had become dependent on this source of energy.

We later returned to Paris for a meeting with representatives of all the major players, including Canada and Japan. But it proved too hard a sell. Unemployment rates in Europe were high, and the subsidized Soviet purchases and work on the European leg of the pipeline would generate large numbers of jobs. Although the British expressed sympathy for our objectives, they could not afford to act unilaterally because any orders they declined to meet would be filled by one of their Continental competitors. Nevertheless, we planted some useful seeds and, over time, the Reagan administration's persistent efforts succeeded in drying up the Soviet Union's dollar reserves and in sharply reducing its trade. Reagan also found alternative ways of impeding the completion of the Siberian pipeline. Former NSC Director Bill Clark told me a few years ago that after I had left the administration, we took advantage of the Soviets' proclivity for industrial espionage by feeding them a design for a critical compression station which, when put into operation, exploded with such devastating force that the resulting fire ball could be seen from space.

These experiences underscored the degree to which Americans and Europeans see the world through different lenses. Yes, we come from the same stocks and subscribe to the same social and political values. But for more than 300 years we have lived an ocean apart and have developed fundamental differences in how we think and how we react to problems. (I first encountered this cultural divide on spending an evening with a young Frenchman in Paris at the time the Marshall Plan was being launched. He kept probing me for the Machiavellian reasons behind the American people's puzzling display of generosity. He couldn't accept the fact that we expected nothing in return.) I won't try to characterize the ingrained differences we encountered on our European rounds beyond saying that I believe Americans, as a whole, tend to be more resourceful than Europeans, more likely to take initiatives to solve a problem rather than simply learning how to live with it.

This is not a novel observation. Alexis de Tocqueville noted these cultural differences when he visited the United States over 170 years ago. He was particularly fascinated by what he described as the uniquely American phenomenon of private initiatives to address public needs. Everywhere he went, he found myriad voluntary organizations created, manned, and financed by private citizens in pursuit of a host of civic goals. The fact is that cultural or ingrained traits do exist; and I think it helpful, in our dealings with our European counterparts, that we keep in mind that we are different peoples despite our surface similarities. This will keep us from being surprised when the other side fails to see the inescapable logic of our positions, and if nothing else, it should make us less inclined to suspect the other's motives when we fail to agree. But because the United States bears unique responsibilities today, we should never hesitate to act alone if we have to.

In this instance, we came to acknowledge that the Europeans had one legitimate concern, and that was to secure a degree of independence from Middle Eastern oil, and they saw access to the huge Siberian gas fields as a logical alternative. It was, up to the point where they developed a far more dangerous dependency on those fields. Bill Clark therefore assigned the Buckley Group the task of identifying non-Soviet sources of energy that might induce the Europeans to keep purchases of Siberian gas to a prudent level; and this in turn included seeing how we could reduce our own energy imports in order to increase the amount of non-Middle East oil available for Western Europe. So, in the interest of advancing our security objectives, we found ourselves investigating a grab-bag of foreign and domestic energy issues ranging from encouraging the development of a new Norwegian gas field, the decontrol of American natural gas prices, streamlining the licensing of nuclear power plants, and even the merits of a federal eminent domain law that would permit construction of a coal slurry pipeline to deliver western low sulfur coal to eastern markets. (Our poaching on domestic turf, needless to say, did not go well with some of the White House's energy advisors.) We met regularly, and in time, we submitted a number of proposals to the president. The most significant result of these initiatives was the development, thanks to Reagan administration prodding, of Norway's strategically important (but then uneconomic) Troll natural gas field. Troll remains a major source of gas for Western Europe.

Some of my happiest times at the State Department were with the Buckley Group. Its members were able men and very good company, and our meetings were both informal and productive. For whatever reason, we were spared a practice which makes it virtually impossible to have just the principals on hand at a meeting on a matter of any importance. In the usual case, each principal will have an assistant in attendance. And then various note-takers and observers will emerge from the moldings. The result is that any time three or four representatives from different departments or divisions want to get together to discuss a matter, the room is filled with eavesdroppers. I suspect that this may be one of the reasons why, in Washington today, there is virtually no such thing as a leakproof meeting. We were a happy exception to that miserable rule.

Comparing notes with Secretary of State Haig.

I still don't understand why presumably responsible adults holding sensitive positions of responsibility find it so hard to keep a confidence. But the phenomenon seems uncontrollable even when the matter leaked is of no public consequence. I recall a meeting of senior State Department officers at which Al Haig made a very funny but derogatory remark about one of his European counterparts. The counterpart was not amused when it appeared in the Washington Post. This leak didn't create an international incident, but others have.

And leaking is not confined to the executive branch. Congressional committee meetings are notoriously porous. But the most breathtaking example I saw of the *inability of at least some senators to keep their mouths shut involved the only executive session of the Senate to take place during my time there. The Senate's Standing Rules state that when acting upon confidential business in an executive session, "[a]ny Senator or officer of the Senate who shall disclose a secret or confidential business or proceedings of the Senate shall be liable, if a Senator, to suffer expulsion from the body; and if an officer, to dismissal from the service of the Senate, and to punishment for contempt." Yet despite this warning, which was read to the assembled senators at the outset of the meeting, the substance of our deliberations was reported in the next day's newspapers.*

Two obvious consequences of this hemorrhaging is a restriction of the number of people who will be consulted in making important executive decisions and a reluctance to commit the reasoning that led to them to paper. This has to result in significant reductions in the expertise that will be brought to bear in reaching them. There are occasions where the public interest in the thoughtful conduct of critical public business far outweighs a putative public "right to know." In such cases, it is enough that the decisions reached be defensible.

The "Science" in my formal title provided me with a limited toehold in certain areas of environmental policy. In 1982, for example, I served as co-chairman of the U.S. delegation to the United Nations conference, in Nairobi, commemorating the tenth anniversary of the Stockholm Conference on the Human Environment, which I had attended as a senator. This enabled me to see what progress had been made in the intervening years. At Stockholm, the great fear had been that Third World leaders would regard the newly emerged environmental enthusiasms of developed nations as a luxury that the rich indulged in at the expense of the poor; a scheme, if you will, to bind them into a permanent status of providers of raw materials to the industrialized nations of the world. By the time of the Nairobi conference, however, most of the world community had become convinced in principle, if not always in practice, that the environmentally responsible management of natural resources went hand-in-hand with economic progress.

Later that year, the United Nations Environment Programme presented me and three other Americans with medals at a Washington ceremony. They were for "Outstanding environmental leadership on the occasion of the Tenth Anniversary of the Stockholm Conference." I suspect that I may have been awarded mine as a prudential measure because I had been responsible, the year before, for preventing a cut in the U.S. contribution to UNEP. The coordination of international environmental efforts is vital for the simple reason that air, water, and wildlife ignore political boundaries. Our ambassador to the UN, Jeanne Kirkpatrick, had assured me that the organization used its money effectively; and so, when I learned that a reduction was being considered, I opposed the cut. What I was able to learn of UNEP's activities at Nairobi vindicated that judgment. But whatever the reason for my award, I was bemused by the fact that among the other recipients was John Oakes who, eight years earlier, had written a blistering editorial in the New York Times *challenging my environmental credentials. I had accepted an invitation to camp on the ice with an Eskimo whaling party from Point Hope, Alaska, and had witnessed the taking of a bowhead whale. Oakes considered this an unforgivable sin against nature, and it didn't matter that subsistence whaling was permitted under international agreements prohibiting the commercial hunting of whales. I suppose it was too much to hope that UNEP's recognition of my environmental purity caused him to feel some pangs of conscience.*

Finally, a word about the quality of the professional foreign service officers I encountered while at the State Department. It was impressive. I found them to be intelligent, knowledgeable, and highly motivated. Given the function of the State Department—to advance our national interests through the art of persuasion—it is not surprising that our foreign service professionals are trained to understand the other party's point of view and to avoid making unnecessary waves. But that doesn't mean that they can't be tough when the occasion requires, and I came to resent an attitude I often encountered on visits to the Pentagon which assumed that only the military knew when and where lines needed to be drawn. (A footnote: I was intrigued by the unusual ability to write clear, expository prose that was shared by the foreign service officers with whom I worked. If the federal government insists on mucking around with education, the least it could do is tell our professional educators the secret of its success in honing writing skills.)

WW: And during that time you were living in Washington.

JLB: Living in Washington.

WW: Was your family still here?

JLB: My wife was here. By this time, my children had all left the nest. At the tail end of my time at the State Department, I changed jobs. Secretary Haig wanted me to move to the position of Counselor, which has nothing to do with the law. The State Department's counselor is essentially an officer without portfolio whom the secretary can deploy to address discrete problems. It can be a fascinating position, but it depends entirely on the nature of the counselor's relationship with the secretary of state. But after the arrangements for the change had been set in motion, Haig resigned and George Shultz was appointed in his stead. Shultz asked me to stay on in that capacity but, unlike Haig, he had not yet determined what role I was to play in his regime. So, about a month after the Senate confirmed my appointment as counselor, I decided to accept an invitation to become head of Radio Free Europe and Radio Liberty.

When Haig asked me to assume the job of counselor, which was a step back in the State Department pecking order, he told me that he wanted to prepare me for the position of deputy secretary on the retirement of the incumbent, Walter Stoessel, which was expected to occur the following year. Haig's subsequent resignation left me in a kind of limbo because Shultz had not yet decided how he wanted to use me and had his own ideas as to whom he wanted to serve as his deputy. Shortly after I was sworn in as counselor, I received a call from an old friend from my Senate days, Frank Shakespeare. Frank was an experienced television executive who had served as head of the United States Information Agency during the Nixon administration. He called me in his capacity as chairman of the Board for International Broadcasting, which was responsible for ensuring that Radio Free Europe and Radio Liberty fulfilled their missions and lived within the rules established by Congress and the Board. He offered me the presidency of RFE/RL, Inc. which, in turn, ran the two radios. The offer was intriguing; and after consulting with Ann, I decided to accept.

WW: Did you move to Germany?

JLB: Yes.

WW: Tell me about that. Was it interesting?

JLB: It was very interesting. I had committed myself for three years and then, towards the end, figured that was enough. My wife and I didn't want to become expatriates. The work was important, and living in Munich was enjoyable. The radios had an important impact on their audiences in Eastern Europe and the Soviet Union. There were, however, some difficult personnel problems. What's happening in Bosnia right now will give you some idea of the tensions that could develop among the nationalities housed in our Munich headquarters. We had 20 national services, including one for each of the Soviet republics, that broadcast in 21 different languages. (The Czechoslovakian desk aired programs in both Czech and Slovak.) Each of the services was staffed by expatriates who had fled Communism, and some of them brought ancient grudges with them. But it was a great experience. I had always done a lot of traveling, but I had never as an adult lived abroad for an extended period under circumstances where I didn't have to pack every other day. It would be hard to choose a more delightful place to be stranded for three years than Munich.

Radio Free Europe and Radio Liberty were complex and historically significant institutions. RFE broadcast to the Soviet's East European satellites while RL beamed its programs to the republics comprising the Soviet Union. Their mission was to frustrate the attempts by the Soviets and their satellites to rewrite history and prevent their subjects from having access to any information or idea that might threaten the regnant regimes. The Radios were funded by the United States Congress through the Board for International Broadcasting, which was responsible to Congress for ensuring that they operated within the BIB's broadcast guidelines. Those guidelines required the stations to meet the highest standards of journalistic integrity. Because, by statute, the members of the BIB board also constituted the board of RFE/RL, Inc., they had direct responsibility for the operation of the radios.

Unlike the Voice of America, whose job is to explain America and its policies to the rest of the world, the task of Radio Free Europe and Radio Liberty was to serve as surrogates for the responsible, uncensored radios that the Communist regimes denied their people. The task of their 21 language services, therefore, was to provide their listeners with full and accurate information on events, conditions, and trends within their own countries and on international developments of interest to them. In addition to reporting the news, they aired the works of banned authors, placed historical events in perspective, broadcast the texts of underground journals, and provided religious programming. Furthermore, because the RFE/RL Munich headquarters housed the most complete research archives on Eastern Europe and the Soviet Union to be found anywhere this side of the Iron Curtain, the Radios' researchers were able to provide sophisticated analyses of events occurring behind that curtain on a daily basis. As a consequence, their audiences came to accept Radio Free Europe and Radio Liberty as their most reliable sources of information.

The Radios, in short, were focused on meeting the informational and cultural needs of more than 300 million people trapped in societies in which the state exercised a monopoly control over every other source of information. A commitment to objectivity in reporting the news, however, is not to be confused with neutrality where human values are concerned; and one of the Radios' mandates had always been to bear witness to the values that undergird free societies. Thus their programs and commentaries were designed to deepen an understanding of those values and to draw the appropriate contrasts between life within free and totalitarian societies. The years of détente, however, had had an effect on at least some of the Radios' programming. The heads of some services had come to accept the division of Europe as more or less permanent. As a consequence, their programs tended to praise and encourage the reform of Communism and to abandon any thought of its ultimate repudiation. The Hungarian service was a case in point. The Hungarian leader, János Kádár, had permitted relaxations on the economic and cultural fronts that had brought a certain glitter back to Budapest. These reforms were applauded while criticisms of the Kádár regime, however warranted, tended to be rejected as counter-productive.

This approach was out of step with the Reagan administration's policy of increasing the pressures on the "Evil Empire," and it chose Frank Shakespeare as its instrument for ensuring that the Radios' programming would be appropriately provocative. When Frank assumed the chairmanship of the BIB, it was understood that he would have a free hand in reconstituting its membership. In relatively short *order, he had put together a truly remarkable team. These included such luminaries as Ben Wattenburg (political analyst, demographer), Michael Novak (Templeton Award-winning author of books on largely religious subjects), Lane Kirkland (president of the AFL-CIO who had strong ties to Europe), James Michener (prolific novelist who had made an in-depth study of Polish history and society), and Steve Forbes, Jr. (editor of* Forbes Magazine *and prize-winning economic analyst). Each of these men became actively engaged in the work of the Radios; and because, by law, they also served as the directors of RFE/RL, Inc., the Delaware corporation that operated the Radios, they had the authority both to establish broadcast policy and ensure that it was carried out.*

With Board of International Broadcasting members
Forbes, Kirkland, Novak, Wattenburg, Madsen, Ney,
Shakespeare, and Michener. Munich, 1984.

Shakespeare's first order of business was to make changes in the top management of the Radios. To head Radio Liberty, he recruited a veteran journalist, George Bailey, who had worked in Europe during most of his adult life and had developed a close association with some of the Russian émigré groups. George was a large, gruff, amusing man who could absorb languages through his pores. His Russian was fluent, and it had to be because all the internal business of Radio Liberty was conducted in that language. George Urban was brought in to take charge of Radio Free Europe. He was a Hungarian who had emigrated to England where he initially worked for the BBC. He became a prominent member of the British anti-Communist intelligentsia and developed a fascinating series of in-depth interviews for RFE on the subject of Communism.

Both Georges were passionate anti-Communists who agreed wholeheartedly on the need for more muscular programming, and it would become part of my job to keep their enthusiasms within the limits of the BIB's guidelines. Neither would broadcast anything he believed to be untrue, but at times George Urban in particular would bridle at the guideline requirement that nothing be broadcast as fact that could not be verified by an independent source. He would come up with a story smuggled out of a prison at great risk which detailed a particularly outrageous act of official misconduct and plead for permission to broadcast it. It would have the ring of truth; but as it would be incapable of corroboration, I would have to say, "Sorry, George, but rules are rules." And these were prudent rules because Communist agent provocateurs were ready to trick us into mistakes that could be used to discredit the Radios.

I joined RFE/RL in late November 1982, and Ann and I moved to Munich the following January. It was an interesting time to be there. Changes in the Soviet leadership were taking place, and the turmoil in Poland triggered by the Lech Walesa-led shipyard strikes provided a case study of the ability of the Radios to shape events simply by reporting news that the official media deliberately ignored. It was because of RFE's reporting of seemingly isolated events that the emerging Solidarity movement leadership realized the nationwide dimensions of the protests that were taking place. And when the movement was driven underground by the imposition of martial law, its leaders were able to keep one another informed by issuing news bulletins that our Polish service obligingly broadcast. This coverage proved of such importance that the Polish government's spokesman, Jerzy Urban, paid RFE this supreme compliment: "If you would close Radio Free Europe, the underground would cease to exist."

I was soon caught up in a kind of generational guerrilla warfare within the Russian service that spilled over into the American media. The oldtimers consisted largely of ethnic Russians who yearned for a restoration of a pre-Marxist culture which was neither rooted in the values of Western liberalism nor noted for its tolerance of outsiders. The newer arrivals tended to be dissidents of a different stripe. They dreamed of a new Russia on the West European model, and a number of them were Jews who were leery of programming that dwelt on Russian nationalism. This *was a potentially explosive mix; and in the late '70s, someone thought to be an agent of Soviet intelligence posted anonymous anti-Semitic letters on the RL bulletin board that set off a torrent of charges and countercharges that continued on into the '80s. The infiltration of the Radios by Soviet bloc agents and provocateurs was an endemic problem.*

Some of the newcomers took umbrage at George Bailey's decision to increase the share of historical programs devoted to Russian nationalist and religious themes, and borrowing a leaf from Washington bureaucrats, they expressed their displeasure by leaking what they described as anti-Semitic or anti-democratic texts to American journalists who were out of sympathy with the Radios' more aggressive programming. My desk was soon covered with clippings from the American press charging Radio Liberty with a reckless disregard for values it was supposed to champion. Radio Liberty was criticized, for example, for broadcasting a speech by Aleksandr Solzhenitsyn which included criticisms of Western democracy that he had voiced at Harvard some years earlier. We had made a point of broadcasting all of his writings, and we declined to censor this towering witness to Soviet repression in order to appease the critics.

The charges of anti-Semitism were a more serious problem. These were often based on snippets from arcane historical texts and other materials that the critics had taken out of context or reflected a failure to understand the cultural differences that existed between RL's audiences and the New York Times's readership. A program that created a particular uproar illustrates the latter problem. It involved the broadcast of a czarist official's memoir which contained a passage describing a pogrom in a Ukranian village. The passage may have raised American eyebrows, but Ben Wattenberg's Jewish father, who had grown up near that village, found nothing in the story that was either offensive or anti-Semitic. It was simply history. The crescendo of accusations reached a point, however, where even our friends in Congress became alarmed, and I had to spend a fair amount of my time reassuring congressional committees that things were not out of control while making a pitch for the increased funding we needed to modernize our transmitters and upgrade staff. It was a hairy time for the Radios — and for me.

In due course, Congress asked the General Accounting Office to make its own assessment. The GAO examiners went about the job with typical thoroughness. After scrutinizing over 10,000 hours of Radio Liberty and Radio Free Europe programming during the first half of 1954, all they were able to find were 18 violations of the BIB's guidelines, which included some relatively trivial questions of taste. Not a bad record, all things considered. The GAO recommended, however, that the Radios adopt stricter controls over broadcast content, which was prudent advice if only to protect their political flanks in Washington. The more fundamental difficulty lay in the history that it was part of our job to report. As former RFE/ RL employee Arch Puddington observed in his excellent book, Broadcasting Freedom, *"as in most RL programming controversies, matters of historical interpretation were involved. Nationalism, chauvinism, and anti-Semitism were ingrained in the history of Eastern Europe; it would have been impossible to limit programs on historical themes to a discussion of figures who had championed the ideals of Western democracy." The important thing was to place the material in its proper context, which we tried to do.*

But the media remained hard to please. A Washington Post article suggested that we might have violated the prohibition against inciting the natives to violence because we broadcast, in their entirety, statements made by Ronald Reagan in the course of an RFE/RL interview. The broadcast had its genesis in a letter written in a tiny script on tissue paper that had found its way to our Munich headquarters in the spring of 1985. It was addressed to Reagan by a group of women in a Soviet prison who wanted him to know that they were praying for him. As I was planning to visit Washington in a few weeks, I asked the White House whether I might present it to the president in person. Permission was granted. More than that, the White House suggested that I take the occasion to interview the president. So in early June, I found myself in the Oval Office, microphone in hand, prepared to conduct my first (and only) interview on behalf of the Radios. While we were waiting for the tape recorder to be plugged in, Reagan muttered that it was indeed an Evil Empire, and we then proceeded with what had been a carefully scripted exchange of questions and answers in which Reagan told the people of the Soviet Union and Eastern Europe that America intended, by its example, to "show the captive nations that resisting totalitarianism is possible" while cautioning listeners that "[w]hat the people of Eastern Europe choose to do to achieve their freedom, of course, is their own business." The Post, it seems, would rather have us censor a message from the president of the United States to our audiences than trust them to decide for themselves what risks, if any, they should be willing to take in order to achieve their own liberation.

The press and Congress were not the only ones who were looking over our shoulders. From time to time I would receive a visit from a genial foreign service officer who was stationed at the American Consulate in Munich. It was his task to pass along the occasional complaint from an American ambassador to a Soviet bloc country who had received official objections to some of our programs. Being Communists, the complaining officials could not accept the fact that the United

A cub reporter's big break.

States government exercised no control over their content. I would explain each time that while I sympathized with the ambassador's problem, we were surrogate radios. As such, our responsibilities were to our listeners. The one restraint imposed by the guidelines was that we take no position that was contrary to American foreign policy. There was no requirement that we make life easier for our embassies. The principal complainant in my time was our ambassador to Budapest, who objected to broadcasts that reminded Hungarians that while they might be living in a Communist paradise, "Communism with a human face" (as it was called) was not to be confused with freedom.

These frustrations notwithstanding, my work was interesting, and I had the satisfaction of knowing that I was associated with an enterprise that was of critical importance. I confess, however, that my enjoyment of those years came in large part from the pleasure of living in Munich and having easy weekend access to an extraordinarily beautiful part of the world. We were within a 40-minute drive of the Alps, and a half-days' excursion in any direction would take us to a village, or monastery, or other site of major interest. Munich itself was a gem: wonderful museums, old quarters to wander through, and music. Ann and I often chose which church to attend on Sundays based on whether the music would be by Mozart, or Vivaldi, or some other master of the Catholic Mass. The city also boasts what must be the world's finest park, the Englishcher Garten, which was adjacent to our headquarters. It is about three-quarters of a mile wide and over four miles long. It contains fields, brooks, woodlands, miles of bike paths, and, of course, a scattering of beer gardens. I would spend endless weekend hours wandering though it, binoculars in hand, trying to identify the birds; and on the rare occasions where there was enough snow, Ann and I would go cross-country skiing there on grooves obligingly pressed into the snow by the city fathers.

WW: How's your German?

JLB: Zero.

WW: How was your German when you were over there?

JLB: Zero. I am very, very poor at picking up languages. My wife is fairly good, and she took lessons. The in-house work of Radio Free Europe was conducted in English. The work of Radio Liberty was conducted in Russian, but the principals all knew English anyway. Nothing in my daily work would have required me to use German.

WW: I think that this brings us to your appointment to the bench. Am I right?

JLB: Yes.

But before I leave Germany, a word about a detour to Mexico City. We are all familiar with the cliché about the world working in strange ways. I learned in Munich that it really does because it was there that I was able to achieve a foreign policy objective that had eluded me while I was at the State Department. During my tenure there, I had spoken with Secretary Haig and Deputy Secretary Clark about the need to ensure that United States funds were not used to encourage or pay for abortions overseas. What concerned me was that although it was against U.S. policy to do either, it was widely believed that the very large contributions we were making to UN agencies and private groups for family planning purposes were having the indirect effect of subsidizing Third World abortions. They agreed wholeheartedly, and encouraged me to pursue the matter.

To initiate the process, my staff and I began to assemble information relating to U.S. contributions to international family planning programs and invited several academics to contribute papers dealing with population dynamics. These activities gave rise to bureaucratic heel dragging within one division of the department and turf skirmishes with AID that impeded our progress. In the meantime, Bill Clark left the department to become director of the National Security Council and, some months later, Al Haig resigned as secretary of state. I dealt with Bill on some initial formulations for a new family planning policy, but the project became the victim of more immediately pressing national security concerns; and then I moved to Munich.

Our work, however, had focused attention on certain fundamentals. U.S. resources earmarked for traditional family planning services abroad had significantly facilitated the financing or encouragement of abortion because contributions to such groups as Planned Parenthood International enabled them to spend more of their own money to support abortion clinics throughout the Third World. We were also able to show that the most effective way to achieve reductions in fertility rates in developing countries was to improve the economic lot of their citizens, as evidenced by the sharp declines experienced in countries like South Korea that had risen from abject poverty to affluence in the years following World War II. The reason is simple. Family planning enhances the ability of parents to have the number of children they want; it doesn't make them want fewer of them. In subsistence farming societies, children are economic assets because they help with the chores and, in time, look after their aging parents; in affluent societies, children *are a considerable expense. It is for this reason that so many industrialized countries are now concerned about their projected population implosions.*

When I left the State Department, I thought that that was the end of my involvement in population policy. But in the spring of 1984, I received a call from a former member of my Senate staff, Bill Gribbin, who was now lodged in the Reagan White House's Office of Policy Development. He told me that the White House had begun work on a statement of United States population policy that was to be announced at a United Nations Conference on Population in Mexico City later that year. He also said that someone had suggested that I be appointed chairman of the U.S. delegation to that conference. President Reagan had so informed a group of pro-life leaders, who expressed their delight because of my work in the Senate on a constitutional amendment to reverse Roe v. Wade. When I told Bill that I doubted I could take the necessary time from my RFE/RL duties, he suggested that the mere possibility that I might head the delegation would give me considerable leverage over the structuring of the U.S. position. So I agreed to consider the appointment provided that I could support the position developed by the administration.

Two weeks later, I received a "Draft Statement for World Population Conference" from the White House that was seriously flawed. As I wrote in response, "I believe it important to include an explicit statement that the Administration will not fund family planning programs conducted by public and private groups that advocate abortion. Because money is fungible, a morally responsible donor cannot ignore the collateral activities of the donee." Then in July, Reagan's chief of staff, Jim Baker, cabled me "the final version" of the policy statement, which he described as "a good statement along the lines we discussed." It was in most respects. It declared, in part, that "the United States will no longer contribute to separate non-governmental organizations which perform or actively promote abortion as a method of family planning in other nations. With regard to the United Nations Fund for Population Activities (UNFPA), the U.S. will insist that no part of its contribution be used for abortion. The U.S. will also call for concrete assurances that the UNFPA is not engaged in abortion or coercive family planning programs; if such assurances are not forthcoming, the U.S. will redirect the amount of its contribution to other, non-UNFPA family planning programs."

The problem with the last sentence was that it did not encompass the pro-

*grams conducted by UNFPA's grantees. Accordingly, I sent Baker a cable request-
ing that it be amended "to read as follows (added language underscored): 'The
U.S. will also call for concrete assurances that the UNFPA is not engaged in, <u>or
does not provide funding for,</u> abortion or coercive family planning programs. . . .'"
The requested change was made and, in due course, the new language was invoked to cut off funds from UNFPA when it was established that China (to which
it made substantial grants) compelled women to have abortions. A few weeks later
I was on my way to Mexico as chairman of the U.S. delegation with the temporary
rank of ambassador.*

*At the substantive level, we accomplished far more than anyone had a right to
expect, especially in light of the near hysteria with which the press and abortion
apologists greeted what has come to be known as the "Mexico City Policy." On the
eve of the conference, former defense secretary and latter-day environmentalist
Robert McNamara assured a national NBC television audience that our delegation would be laughed out of Mexico City. Instead, we emerged with some
significant achievements.*

*As the result of our initiatives, the report adopted by the conference affirmed
the right of parents to determine the size of their own families, condemned the use
of coercion to achieve state-defined population objectives, acknowledged that government is not the sole agency for the achievement of social objectives, and noted
the coincidence of economic progress and falling birth rates in the developing
world. Also, given the intensity of the attacks on the U.S. position that abortion is
not "an acceptable element of family-planning programs," we took considerable
satisfaction from the adoption of an almost identical position; namely, that abortion "in no case should be promoted as a method of family planning."*

It was a satisfying close to a very brief diplomatic career.

WW: Tell me how your appointment to the bench happened. Were you in
Germany?

JLB: I was in Germany, and I received a telephone call from my brother Bill.

WW: He'd called before—I remember that earlier. That's how you ended up
in the Senate.

JLB: This time he said that he had been asked to do so by a guy who had once done some work for *National Review* and knew Bill, and who was currently a member of a group in Attorney General Meese's shop that worked on the selection of judges. [*The "guy" was Joseph Reese who, while a student at the Yale Law School in the fall of 1970, spent his weekends in New York City working as a volunteer in my senatorial campaign. I had never met him, but he followed my subsequent career with care while he pursued his own as a professor of law before being recruited to serve in the Reagan administration. For whatever reason, he thought I would make a good judge and suggested that I be considered for a vacancy that had occurred on the Second Circuit, whose jurisdiction includes the states of New York, Connecticut, and Vermont. I cannot believe that the idea would have occurred to anyone else in his group, and have no idea why it occurred to him—but this is just one more of the unexplainable circumstances that have continued to shape my life.*] Bill was asked to ask if I would be interested in being a circuit judge. I told Bill it was the most outrageous idea I had ever heard.

WW: No, it wasn't—you said that when you thought about going to the Senate.

JLB: I thought it all over again. I had never given the matter a single moment's thought. My first reaction was that I wasn't competent to do the job. But as I have never believed in turning any offer down without giving it careful thought, I decided to do just that. At the time, I had started making the rounds of Washington law firms to see if I could get an "of counsel" relationship that would involve international work and negotiations, which I felt very competent to handle. But I hadn't done any legal research in 30 years, and I had never done any trial work. In any event, I figured I would have to do a little investigating before rejecting the idea. It happens that I knew Justice Potter Stewart pretty well, so I called on him and said, "An astonishing thing has happened to me. I have been asked if I would be interested in being on the Court of Appeals for the

Second Circuit." His answer was, "Grab it!" I told him I hadn't practiced in any traditional sense in over 30 years. He countered that I had spent six years in the Senate, which would prove most valuable. He said that I was competent to do the job, but that I would have to put in a tremendous amount of very hard catch-up work for the first couple of years. Yes, I hadn't had 15 years of antitrust experience or whatever, hadn't done trial work, but I would bring to the table other experiences that would prove equally valuable, always assuming that I had the necessary judicial temperament and basic intelligence, which he thought I had. So I heard him out and then talked to four circuit judges, two of them on the Second Circuit and the others on the D.C. Circuit. They all said the same thing. Then the question was, would I enjoy it? I was then 62 and I figured this would be my last job. What impressed me was that the judges I talked to had all come from different backgrounds—academia, elective office, the traditional Wall Street type of practice. They all said, "Yes, it's a cloistered life; yes it's this; yes, it's that; but it is intellectually very interesting, and you have the satisfaction of knowing you are doing important work." The telling argument in the end was that if I found in two or three years that I didn't like the work, I would have little difficulty, as an ex-judge, in moving on to a law firm.

WW: The question on my outline, which I wrote before we actually started talking, was long-time ambition. I take it the answer to that question is no. It never occurred to you that you might do that. In telling your story you said you were thinking about being a judge on the Second Circuit. But of course, as you and I know, you are not on the Second Circuit.

JLB: When the possibility of becoming a judge was first broached, I asked the people at Justice whether there was a vacancy on this court because I thought my Senate experience made me better suited for the D.C. than the Second Circuit. But there was none at the time. It was only after Judge Tamm's death created a vacancy here, which was after my nomination had been sent to the Senate, that I was redirected to this court.

I felt the D.C. Circuit would be a better fit because a substantial part of its workload involves appeals from decisions of the scores of administrative agencies that are located in the District of Columbia. Thanks to my work in the Senate, I was familiar with the kinds of laws they are required to apply as well as the problems they face in doing so.

WW: Wasn't there opposition to your nomination for the Second Circuit?

JLB: Yes, there was, and it came primarily from one of my own senators, Senator Lowell Weicker, and this created some formidable, although not insurmountable, problems. As I had become a Connecticut resident again in 1979, he was in a position to exercise one of the traditional senatorial prerogatives—that of placing a hold on consideration of a presidential nominee from his state. He raised large questions as to whether I'd be competent to do the job for all the very understandable reasons—I hadn't practiced law for over 30 years; I hadn't taught law; I hadn't done trial work, etc. His ability to obstruct my confirmation, however, was defused by Judge Tamm's death, which enabled the White House to redirect by nomination to the D.C. Circuit.

WW: Then it was easy. Tell us about the confirmation process. Did Senator Weicker voice any objections once the nomination was for the D.C. Circuit?

JLB: Yes, on the floor.

Lowell Weicker had maintained his hold even after my nomination had been switched from the Second to the D.C. Circuit. Although he ultimately lifted it, during the debate over my confirmation he argued that I had neither the legal experience nor the judicial temperament required for the job, that I was an ideologue who could not be trusted to make objective judgments. The first objection was a fair one, the second merely established that poor Lowell had never figured me out even though we had both entered the Senate at the same time and served six years together as members of the Republican caucus. My other senator, Chris

Dodd, also voted against me; but he later sent me a hand-written note of apology, which I greatly appreciated. The Senate confirmed me by a vote of 84 to 11. All but five of the senators I had worked with found me qualified, as had the American Bar Association.

In those days, the ABA played a semi-official role in the screening of candidates for federal judgeships before their names were submitted to the Senate. When the Reagan administration asked the ABA to review my credentials, I was still being considered for a vacancy on the Second Circuit. As a consequence, the man placed in charge of assessing my competence was Robert MacCrate, a prominent New York City lawyer who later served as president of the ABA. This was providential because such qualifications as I had were anything but conventional, and Mr. MacCrate proved willing to go to extraordinary lengths to ferret out the evidence that would enable the ABA to declare me qualified for the job. To this end, he interviewed the staff counsel of the Senate committees on which I had served, lawyers of companies with whom I had negotiated business deals, the circuit and district court judges whose appointments I had recommended while in the Senate, and even the associates at Wiggin & Dana with whom I had shared brown bag lunches 35 years earlier.

I must have received some good report cards, although there was at least one qustionable one. After he had completed his investigation, Mr. MacCrate came to see me at the Radio Free Europe/Radio Liberty office in Washington. He began by telling me that he had heard I could be rigid, unwilling to compromise. I replied that that was a fair comment because I have always been wary of the ability, over time, of seemingly inconsequential accommodations to erode important principles out of existence. My answer appeared to satisfy him. He then said that my judicial nominees were "money in the bank," presumably because they had informed him that when I had interviewed them, I never asked for their views on matters of public policy. Rather, I limited my questions to those bearing on their understanding of the role of a federal judge. Finally, he asked how I had come to be nominated for the position. When I described my serendipitous connection with Joseph Reeves, he remarked that my selection was "prescient." I concluded from this that he had found me qualified.

I began my judicial career with very shaky knees, but am grateful that, in time, I was able to vindicate MacCrate's confidence in me. In June 1996, Washingtonian *magazine published an article on the judges of the D.C. Circuit which contained the following statement: "James Buckley, 73, . . . has emerged by consensus of liberals and conservatives alike as the finest appellate judge." That happens not to be the case (and I am in a far better position than the* Washingtonian *to make that judgment), but it did confirm that I approached my work as a judge and not as an ideologue.*

WW: In those days the confirmation process, I think, was quite different than it is now. You might agree or disagree. That was one of the questions I was going to ask you.

JLB: Yes. It still tended to be a formality, but the process was not nearly as perfunctory as it was when I was introducing New York judicial nominees to the sole member of the Judiciary Committee who would be on hand to conduct the confirmation hearing. I'd introduce Mr. So-and-so, the candidate for the Southern District of New York, and the ranking minority member, Senator Roman Hruska of Nebraska, would in effect say, "Mr. So-and-so, do you believe in the Constitution of the United States?" "Yes, sir." "That's fine. I know you'll go out there and have a wonderful career." And that was about it. At my hearing, three or four senators were on hand at one point or another. I had served with all but one of them, Senator Paul Simon. The hearing was opened by the committee chairman, Senator Strom Thurmond, who mentioned that he had known my parents back when he was governor of South Carolina and said that they were fine people. He congratulated me on my nomination; said that the president had made a fine choice. He threw a few very soft questions my way and then asked whether I felt my lack of trial experience would be a problem. I answered that I had myself been worried about this, but that conversations with several appellate judges had satisfied me that I could handle the job despite the lack of this experience. Senator Simon was the only other senator to question me, and his questions were also friendly. I received several follow-up inquiries, however, while bouncing around Europe.

The questions that were forwarded to me raised legitimate concerns about my experience as a lawyer. Even when they touched on controversial positions I had taken in the Senate, it was to determine whether I had a "judicial temperament," namely the ability to subordinate personal feelings and beliefs to the constitutional duties I would be assuming. Unfortunately, the confirmation process has since deteriorated to a scandalous degree, and neither political party is blameless.

WW: You hadn't finished your three years with the radios yet.

JLB: No. No, I was still there. I do recall that we were taking a holiday, my wife and I were in Austria, and a list of questions was telephoned to the desk of our hotel that I was supposed to answer forthwith. I had a devil of a job drafting my answers in our poorly lit attic room using the little pieces of tissue paper that passed for stationary.

Senator Mac Mathias's secretary had sent three pages of questions to my Munich office with instructions that they be answered "today." My answers, which I read over the telephone to my secretary in Munich, filled five typewritten double-spaced pages. They were addressed to three topics: my well-known position on abortion, my lack of trial experience, and my lack of familiarity with the folkways of the District of Columbia bar and the D.C. Circuit court. Mac was a friend, but I suspect he never quite believed I would be able to set strongly held views aside when deciding a case.

WW: You didn't have your notebook with you or your Apple?

JLB: No, none of those things. So, there was a certain amount of follow-up — for example, would I recuse myself from any cases involving abortion in light of my strong pro-life stand while in the Senate? I answered that my introduction of a constitutional amendment to protect unborn life should be evidence enough that I fully understood the implications of *Roe v. Wade* and, further, that I fully understood that it was not the province of a circuit judge to overrule the Supreme Court. Therefore, there would be no reason for me to recuse myself.

WW: So that was an issue even back then?

JLB: Oh, yes [*but not the critical one it is today*]. It was also suggested that I gain some trial experience by actually handling some trials. I replied that I was so inexperienced in trial work that it would be a disservice to the parties if I were to do so. Having since learned the pressures under which trial judges work and the command they have to have of the relevant rules, I know I was right. I have a tremendous admiration for trial judges.

WW: They have to make a lot of decisions fast—and be right.

JLB: Yes, and without having people second-guessing them.

WW: Who never did a trial. I suspect that ultimately the confirmation process for you must have been rather genteel—these were your colleagues, and they must have been very supportive.

JLB: It was genteel. There was frankly some question as to whether Weicker's delaying tactics would still be able to block it. There was a long delay between the time that the committee signed off on me and the time that my nomination was taken up on the floor. The administration was getting very nervous about the matter because it was getting close to the time when Congress would adjourn for Christmas. It is reported, I don't know whether there is any truth to it, that my nomination served as leverage for securing millions of extra federal highway dollars for Connecticut.

WW: That would not be inconsistent with what often goes on. Right?

JLB: It's inconsistent with nothing that goes on, but I always objected to that sort of thing.

WW: Well, but it is what goes on.

JLB: Yes.

WW: Having been in the Senate and gone through the confirmation process, I suspect you have views about what has happened to the confirmation process. It is dramatically different.

JLB: I think that much of it is outrageous.

WW: Do you think it's outrageous on all sides? Do you think that more deference ought to be given to whoever the presidential choice is, without political considerations interfering?

JLB: I don't think you can ever do away with political considerations, but I think there are licit and illicit ones. Take the matter of judicial philosophy—a [*Justice William*] Brennan's living Constitution versus a [*Justice Antonin*] Scalia's focus on original meaning. That issue can be described as political.

WW: That's true.

JLB: I think that's a legitimate inquiry. Questioning a candidate on how he or she would rule on substantive matters is illegitimate. Questions dealing with such things as professional competence and judicial temperament are proper. If I were a president who had a Supreme Court vacancy to fill, I would sacrifice two or three first rate candidates by instructing each to open his testimony on the first day of the confirmation hearing with something like the following, "Mr. Chairman, members of the committee, I think it's important that we understand our respective roles here. I respect your right to ask me anything that will enable you to assess my competence to serve as a Supreme Court justice. By the same token, you have to understand the constraints on my ability to answer questions. Specifically, it would be improper for me to answer any question about my views on any issue that might ever come before the court because if I were to do so, I would be compromising my ability to objectively assess and rule upon arguments that have yet to be presented in cases and controversies that have yet to arise." And then every time a senator asked for the candidate's position on the relevance of natural law, or to rank the importance of property rights, or for a view on abortion, the candidate would reply, "Sorry, Senator, I can't answer that question. It is inappropriate." I think that after four, five, or six televised confrontations of this sort, the country might begin to be educated as to the role of a judge and perhaps the Senate would learn to limit its questions to those bearing on the nominee's competence to serve.

WW: Which is generally to advise and consent in the process. I think everybody would agree that the process has dramatically changed.

And dramatically for the worse. To my mind, there are only four areas that senators may legitimately examine at a judicial confirmation hearing: Does the candidate have the professional competence required for the job; does he have the judicial temperament that will enable him to apply the law objectively to the facts of a case; does he understand the limits of a federal judge's constitutional responsibilities; and does he have the character, the personal integrity that is the best guarantee that he will honor those limits once in office? If those criteria are met, the strength and nature of a candidate's views are irrelevant because, if confirmed, he can be counted on to seek an objective assessment of the relevant law's meaning and apply it fairly to the facts of the case at hand.

JLB: I really preferred the old system—the one that was in effect until about 60 or 70 years ago—when a candidate for the Supreme Court was never asked to appear before the Senate.

WW: We're a long way from that. It's about 6:15—I don't know how much longer you want to go.

JLB: I'll go five minutes more if you want.

WW: OK. You were confirmed. You put on your robe. You came to the courthouse. And what did you do next?

JLB: I needed to find law clerks. I was rather desperate because I was sworn in in December and this was out of the clerk hiring season. What I had to do was raid some law firms. Fortunately, I had a friend at Covington & Burling [*a pedigreed Washington firm*] who passed the word around that I was in the market for bright young lawyers who would welcome the opportunity. I ended up hiring two excellent associates from Covington, and my third from a New York law firm. While I was interviewing and hiring, I had to make do with the help of other judges' clerks and one or two staff attorneys. But by the end of my second month I had three very good people.

WW: And who were your first clerks? Who were these three?

JLB: They were Jeff Holdaway, Steve Rademaker, and Steve McCowin.

WW: What happened to them? Where are they now, do you know?

JLB: None of them went back to their firms.

WW: That's very interesting.

JLB: Two of them—one from the New York firm and one from Covington — had roomed together at Columbia Law School. They were Mormons, and one of them went from me to Salt Lake City, where he's in practice, and the other one went to work for Marriott International. And the third, who was very interested in foreign policy, went to the State Department where he worked on Central American problems and ended up attached to the Office of the Legal Counsel for the President while spending a fair amount of time with the NSC. He is now chief counsel for the House Committee on International Relations. [*And has since served as an assistant secretary of state in the George W. Bush administration.*]

WW: Now, you get to hire them in their second year of law school, right? You don't have to wait until they're at Covington. When did you hire your first clerk—how long had you been on this job before somebody showed up?

JLB: I took the oath of office in the middle of December 1985, the 19th to be precise. My first clerk came on board the third week of January; but because he was scheduled to be married the first week of February, I graciously granted him two weeks for a honeymoon. My second and third clerks came in late February. So I was understaffed during my first two months.

WW: Were there any of your colleagues whom you were particularly close with who were mentors as you started this job?

JLB: They were all ready to help. Spottswood Robinson helped me out—he was just down the hall. He was sitting with me on a couple of cases and let me have his clerk's bench memos. I turned to Judge Scalia a couple of times, and Judge Silberman was always very, very helpful. But the key to my survival has been someone called "Dee."

WW: I know who Dee is. Did you hire her or was she here?

JLB: She had been Judge Tamm's secretary.

WW: I see.

JLB: And she called on me at the Radio Free Europe/Radio Liberty office here in Washington while I was awaiting confirmation. She's just a gem. She started out in the Clerk's Office, and she knows how all of the court machinery works. She has a wonderful sense of language, and she will go through a draft opinion and will say that this or that sentence doesn't make sense; and she is almost always right. And finally, she has a proofreader's eye that is just extraordinary — she can find mistakes in opinions that two or three clerks have gone through 12 times and I've gone through 15 times. Well, anyway, she gave me a real head start.

WW: And she'd been here so she knew how things really worked. [Laughter]

JLB: Exactly.

WW: That's wonderful. She was here from the beginning. OK, why don't we quit for now.

The indispensable Dee Barrack.

Experiences and Reflecions of an Appellate Judge

WW: This is the beginning of our fourth session. Today is November 29, 1995, and we'll start with some memories that you have about the Senate that you have recently recalled.

JLB: When I was in the Navy in officers' training, I was taught that "forehandedness" was the hallmark of a good officer — the ability to foresee the future and prepare for it. But only after my appointment to this court was I able to realize how very forehanded I had been in the Senate. In the years immediately before my election, Congress began giving the D.C. Circuit exclusive jurisdiction over appeals from agency decisions implementing key regulatory statutes. I had a close collaborator in the Senate, Jim McClure of Idaho, who served with me on both the environmental subcommittee of Public Works and the energy subcommittee of Interior. As I mentioned earlier, these subcommittees were engaged in drafting important new bills. We were sufficiently alarmed by the activist reputation of the U.S. Court of Appeals for the District of Columbia Circuit that we made a point of ensuring that it not have exclusive jurisdiction over any of the legislation being reported out by our subcommittees. This was a controversial circuit in those days, and we thought that people who felt abused by this agency or that in Idaho or Arizona or Florida or New York should have the option of bringing their appeals in their home circuits. As a consequence, I saved myself and this court a great deal of future work.

WW: Now in hindsight, looking back from where you now sit, do you think that was such a wise decision after all? I won't cross-question you about that. Last time, if you will recall, we had just had you appointed to the bench and were talking about what you first did when you got here. When you first got here, what did you feel you were comfortable with, that you knew how to do, and what was it that you thought you were going to have to learn the most about in order to do this job?

JLB: Well, I was obviously dropped into a great big cold bath and assumed responsibilities for which I had little traditional preparation. Nevertheless, after talking to one Supreme Court justice and several circuit court judges, I was satisfied that I was competent to do the job. I had been warned that I would have to spend a great deal of extra time at the outset getting up to speed on various aspects of the job, but that was doable. What I hadn't counted on was the problem I would be facing as a result of my being a very slow reader with a very poor memory for details. I was overwhelmed by the volume of reading I had to do in preparing for my first hearings—the job of having to absorb and sort out quantities of factual information and questions of law that were completely new to me. So, it was a little bit like going to law school and plunging into your first assignments in which you were required to read a dozen difficult opinions and start making some sense out of the law. I found, however, that I hadn't forgotten how to think like a lawyer and was soon satisfied that I had nothing to be scared of in terms of my ability to do the job. But there were a myriad details to be absorbed and learned—the ABCs of the FCC, FERC, ICC, and things of that sort. And initially I had to get on top of all this without the benefit of a clerk, because my first clerk didn't report for duty until after I had heard my first cases. I guess what this all adds up to is a huge amount of concentration on a type of work that I hadn't been exposed to in years in the hope that I would get to the root of the key questions with sufficient confidence not to make a fool of myself when I asked my first question in open court.

I misspoke. It is not quite true that I "was soon satisfied that I had nothing to be scared of." For several years I suffered periodic attacks of panic in which I felt that I had taken on responsibilities that lay beyond my competence. I experienced my first attack a month or two after I had been sworn in when, at a judge's meeting, I sat transfixed as Judge (and former law professor) Ruth Ginsburg and Judge (and former law professor) Antonin Scalia discussed an esoteric but critical legal principle I had never heard of. It was clear to me that I was the only person in the room who didn't, and couldn't, understand what they were talking about. But during the course of my work, every time I felt I was over my head, I was ultimately saved by concentrated effort. Those moments became increasingly rare, but they never entirely deserted me.

WW: Do you remember anything about the early cases that you heard—anything come to mind in particular?

JLB: The first case involved WMATA [*Washington Metropolitan Area Transit Authority*]—

WW: Yes.

JLB: —and it had to do with workman's compensation.

WW: Anything in particular that you remember about it? Suddenly you're listening to arguments, you're listening to cases, you're reading the law, you're learning again about Shepard's [*a legal research tool*]. Did it all come back to you?

JLB: A surprising amount of it did, yes.

But nothing prepared me for what occurred at my second sitting. One panelist called in sick, which left two judges to hear the oral argument—the court's longest serving judge and its newest. Halfway through the presentation of the first case, the other judge picked up a piece of paper and asked a question relating to an issue in the next case. It was the first indication that he had been overtaken by a galloping case of Alzheimer's Disease. I was on my own. It was an unnerving experience.

WW: Did you find that the other judges were helpful in getting you oriented?

JLB: Very willing, but not all that helpful. As I had found on several previous sink-or-swim occasions, there is precious little that someone else with all the good will in the world can do to help you. They're there to listen and give advice on this, that, and the other detail, but you are essentially on your own.

WW: And so you had to find your own way.

JLB: Exactly.

WW: Did you find that whatever style you developed early on is what you carried through in the way you prepare for cases or has that changed over time?

JLB: It has changed to a degree. From the beginning, I have required my clerks to prepare fairly detailed bench memoranda, but I nevertheless used to read each of the briefs from beginning to end and to duplicate a lot of the other work my clerks were doing. I now begin by reading the bench memoranda and then check those portions of the briefs that address the legal questions at issue in the case. In this way, I have a first hand knowledge of how each of the parties frames the argument but spare myself an awful lot of the background and excess verbiage. In other words, I've learned how to make more intelligent use of my clerks' bench memoranda. This in turn has freed up time for a closer scrutiny of cited sources, which can often prove misleading.

WW: Tell me about your early relationships with your clerks. How did you use them, how do you relate to them, how much time do you spend with them?

JLB: First of all, it has to be understood that this is a solitary business. Appellate work consists about 99 percent of reading and writing. These are hardly group activities. I have my work to do, and the clerks have theirs. But I quickly establish a relationship with my clerks where they know my door's always metaphysically open even though I keep it shut because I am usually playing music on my CD player. But they can barge in whenever they have a question they need to discuss with me. And as I get into my preparation for oral argument, I will call in the clerk who is assigned to the case to discuss a particular point or to ask for additional research. I end up with very close relationships with my clerks, and one of the best things about this job is the chance to know some very bright young people who are fresh out of school and beginning their careers. I'm more of an introvert than an extrovert, so I'm not a glad-hander. Anyway, the relationship evolves very naturally. My clerks seem to be pleased to have been associated with me, I'm happy to say. Because I spend so much time with them, to the exclusion of anybody else, I have always made a particular point of trying to find people who are agreeable as well as competent. I try to be aware of the intellectual arrogance that afflicts some very, very bright individuals, so when I interview candidates for clerkships, I place particular importance on what I call the "chuckle factor."

WW: And have you generally been successful?

JLB: Yes, I have.

WW: Do you have reunions of your law clerks?

JLB: Yes. About two a year. One at Christmas time and one in the summer.

WW: Do you do it here? Somewhere in Washington?

JLB: Yes. Actually we have three occasions—one is a Christmas party my wife and I give for current and past clerks. The clerks tend to stay in the Washington area—I've had 70 percent of my alumni show up. Then my past and present clerks will have a lunch for me around the time of my birthday. Finally, there's a barbecue which the current clerks organize, but it's for the alumni as well. Usually it's at the home of a former clerk. In my first full term, one of the clerks and two friends had rented a house with a substantial yard, which was used for the purpose. It started the tradition. The clerks did all the cooking, messing up the dining room and yard. Anyway, they organize it.

A Christmas party for clerks, past and present.

WW: Organized—and has that become a ritual?

JLB: That has become a ritual. This is one of the great pleasures of this job. You get to spend some serious time with very bright young people, and it gives you some faith in the future. Some people are still getting very well educated in this country.

WW: How long would you say it took you until you felt as though you'd really settled in and were comfortable with this job?

JLB: Close to a year.

WW: Do your clerks generally write drafts of opinions?

JLB: Yes. Then how it goes from there depends on a lot of things, including the clerk. Clerks come in different varieties. In terms of writing, there are those who write and frame an argument the way I do, and those who don't. In those few instances where I have had a very close fit, I have had relatively little reworking to do. In other instances, even when I am presented with a draft that is competently written, I find the style and approach so foreign to mine that I end up completely rewriting the opinion. In only a few instances have I signed off on an opinion without having made significant revisions in both the style and substance. As a rule, I do a major rewrite that will involve a half dozen or more drafts to get things just right. I'm a heavy editor and very conscious of the fact that the opinions will appear over my signature. One thing I strive for is what I call "reader friendly" opinions. That is one of the reasons I have banished footnotes. I tell my clerks that a reader should never have to read a sentence a second time, or flip though the pages, or look up a case or statute in order to understand what is being said. I also emphasize the need to avoid any asides, dicta, things of that sort which, in my experience, have the effect of strewing the legal landscape with land mines. I am aware, however, that the quality of my writing can be uneven. Polishing takes time. You may or may not have read some of my opinions.

WW: I have.

JLB: Is there a consistency in style?

WW: Yes. I would say there really is.

JLB: Anyway, that's—I would like to think it ends up as my work.

WW: I would have guessed that you have clerks do a first draft and then essentially after that it's pretty much your work and you write it in your way. My perception is that your approach is to take the problem, to take it apart, to analyze each issue, one at a time, and reach your conclusions. It's very linear. There aren't a lot of asides or byways and other analyses. It's just very straightforward and clear. Your opinions tend not to be very long, as D.C. Circuit opinions sometimes can be. You tell the reader where you're going and then you get there. It looks like a style that is yours.

JLB: For better or worse, anyway.

WW: When you are reaching a decision, do you think at all about what the Supreme Court will do or how it will react to the decision you make?

JLB: No. On certain issues I assume that the Supreme Court is going to be given a crack at my handiwork and assume that the Court might very well grant certiorari [*agree to hear the case*], but I do my job and they do theirs. If you are asking whether I will change anything because of the prospect of Supreme Court scrutiny, the answer is no. In arriving at my conclusions about a case, I will apply, to the best of my ability, what is binding Supreme Court precedent, but I am not going to second guess where the Supreme Court goes next.

WW: What do you think makes a good judge, as you look back on your own experiences?

JLB: You've got to rid yourself of your own prejudgments. My job is to apply the law. I didn't write the law. I think a lot of the law I am required to apply is awful, but I view my oath as requiring me to use my best understanding of what the law is and, in applying it to the facts, to come out with the result that the lawmakers intended.

WW: And do you think that's the most important thing that a judge does?

JLB: Yes, if you're talking about a federal judge. Common law judges, of course, will at times evolve substantive law. [*In contrast with statutory or constitutional law (with which federal courts are almost exclusively concerned), the common law, which we inherited from England, is based on legal principles distilled by judges over the centuries. These govern the bulk of the issues (such as contract and commercial law, property rights, criminal prosecutions) with which state courts are concerned.*] But it isn't my prerogative to act as a philosopher king. That's not the job that I was sworn to perform. A good judge has to resist the temptation to write his political preferences into the law. And so what else makes a good judge? Obviously, a good judge will have to have certain intellectual credentials, such as the ability to grasp sometimes complex concepts and to relate them to the facts. I am aware, however, that people of the same intelligence and the same commitment to objectivity may nevertheless perceive reality in different ways. There's a book by Thomas Sowell that elaborates on this. One of these days I'll find the time to read it. In it he sorts mankind into two categories based on their perceptions of reality. What seems reasonable to "X" percent of humanity in any given situation will not seem reasonable to "Y" percent. People who believe in original sin will see things one way and those who believe in the perfectibility of man will see them in another. According to Sowell, political conservatives will fall in the first camp while liberals will fall in the other. And so I think it may well be this different perception of reality that explains why, in a very small percentage of cases, politically conservative and liberal judges of equal intelligence and probity will come to different conclusions as to what the law requires.

I have since read Sowell's book, A Conflict of Visions. *I have oversimplified his thesis, but it is essentially as I have described it. Those whom he describes as having a "constrained vision" tend to distrust instant cures of age-old human problems and prefer, instead, to rely on folk experience as reflected in a society's slowly evolving institutions, traditions, and values as the surer guide to a productive and equitable society. Those who have an "unconstrained vision," on the other hand, tend to have an infinite faith in the ability of human reason to solve hitherto intractable problems by devising (and enforcing) sweeping changes in human institutions and*

practices. The first camp, for example, instinctively distrusts the regulatory state;
the other sees it as necessary to the achievement of its concept of the ideal society.
Sowell demonstrates how these contrasting perspectives tend to place individuals
on the conservative or liberal side of a host of current political issues. According to
his analysis, we tend to align ourselves as we do because we see reality through
different lenses. It explains, I think, why, in our en banc cases, the court will tend
to split along ideological lines where the critical issue involves the application of an
essentially subjective standard, such as reasonableness or whether a particular
government interest is sufficiently compelling to override a First Amendment right.

WW: Is that something that becomes clearer as you deal with your colleagues
on the various cases that you've handled?

JLB: Yes, yes. Although I think one or two of the judges I sit with may be
influenced by what they think the outcome ought to be, but I won't
name names, I am increasingly persuaded that Sowell may have the
answer to why I will reach a different conclusion than somebody else
when I believe that both of us are trying to apply the law as objectively as
we can.

WW: How often do you think the oral argument makes a difference?

JLB: Maybe one out of five cases, one out of four cases. You never know in
advance which case it'll be.

WW: But generally you find that whatever tentative conclusion you bring to
the argument, when you leave the argument you probably are pretty
much in the same place?

JLB: Generally speaking, yes. But judging ought to be a leisurely profession
with a lot of time to think these things through and rethink them, to
make sure that some critical factor hasn't escaped you and that the precedent you are about to establish won't prove pernicious in the longer
run. From time to time, when working on an opinion, I have become

convinced the panel had reached the wrong conclusion, and I have been able to persuade my colleagues that we needed to dispose of a case in a different way. (The reverse, of course, has also occurred—my eyes have been opened by a more perceptive colleague.) This has happened often enough to lead me to believe that if we had more time to mull over a case, we would gain a better understanding, better perspective on the real issues that were presented to us. I had lunch today with a fellow who had just finished reading a biography of Learned Hand, and he told me that Hand would invite members of his panel to spend a weekend at his country home where they could discuss the fine points of a case they'd heard three or four days earlier. There is no opportunity to do that sort of thing today.

WW: Because there's no time—

JLB: Yes. Which reminds me of a comment I heard a few years ago at a convocation of appellate judges. When one of them held Learned Hand up as an example to be emulated, another judge replied, "If Learned Hand were on the bench today, he wouldn't have the time to be Learned Hand."

WW: Do you find it more difficult to decide some cases quickly than others?

JLB: I find the more difficult cases to be those involving highly technical regulations applying a statute that draws arbitrary lines and where the particular situation to which the regulations are being applied had not been anticipated by Congress, and where there is no guiding principle that allows you to bring order to the chaos. Does this make any kind of sense to you?

WW: Yes. What you're saying is the hardest cases are those where there's no underlying public policy or philosophy that guides you in understanding the statute or its application.

JLB: Yes, exactly. There are too many of those.

WW: I was going to ask whether those are most of the cases that you get. They're most of the cases that I have.

JLB: What is your field?

WW: I do some appellate litigation, I do some environmental and labor work, products liability, a lot of different things. But the case that you just described is similar to a case right now that I'm working on where the issue is one that nobody thought of; it could come out either way.

JLB: I have my own views on a number of Supreme Court decisions, but I find *Chevron* very troubling; and I say that in significant part because of my own experience in the Senate. [*The Supreme Court held, in* Chevron USA v. Natural Resources Defense Council (1984), *that courts must defer to reasonable interpretations placed on a statute by the agency entrusted with its administration.*] In *Chevron*, the Supreme Court assumes that because Congress has assigned a particular agency with the responsibility for administering a program, Congress expects judges to defer to that agency's interpretation of the relevant statutory language. I recall markup sessions when this very new senator would ask, "What does this language mean?" And the old-timers would say, "Well, we don't have time to fiddle with this. Let the courts decide." I never heard anyone say "let EPA decide" except with respect to those highly technical matters that fall within the agency's area of expertise. So I think that the Supreme Court got this one wrong; it creates a terrible burden for a court that is persuaded that Congress intended something else.

WW: Although I generally find that if the court believes that, it can find a way around *Chevron*.

JLB: It does encourage a tendency to find a statute unambiguous. [*The Supreme Court states, in* Chevron, *that a reviewing court need not defer to an agency's interpretation when the statute is unambiguous.*]

242

WW: Precisely. This is clearly what Congress meant. Which leads me to another question, which is, having been in the Senate and knowing what legislative history is all about in the real world, how much do you defer to legislative history, how much do you rely on it, what do you think of it?

American courts have developed the questionable habit or looking at all stages in the development of legislation for clues to its meaning. In its broadest sweep, "legislative history" will include statements by witnesses at legislative hearings, committee reports, and, of course, statements made — or putatively made — in the course of legislative debates. I say "putatively" because in my day, at least, a senator was able to have a statement included in the Congressional Record's report of a debate even if he was not on hand to deliver it.

JLB: I prefer the British system [*which ignores legislative history*], but I understand the British system is getting corrupted by American law.

WW: It always has.

JLB: One of the opinions I referred you to laid out my views on legislative history.

WW: Which one? I have not read them all, only a sampling of them.

JLB: OK. The first one I cited, *International Brotherhood of Electrical Workers*. I have scant use for most legislative history. First of all, statements made by a particular senator or representative in floor debate can hardly be taken to reflect the body's understanding when there is virtually nobody on the floor to hear what is being said. Number two, Congress is a political as well as a lawmaking body, and a lot of things will be said on the floor that are directed to a home audience and cannot be taken as a serious explanation of what a statute means. Number three, because legislative history has assumed the importance it has in so many court decisions, people who've lost a fight in Congress will try to win it in the courts by salting the Congressional Record with self-serving interpretations. For these and other reasons, I will ignore the whole body of legislative history with the exception of the committee reports, which can be very useful in determining what meaning is to be given a particular word or phrase. But committee report discussions of policy objectives can be deceptive. In interpreting a statute, I take the same approach I do in interpreting a provision of the Constitution. What is significant is not what this or that delegate in Philadelphia may have thought, but what the people who ratified the Constitution understood the language of the document to mean. Similarly, it seems to me that in order to interpret a statute of Congress, it is ultimately irrelevant what the sponsor or reporting committee intended; we need to give the statute the meaning that the majorities in each house believed it had when they voted it into law. In deciding how to vote, they have access to the committee reports and therefore it is not unreasonable for a court to take those reports into account in deciding what a particular provision means. But nowadays, a knowledge of what is said on the floor or at committee hearings cannot be imputed to the average member of Congress.

WW: But it's very hard to figure out what the majority thought—

JLB: Therefore you look at the language. Surely that's the best clue to what they understood the statute they were voting on to mean. There is another reason why the focus should be on the statutory language. Ours is supposed to be a government of laws, and the law is made intelligible to laymen by lawyers. Take a lawyer in a small town in North Dakota. He doesn't have the Congressional Record at his elbow; he certainly doesn't have transcripts of the committee hearings. He ought to be able to look at the language and advise his client.

WW: Do you think it's also true that the legislative history is often written from whatever political vantage point you have and therefore may or may not shed light on what anybody really thought they were doing?

JLB: That's one of the problems. It can be manipulated. Committee reports can also be unreliable. I remember a lunch I had with Senator McClure shortly after he left the Senate, where he had served as chairman of the Interior Committee. He told me that he took the trouble of reading the committee report on one of the bills that had been reported out by his committee and found something like 18 errors in it, significant errors, including a couple of assertions that had been expressly rejected by the committee.

WW: I'm not surprised. I'm sure you're not either.

JLB: No. So, anyway, for all of these reasons I think that courts ought to rely on the language of a statute or of the Constitution as it was understood contemporaneously by the people who enacted or ratified it.

WW: This is all consistent with the opinion that you wrote in *Chastain v. Sundquist* where you went back and looked at *The Federalist Papers* and what the Speech and Debate Clause was thought to mean at the time. [*The Constitution's Speech and Debate Clause grants senators and representatives immunity from suit or prosecution "for any Speech or Debate in either House."*] Was that opinion fun to write? I bet it was.

JLB: It was. The work on the constitutional issue was indeed fun.

Because this case is the subject of the next half dozen questions, I need to explain what it was about. It involved a libel action brought by a lawyer, Wayne Chastain, against Congressman Don Sundquist based on certain charges contained in a letter the congressman had written to the attorney general and released to the press. The trial court dismissed Chastain's complaint on the basis that Sundquist was protected from suit by the Speech and Debate Clause, a defense that Sundquist had not raised during the course of the trial. Rather, he had argued (and continued to argue on appeal) that he was entitled to the protection of the common law doctrine of official immunity that enables judges and certain executive officials, for example, to discharge their responsibilities without fear of retaliatory suits. The historical research alluded to by my questioner was directed to the scope of the Speech and Debate Clause. Most of my opinion, however, was concerned with Sundquist's claim of official immunity, which I rejected.

WW: That's why I was going to ask you about it. Because you could use all of the history of that time and go back to research it. Did you do that yourself, did you go back and read that history or was that given to you in the briefs?

JLB: Most of it was the result of original research by a very bright clerk using a set of books that I'm now the proud owner of. Four volumes published by the University of Chicago called *The Founders' Constitution.* Are you familiar with them?

WW: No.

JLB: Those volumes take up one clause of the Constitution at a time and follow it with quotations from dozens of relevant sources that relate to it—commentaries on the common law such as Blackstone, royal edicts, writings by various of the Founding Fathers, and so on, so as to place the clause in its historical and philosophical context.

WW: What a fabulous tool for a judge in deciding a Speech and Debate Clause issue. Did your clerk find that book or did you have it? I bet he had a wonderful time working on this case. I wondered whether or not the historical work was something that was presented to you by the advocates or something you had developed. My guess is that you had done that work.

JLB: Yes. [*Actually, my clerk had done it.*]

WW: In writing that opinion, Judge Mikva, as you may or may not remember, was concerned about the policy issue of limiting the definition of what a legislative duty was. Did you struggle with that issue?

JLB: I lost no sleep over it. I left open the possibility that somebody might find certain congressional activities protected by a principle of qualified or official immunity under state law; but that is quite different from the immunity provided by the Speech and Debate Clause.

I should note that Judge Mikva (who had served in Congress) agreed that Sundquist's actions were not protected by the Speech and Debate Clause. He felt strongly, however, that congressmen were entitled to official immunity for all actions taken in the course of non-legislative duty, a position with which the House of Representatives emphatically agreed. The House, in fact, passed a unanimous resolution asking the Supreme Court to hear an appeal of the case, which the Court declined to do; but a year later, the Court addressed the issue in another case and agreed that members of Congress were not covered by that immunity. Congress, however, has had the last laugh. In 1998, it enacted the Wesfall Act, which immunizes its members against suits for defamation and other common law torts for acts committed while "acting within the scope of his office." This may not be unreasonable in these litigious times, but it is a far cry from the probity that informed the Constitution's framers. As one of them, Charles Pinckney, observed, "They knew that in free countries very few privileges were necessary to the undisturbed exercise of legislative duties, and those few only they determined that Congress should possess: they never meant that the body who ought to be the purest and the least in want of shelter from the operation of laws affecting all their fellow citizens should be able to avoid them; they therefore not only intended, but did confine their privileges within the narrow limits mentioned in the Constitution." Needless to say, I found this quote in The Founders' Constitution.

WW: Limited immunity—I know what you're talking about. Did you and Judge Mikva have a debate in a conference about this or was it clear?

JLB: We had a discussion and I just said I disagreed; and at the time, I was in the minority. What I originally wrote was the dissenting opinion, which persuaded the third judge.

WW: That's very interesting.

JLB: Which is always fun. What won over the third judge was the distinction that I drew between executive and legislative functions. A public official is granted immunity in order to protect his ability to perform his constitutional duty; to do the job assigned. Members of the executive branch or the judiciary are required to make hard decisions without fear or favor, and they have the benefit of broad immunities. The obligations of a legislator are more discrete. If a legislator is to be effective, he must be free to say anything he wants to with respect to the making of laws and the formulation of law without fear of being hauled into court. The Constitution doesn't protect a member of the House or Senate from being sued for libel for speech that is unrelated to the function of legislating.

WW: Is that a distinction that you drew in your own analysis? That was not something that you found in the briefs?

JLB: That's right.

WW: I also take it that this was an opinion that even if you'd gotten a first draft from a law clerk that you wrote pretty much start to finish. That's how it read. And it was one of your earlier decisions.

JLB: Yes.

A postscript. Between the time I had finished writing my opinion and the time it was published, I ran into Congressman Sundquist at a Washington reception. He reminded me that we had met 15 years earlier when he served as my escort at the University of Washington in 1974 or '75 where I was addressing a meeting of the Young Republicans organization. I don't know whether he was aware that I was a member of the panel that had heard his appeal, but it was an awkward moment. I have no idea what happened to his case on remand, but it obviously didn't hurt his political career because he went on to become governor of Tennessee.

WW: I take it you probably haven't done any Speech and Debate Clause work since?

JLB: I've done several.

WW: Really? Do you remember which cases they were? Not the names necessarily but what the issues were?

JLB: A couple of the recent cases involving the prosecution of congressmen for violations of the Ethics in Government Act.

WW: How did this early opinion, when you went back to use it in analyzing these later issues, how did it hold up? That's the question I want to ask.

JLB: It held up well. The speech and debate issues were not close; the larger focus, as I recall, was on questions of separation of powers.

WW: I take it you didn't find the conduct to be protected by the Speech and Debate Clause?

JLB: I didn't.

As the foregoing suggests, I have had an unusual exposure to one of the Constitution's more obscure provisions. The resulting expertise has not gone to waste, however. It has been distilled and refined, and is now enshrined in The Heritage Foundation's primer, The Heritage Guide to the Constitution.

WW: I want to go back to one of the answers you gave me earlier about what makes a good judge—that you have an open mind and that you look at the issues. That being true, and recognizing that everyone is trying to do that, it was interesting as I looked at the opinions you identified as significant that I could have told you in advance, pretty much in every case, how the court would be aligned. Does that surprise you?

JLB: I hadn't thought about it in those terms.

WW: I didn't think of it when I asked for it, and I certainly didn't ask for it for that reason; but when I read four or five of them, it did strike me as interesting. I read about half of them before I came today—some of the early ones and some of the later ones—and was struck by my guess that you had done a lot of independent work on each decision. Your opinions start with first principles and work through the issues and come out at the end. It was also interesting to me that judicial philosophy somehow seemed to play a role in most of these significant decisions. Now why did you pick these? What criteria did you use?

JLB: Well, I guess because more often than not they dealt with an area that was not squarely predetermined by 83 nearly identical cases and because a certain amount of "original work" was required. *Association of American Physicians and Surgeons* is one example. There you find me disagreeing with two very conservative judges, namely Judges Silberman and Williams.

The key issue in that case was whether a "First Lady" is a "full-time officer, or employee, of the Federal Government." If so, the proceedings of a health care task force presided over by Mrs. Hillary Rodham Clinton were exempt from a statute requiring full disclosure of its proceedings. My friends Larry Silberman and Steve Williams insisted that she was an officer of the United States, hence entitled to the cloak of secrecy. As I demonstrated, at least to my own satisfaction, they were dead wrong; but I admired their chivalry.

WW: That's right. Silberman, Buckley, and Williams. Judge Silberman wrote the opinion and you wrote a concurring opinion.

JLB: You read that one too?

WW: Of all these cases on your list, or any others, is there a case or cases that you thought were the hardest to decide, that you really did lose sleep over?

JLB: Are there cases where years after I'm still not sure if we got it right? Yes, there are such.

WW: But you don't lose sleep over them.

JLB: You can't.

WW: Because you've got to move on. Are there any cases, as you sit here now, that you can remember at the time you were deciding them you found very hard to decide either because of policy reasons or because you couldn't sort out what the law really was or ought to be or for any other reason?

JLB: Yes. First of all, I don't think I have any right to impose my own views on policy. But I don't think that's what you are talking about.

WW: No, it's not.

JLB: Incidentally, would you be interested in a written statement of my philosophy as a judge?

WW: Yes.

JLB: Would that be helpful? OK, I can give you that. [See Attachment.]

WW: In what context did you write this?

JLB: It was originally for presentation at a Senate prayer breakfast. It ended up as an article.

WW: Good, yes.

JLB: I have had plenty of cases where I think the correct application of the law has done American society significant harm. But our understanding of the law was clearly what Congress intended, and making policy is its job, not ours. So that sort of thing doesn't bother me.

I must qualify that statement. Two cases did indeed bother me, and they bothered me profoundly because of their implications. In each of them, the defendant was a victim of Congress's recent impulse to criminalize breaches of statutory or regulatory law involving conduct that is not inherently immoral or unethical; and to compound the injury. Congress has often suspended the usual requirement that a person be aware that he is breaking the law before he can be convicted of a crime. As a result a person may now be thrown in jail for an innocent failure to comply with any one of hundreds of fine print commands. This provides prosecutors with formidable weapons with which to coerce or intimidate morally blameless men and women. (In one of the cases I heard, we vacated a jail sentence because of a statutory ambiguity; in the other, I had to agree to what I felt was an unjust sentence. The law is the law; but in the immortal words of Dickens' Mr. Macawber, the law can also be "a ass.")

WW: But it must also be the case that sometimes the law is not clear.

JLB: Unfortunately, that is too often the case. A law is poorly drafted and difficult to understand, or it may be very difficult to determine whether it was intended to be applied to the situation at hand, or the case involves a number of intellectually difficult concepts, or there is no underlying principle that can be relied on for guidance. For whatever reason, it can be devilishly difficult to come to a conclusion with any degree of certainty that it is the right one.

WW: The court, as we talked about a few minutes ago, does divide in some sense by judicial philosophy.

JLB: I'm not sure you would get anyone to say that.

WW: Well, I was just going to ask you whether you would agree with me. Other than my looking at the way these significant opinions were decided, what do you think about that? Let me just ask the question straight. Do you think there is a division of judicial philosophy on this court?

JLB: At the margins. Law schools will talk about the Constitution as a living document that must be constantly massaged and changed and kept up to date, and so on. Insofar as there are judges on this court who are comfortable with this view, their decisions will, I think, inevitably test the limits in pursuit of what they believe to be the correct result. But on this court, at least, any "activism" of that sort is held within rather tight limits, bound by a perception of the latitude the Supreme Court will allow in a particular field. I don't believe that our judges will claim any latitude with respect to a statute. At times, however, some of them will read something into a statute that I can't find. That is why I prefer to attribute differences in results to differences in perceptions of such intangibles as what is reasonable. People reading the same words will at times understand them quite differently. Especially when you have to come to grips with things such as "compelling government interest" or "reasonable due process." These are spongy concepts. I think probably we would all define our jobs in pretty much the same way—yet we will reach these quite different conclusions in a very narrow set of cases. I think this sort of thing will manifest itself in less than 1 or 2 percent of the cases.

Action for Children's Television v. FCC, a 1995 en banc case for which I wrote the majority opinion, is a classic example of one that turned on the individual judges' necessarily subjective assessments of intangibles. It involved a challenge to the constitutionality of a statute whose purpose was to protect children from indecent programs by forbidding their broadcast between the hours of 6:00 A.M. and midnight. The test established by the Supreme Court was whether the public interest Congress sought to protect was sufficiently compelling to override the exercise of a First Amendment right. As a Sowellian analysis might have predicted, the conservatives on our court all concluded that the public interest in protecting the innocence of children was more compelling than that of protecting the right of adults to view indecencies at their convenience.

One aspect of Action for Children's Television *that has always intrigued me is that this challenge to a law designed to safeguard children was brought by the same organization that twenty years earlier had brought a suit demanding that the Federal Communications Committee be more vigilant in protecting children from indecent programs—which provides striking support for the dictum of one of*

National Review's founding editors, James Burnham, that holds that any organization not explicitly conservative will, in time, be controlled by liberals.

WW: OK. To the extent that there are differences on the court of what we will call a worldview, do you find that there are personality conflicts that arise or are you all pretty much able to accommodate the different worldviews that you have?

JLB: I think we do a pretty good job of that. I know that there are those who assume, from the great differences in our political backgrounds, that we must engage in all kinds of clashes, but it's not true. I understand that in earlier years, there were some legendary battles among the judges of this court, but I haven't experienced any. There are individuals of all different types here, and they are all extremely capable. Occasionally some sparks will fly, as they will in any human situation, but these flare-ups are short-lived and have left no bruises, at least I am not aware of any.

WW: I would hope that would be true, but I can see that people with very different personalities could find it difficult to accommodate one another.

JLB: One of the strange things about this job is that we almost never see one another. I can literally go three weeks without laying my eyes on another judge. It's a very weird situation. In my first years on the job people asked me what it was like, and I said it's like entering a monastery. And then after a while I realized this was wrong because monks get together about five times a day, at inconvenient times, to pray. By contrast, this court consists of a series of hermitages. We each live our own quite separate existence.

WW: Do you find that to be a good or difficult part of the job?

JLB: It's a limitation. There are wonderful people here that I just don't get to know as well as I would like. We don't have sufficient numbers to support a dining room where you could drop by to have lunch and have a chance to get to know each other in a three dimensional way outside the context of the legal issues that we discuss during those four days a month that we hear cases with two other judges.

WW: We'll get to that. Do you think that there are judges on this court who are particularly good at consensus building?

JLB: Unlike the Supreme Court, we have very few cases that offer the opportunity to build a consensus. We have *en banc* hearings, but only two or three of them a year. So basically you come down to a situation in a three-judge panel where some individuals prove more persuasive than others in presenting a particular point of view. So the answer is yes, but you won't get me to name them.

WW: Do you think that the court is overloaded? You said earlier that there is no time.

JLB: I think it is more accurate to say that I have no time. I am a very untypical judge in that I am truly very slow. It takes me significantly more time to do my job than it takes the other judges here. When I mention this, people say that I must be more thorough than the others. But that is not so, I'm not better prepared. I am often less well prepared than other members of the panel. I am just painfully slow at reading and writing. I have always been a workaholic, but I have never put in more hours in any job in my life. I work most weekends and I get here at 8:15 in the morning, and I leave at 6:30 in the evening, and I usually put in an hour or two at home at night. On the other hand, there are three or four judges here who teach on the side, who do a fair amount of lecturing, who take off to Eastern Europe and help people write constitutions, and so on. So from my perspective, the court is way overloaded. Taking the court as a whole, I think we are probably at the level where we can handle our work without falling behind. [*At the time, there was one vacancy on the court and the consensus among the judges was that a replacement was not needed.*]

This was the most arduous and demanding work I had ever undertaken. My remark, at the outset of these interviews, that "I actually live in these chambers," was not an exaggeration. It was not unusual for me to work in my chambers 30 days or

My court in 1991. Standing: Judges Robinson, Henderson, Sentelle, Ginsburg, Thomas, Randolph, and McKinnon. Seated: JLB, Ginsburg, Mikva, Wald, Edwards, Silberman, and Williams.

more at a stretch. Month in and month out, I would be at my desk reading briefs and cases, deciphering murky regulations, and writing opinions that I hoped would explain the reasoning behind the court's decisions in a reasonably readable and persuasive way. The only relief from this routine was the four mornings every few weeks, from September through May, when I would hear oral arguments. The work, however, was often very interesting and, at times, extremely important. But it could also be extremely tedious. Unraveling the intricacies of regulations governing the rates that may be charged for the interstate transportation of natural gas can lose its charm the 12th time around, and candor requires me to acknowledge that after

four or five years on the job, I was tempted to bail out, and I might have if I had been
young enough to start a new career. But I have no regrets. I have been able to put
such talents as I have to good use, and that is reason to be satisfied.

WW: Are there any lawyers that you can think of now who struck you as particularly good appellate advocates?

JLB: Yes, but I can't think of their names.

WW: Do you remember any of the cases or the nature of the cases that they argued?

JLB: I'm sorry, specific cases don't spring to mind. There are some lawyers who have a way of explaining complicated issues, and they do it in an agreeable way—they answer questions directly. They display a certain amount of artistry, they can really give you a feel for an issue and an argument. There is the art of persuasion that some people have in greater abundance than others.

WW: Partly related to being smart and it's partly just a talent. It is wonderful to see somebody who you think is really good at advocacy. There must be times when you sit on the bench and think to yourself—this person is really good at this.

JLB: And then it's wonderful when both sides are really good at it.

WW: Do you find at the end of the day that you go home and share with your wife either interesting cases or particularly good advocacy or bad advocacy that you have seen?

JLB: No.

WW: Do you share it with friends or colleagues?

JLB: No. For better or for worse, I've taken very literally the injunction that nothing that goes on here ever gets repeated elsewhere. Of course public argument is public argument.

WW: This is a good place to break. I think we have about one more session of questions. Whenever it's good for you, we should meet again.

Life as a Judge, Role of the Judiciary, Retirement

WW: I think that this probably will be our last, our fifth session. Today is January 15, 1996. When we left off we were talking about the courts and the court system here. One of the things that I think we talked about briefly and you were going to think about more was whether, as you think about your judicial career, there were any memorable arguments or advocates either because they were particularly good or particularly not good

JLB: There have been times when I have been overwhelmed by the quality of the lawyers. I have also been surprised that sometimes you have somebody from a very big name firm who would fly all the way across the country to argue a case—and would bomb.

WW: I suppose I could ask a question this way. I have found that it is often the case that when a case reaches the Court of Appeals, the clients think they have to bring in some big name, and they will bring in somebody, someone who is not familiar with the record, someone who is not familiar with the case below, and the argument is not as excellent as the advocate thinks it is and the client had hoped, despite all the money that the client paid. Do you think that's right, do you find that?

JLB: I think that is a very good analysis. I have also had cases where you wonder how the lawyer ever passed the bar or received a law degree.

WW: What do you find generally when you sit on the bench? Are the arguments generally what you would expect or are you often impressed or are you often amazed at the quality of the argument?

JLB: Well, you expect competence and you usually get it, but sometimes you get someone who is exquisite. I do remember one instance—it involved election law and a challenge to the election of some New York judges. The attorney general of New York argued the case, and he came before us three times. He was absolutely masterful. Total command of the law, total command of the facts. The good sense not to pursue a losing argument. The quickness to pick up on an admission made by the other side—wit and grace; and I heard this man in his last argument as attorney general because he had lost his bid for reelection. We heard the case in the first week of January, before he had to step down.

WW: That is a wonderful thing to hear. When somebody is really good, at his or her best, it is a wonderful experience to watch. Who was this? Which attorney general?

JLB: The one who just lost. Couple of years ago, 1994. [*He was Attorney General Robert Abrams.*]

WW: Is this a case about the election of judges in New York?

JLB: Yes.

WW: Yes, I do remember that case. I can't remember what the issue was but I remember.

JLB: The Justice Department was trying to set aside the election of several judges in New York City by expanding the definition of discrimination beyond what the language of the statute and prior judicial interpretations of it could possibly support. The basic argument was that the system by which candidates are selected is such that it makes it harder for a member of a minority to be among the pool from which they are selected.

WW: Let's talk for a few minutes about your personal life while you have been on the bench. Do you find that being a judge makes it difficult to meet new people and be in social situations because of the limits of what your job is and what you can talk about?

JLB: Not because of the limits of what you can talk about. The fact is that I have had a limited social life these past ten years in part because I have been working so many evenings. Another factor is that judges live such isolated lives at work and don't have the occasion to bump into people casually. Therefore people tend to forget that you exist. Even people you are very fond of. If you are practicing law, you are in daily contact with other lawyers and clients. As a result, I have found that I have to take the initiative to call people and say let's have lunch. Otherwise I won't see anybody except my clerks.

WW: How about the judges on this court. Do they socialize? Do you socialize among yourselves?

JLB: Very little, but that little is enjoyable. We have a great group of people, but everyone is very preoccupied with his own work

WW: How does your wife deal with this—your working all the time?

JLB: Philosophically. She has her own activities. And a couple of them routinely take her out an evening or two a week.

Because Ann has wide interests and a remarkable talent for friendship, she has never been at a loss for things to do. While we had children at home, their (and their father's) welfare was her primary concern; but later, when I joined the State Department, she became involved in a number of activities, including the Washington Hospice program. It was there that she began to adopt what she refers to as "my old ladies"—typically, elderly widows who are very much alone in the world. She will visit them at least weekly, see that their basic needs are cared for, and generally jolly them along. Whatever the undertaking, because she combines an amiable persistence with a first-class sense of humor, she achieves her goals without ruffling collegial feathers. Well, she achieves most of them. Ann was an excellent and enthusiastic tennis player until arthritis forced her to shift to golf. To her distress, she has failed to master that game; and the fact that she beats me regularly brings her little satisfaction because my golf is very, very bad.

Unfortunately, the "annotation" format hasn't allowed me to say very much about my wife. I will take this opportunity, however, to smuggle in the following non-responsive observation: Ann hasn't a self-centered bone in her body; she is that rarity, a Christian who consistently practices what Christ preached.

WW: And what about travel? Do you ever get a chance to go anywhere?

JLB: Yes. I've always taken three weeks off in the summer and usually travel someplace. Then we have had a habit of taking about six or seven days off in the spring and go someplace warm.

WW: A favorite?

JLB: No. Gone to different places. No place that we routinely go to. We also take off for four or five days in October to see the New England foliage at its peak. It has become close to a sacred obligation which we missed this year for the first time in God knows how many years. The magic date is October 12.

WW: And where do you go?

JLB: We have friends who live in New Hampshire. And we come back through Connecticut. In the early '80s I spent three years in Europe and swore that I would never again for the few remaining years left to me deny myself this experience.

WW: New England is October. We just came back from New England. We always spend Christmas in New England, which is not the leaf season. How about books?

JLB: I'm reading an interesting one right now, Thomas Sowell's *The Vision of the Anointed*.

WW: Do you read novels? Or do you read more serious stuff?

JLB: I tend to read more serious things which these days I usually do by listening to recorded books while driving. It is astonishing how much ground you can cover during daily 30- or 40-minute trips to and from work. I have managed to cover some pretty heavy stuff—de Tocqueville's *Democracy in America*, Dante's *Inferno*, the *Iliad*, *Moby Dick*. As for traditional reading—sitting down with books and turning pages—this has virtually been limited to long plane flights and vacations, and that reading is usually light.

WW: That's pretty heavy stuff for somebody who is working all the time.

JLB: History, a lot of American history. Occasionally a novel, sometimes trashy novels.

WW: You can buy those on tape too. Any other activities or interests that you have cultivated in the last few years?

JLB: None that I have cultivated in the last few years but I have been able at the margins to continue some interests I have always had. Natural history, birds in particular, and in recent years—meaning going back 30 years—an interest in the Arctic. Since I have been on the court I have watched polar bears on three occasions. If you do something like this, you escape into a totally different world. When out watching polar bears, you have no access to news and therefore. . . .

WW: Just polar bears—no access to people either.

JLB: You have access to other people who like to watch polar bears, who happen to be an enormously congenial lot. In any event, I try to do that sort of thing.

Introducing grandson Jimmy (Jay's son)
to the delights of watching polar bears.

WW: Are you a member of the Audubon Society?

JLB: Yes. [*And I may be among its longest-standing members, having joined what was then the National Association of Audubon Societies in 1935 or '36.*]

WW: OK. Let's talk a little bit about judicial philosophy. Over the last few meetings, you have really talked a fair amount about your judicial philosophy which has been consistent throughout your career. But let me ask you a few questions anyway about that. Let me ask you a general question. Do you think the public's view of the courts and the judiciary has changed over time, and what do you think it is and is there anything we can do to improve it?

JLB: I am sure the public view has changed, and I think there probably are things that can be done about it. Whether we will or not is something else. My impression is that, beginning with the Warren Court, too many Supreme Court decisions have overturned too many settled practices of the American people so that a very large number of Americans have come to view Supreme Court justices and other judges as engaged in making policy rather than concentrating on the objective application of the law. And this perception of the judiciary can only be reinforced by recent spectacles of Supreme Court confirmation hearings which give the impression that the Senate's sole concern is with assessing the political views of nominees for the position of philosopher kings who will have the authority to write their policy preferences into law. I find this terribly disturbing because that isn't what the rule of law is supposed to be about. If this impression is even part way justified, then it should hardly be surprising that significant numbers of Americans have become disenchanted with the judiciary. I don't know if you read my piece on the oath of office. In it I say that the oath administered to judges requires me to apply the Constitution and laws of the United States to the case at hand as objectively as I can. If I deviate from that standard and insert my own druthers into the Constitution or other laws of the United States, I violate the oath and undercut the constitutional principle of the separation of powers.

WW: What do you think the public perception is? Do you think that the public perception is that the judiciary has a broader role because of what it was doing early in the '60s and '70s?

JLB: That it plays a larger role, which is not the same thing as saying that it has a larger role. When organizations like People for the American Way and National Organization of Women wage major advertising campaigns to defeat Robert Bork or some other nominee for the Supreme Court, they reinforce the heresy that judges have a legitimate policy role to play; and presumably, many members of the Senate share that view, judging by some of the questions they ask nominees. Under the circumstances, it would hardly be surprising that many Americans see a legitimate policy role for the courts. But at the same time, because federal judges are not elected and have life tenure, a perception that they are in fact policy makers must inevitably undermine confidence in them as guardians of the rule of law. You can't have it both ways.

I should qualify the above. I am not sure that the American public, or even senatorial inquisitors at confirmation hearings, really believe that judges have a legitimate role in the formulation of public policy. What may be closer to the truth is that because some judges have engaged in formulating policy and have done so in often highly controversial areas, the public may well come to accept the application of political litmus tests in deciding who should be appointed to the federal bench. My fear is that this will encourage the belief that the judiciary is in fact, if not in theory, merely a third political branch of government; and that this in turn may encourage future judges to act as if it were. Liberal activists such as People for the American Way have little problem with policy-making from the bench because, in recent years, they have won so many battles in the courtroom that they could not win in Congress or in state legislatures. They know, too, that liberal judges are more apt to be on their side of the ideological fence.

This is a reflection of the deep division that exists today over the standards that are to be applied in interpreting the Constitution. One school, which is exemplified by Justice Antonin Scalia's focus on original meaning, maintains, essentially, that in construing the Constitution as well as any other federal law, a judge is bound by the meaning of its text as illuminated by contemporaneous usage and tradition; that is to say, its meaning as understood by those who ratified or enacted it. The second school, as epitomized by the late Justice William Brennan, views the Constitution as a "living" document that each generation of jurists is at liberty to adapt to the exigencies of the times. Thus, as Justice Brennan expressed it in an address at Georgetown University in 1985, "The genius of the Constitution rests not in any static meaning it might have had in a world that is dead and gone, but in the adaptability of its great principles to cope with current problems and current needs." Needless to say, such a view of the Constitution will allow a jurist to make rather breathtaking departures from the original understanding of what the Constitution permits. Because conservatives tend to belong to the Scalia school, they are far less likely than their liberal colleagues to read new meanings into the Constitution. I do not claim that there is no such thing as an activist conservative. The temptation to write policy into law can be strong. But if a member of the Scalia school is tempted to abuse his judicial power, he would at least know (or should know) that he is exceeding his authority. Given the Brennan example, however, those who act on the theory that the Constitution is malleable may have no such qualms.

As I have suggested elsewhere, conservative and liberal judges of equal competence who intend to apply the lawmakers' understanding of what a particular law requires may nevertheless disagree as to how it should be applied in cases where an essentially subjective standard must be applied. But such occasions are too rare to warrant the application of political litmus tests to judicial nominees. These can only undermine the public's confidence in the rule of law, which is based on the assumption that laws are capable of objective application and that the function of the federal judiciary is to do precisely that: to apply the law objectively. The answer to the problem of activism is to use the confirmation process to weed out candidates who either do not understand the constitutional role of a judge or who cannot be trusted to live within its bounds.

WW: What do you think about how the courts are doing in the criminal justice system? How is this court doing, do you think?

JLB: Well, I think that we are doing a competent job of applying the Constitution as the Supreme Court tells us to. I'm not necessarily in agreement with some of the Supreme Court's rulings. The exclusionary rule has never made a great deal of sense to me. [*The exclusionary rule forbids the use of illegally secured evidence in a criminal trial.*] I know the public policy rationale for it, but if you have somebody who has been certified a career rapist and murderer and you have the goods on him but can't use them because some policeman made a mistake, punish the policeman but don't punish society.

WW: I suspect that's what the public generally thinks about the exclusionary rule. Especially those who are mostly concerned about crime. And if you were on the Supreme Court and had that case before you, would you reverse it?

JLB: I might, I might. This of course gets into the whole difficult area of. . . .

WW: Right. I know I am asking you a complicated question. Here's something you feel fairly strongly about. I take it that in the first instance if this had come to you, you would not have developed an exclusionary rule. Now that we have had it for 20 some years. . . .

JLB: I guess at the federal level it's been there for eons, hasn't it? And this in effect is federal common law. The exclusionary rule does not represent an interpretation of the Constitution as such. But I have questions about the view that the Fourteenth Amendment has required the substitution of federal law for traditional state law in many of these areas. This is more a gut feeling than a studied conclusion as I have never had to address the matter. I also have a problem with the use of a common law methodology, i.e., the development of law case by case, to the interpretation and application of written law. Oliver Wendell Holmes demonstrated early on that the common law was an evolutionary process that, over time, could result in radical changes in what had earlier been considered immutable rules. Courts would build precedent on precedent, and over time a particular rule of law would be transformed into a beast of quite a different kind. But our Constitution is the instrument by which the people, in their ratifying conventions, delegated specific powers and authority to a new government and established the rules for conducting their new nation's future business. And while the common law principle of *stare decisis* is important in lending predictability to the law, if with benefit of hindsight it can be seen that a chain of precedents has turned a constitutional principle on its head, I am not satisfied that the Supreme Court doesn't have the duty to revert to the original understanding.

For the benefit of the uninitiated, stare decisis *(Latin for "to stand by things decided")* is a sacred principle of the British system of common law that we have inherited. Unlike the Continental or Civil Code, which is based on written statutes, the common law consists of legal principles established by judges in the course of deciding cases. A court will review decisions in earlier cases to determine whether a precedent exists that is applicable to the case before it. If one does, the court is required to apply it. Until relatively recent times, common law judges believed that the resulting rules were based on immutable principles of justice. They spoke of the "seamless fabric" of the common law; and when they found it necessary to go beyond existing precedent in order to resolve a case, they thought of themselves as doing no more than unveiling principles of natural law that had yet to be applied. But as Oliver Wendell Holmes demonstrated in his book, The Common Law, *common law courts were unconsciously engaged in creating new laws, however imperceptibly.*

While it is true that stare decisis *is conducive to stability and predictability in the law, I have come to question its utility in cases involving constitutional or statutory issues precisely because, over time, judges adding another link to a precedential chain can become so intent on exploring the implications of the last preceding case that they lose sight of the underlying text and its inherent limits. This is what happened in a recent highly controversial Supreme Court case, Keno v. City of New London (2005), challenging the constitutionality of the city's condemnation of some modest houses so that a private developer could proceed with a project that the city fathers believed would improve its economy. The case required a construction of the Fifth Amendment's command that "private property [shall not] be taken for public use without just compensation," which New London was prepared to pay.*

The case hung on the scope of "public use;" but instead of examining what those who ratified that language reasonably understood it to mean, the Supreme Court's majority opinion focused exclusively on an examination of recent cases which had substituted the phrase "public purpose" for "public use." Although those precedents at least had the merit of restricting a lawful taking to the removal of urban blight or other conditions that resulted in a demonstrable public harm, a slim majority ruled that enabling a private entrepreneur to create jobs and increase a city's tax revenues represented a licit "public purpose." And so, freed from textual restraints, the Supreme Court has transformed the Constitution's "public use," which has discernible limits, to an open-ended "public purpose" that knows none beyond those a particular majority of the Court may choose to impose. That's a substantial departure from at least my understanding of what the rule of law permits.

If I am right about the hazards of stare decisis, *one solution might be to require that every court decision include an explicit demonstration that its precedent-based holdings fall within the scope of the applicable constitutional provision or statute. This would ensure that its analysis remains tethered to the texts. In the New London case, only Justice Clarence Thomas bothered to determine whether the authors of the Fifth Amendment would have condoned the taking.*

WW: Give me an example of an area where you think the Supreme Court should revert to an original understanding of the Constitution

JLB: First Amendment and pornography, for example. First Amendment as applied to religion.

WW: Well, why don't we focus on that. Let's look at religion.

JLB: The establishment of religion had a precise meaning in the 18th century. The Church of England, the Anglican Church, was the established religion of Virginia. Other denominations were publicly supported in other states. I think a straightforward reading of the First Amendment supports the view that all that the Establishment Clause was intended to do was to prohibit the federal government from establishing an official religion of the United States and, conversely, that the Free Exercise Clause was intended to keep the United States from prohibiting the practice of any religion. It seems to me that it is less than self-evident that these provisions prohibit the saying of a nondenominational prayer at a public school. At least it never occurred to anyone during our first 170 years that school prayer was forbidden by the Constitution. But I take my orders from the Supreme Court.

I note in passing that the Congress that adopted the First Amendment's religious clauses also reenacted the Continental Congress's Northwest Territories Ordinance

(with modifications not here relevant), which contains the following provision: "Religion, morality, and knowledge being necessary to good government, and the happiness of mankind, schools and the means of education shall forever be encouraged." Thus early Congresses made grants of land in support of religious purposes and funded sectarian education among the Indians.

WW: Well, I am giving you a chance to be a little more expansive; if you were on the Supreme Court, would you cut back in that area do you think? Or has the law moved to a place where it would be very difficult now?

JLB: There are always difficulties. But if I am a justice of the Supreme Court and I take an oath to apply the Constitution to the best of my understanding, what am I to do if I conclude after the most thorough study that, contrary to what the Supreme Court has ruled in the past, there is nothing in the Constitution that permits a particular exercise of federal power? Where do I find the authority to enforce what I am convinced is an illegal act by the federal government? But how can one unscramble an omelette. It's a real dilemma.

Some of the Supreme Court's decisions have had such profound institutional consequences that it is hard to see how the Court could return to constitutional purity without causing some formidable disruptions in how we have come to govern ourselves. In such instances, I assume a bemused Providence would excuse the justices' decision to honor misguided precedent rather than their oaths to defend the Constitution.

WW: That's right. But even so, as you said, if you are on the Supreme Court you still have to deal with what has developed into federal common law in an area like establishment of religion where the law has developed over the years. Any other areas in particular as you look at it?

JLB: The most difficult one to unravel is what's been done with the commerce clause.

WW: Well, the Supreme Court is looking at that.

JLB: It is looking at it but with a very narrow focus. I think you are referring to the case last year which threw out a federal law forbidding possession of a gun within X feet of a school. In enacting that law, Congress didn't even adopt the formality of finding an interstate connection. There was no reference whatsoever to commerce. I think it is too early to tell whether we are witnessing a significant reexamination of the Court's commerce clause jurisprudence. One could say that the Supreme Court is now going to insist that Congress claim an effect on commerce, however tenuous. But a real rollback? As a consequence of this jurisprudence, we have, in my judgment, totally discarded what was one of the critical protections of American freedoms in the Bill of Rights, the Tenth Amendment.

WW: Well, how far back would you go in rolling it back? Would you go so far as to say Congress shouldn't be legislating in the area of minority rights, discrimination?

JLB: Congress clearly has that authority under the Fourteenth Amendment.

WW: But you have hesitations about relying on the Fourteenth Amendment.

JLB: Not in terms of protecting minorities against discrimination. The only place where I have hesitation is when you say that the Fourteenth Amendment extends all provisions of the Bill of Rights to the states as opposed to recognizing that the Fourteenth Amendment prohibits discrimination across the board.

WW: Even based on disabilities as opposed to race? Which nobody thought about?

JLB: That requires an assessment of the scope of the class protected from discrimination by the amendment and also of the nature of the discrimination. But if required to guess, I would say that is state business.

WW: So in other words—I'm just looking, exploring the limits of this—we are talking about the American Disability Act. It's hard to rely on the Fourteenth Amendment if you are looking at the Fourteenth Amendment for what it was designed to do, and if you can't rely on commerce, you would really say that it was up to the states.

JLB: Sure. And I think if you did return to a more restricted view of the scope of Congress's authority, we would have far better government at the national level. Congress would once again have the time to think through those things that are necessarily national.

WW: Well, they are not doing a very good job.

JLB: They can't. They don't have time to. A couple of years ago, a researcher accompanied a member of the House of Representatives for an entire week and concluded that he had no more than 15 minutes during the typical day for uninterrupted, consecutive thought, for reflection. It has become an impossible job.

It must be clear, from my answers to the last few questions, that I question the legitimacy of a number of the Supreme Court's decisions, although I am obliged to follow its understanding of the law. This hardly makes me a revolutionary. In fact, some of the Court's severest critics have come from within its own ranks. In 1964, for example, Justice John M. Harlan lamented what he described as the "current mistaken view . . . that every major social ill in this country can find its cure in some constitutional 'principle,'" and noted that "when, in the name of constitutional interpretations, the Court adds something to the Constitution that was deliberately excluded from it, the Court in reality substitutes its view of what should be so for the amending process;" and in his dissent in Roe v. Wade, *Justice Byron White described the majority opinion as "an exercise of raw judicial power" without support in "the language or history of the Constitution."*

For better or worse, that some judges will use their power to shape public policy is hardly new. What is new is the profound impact that some of the Supreme Court's rulings are having on the social and political life of this country. In recent years, it has issued decisions based on newly defined rights that millions of Americans see as threats to their most deeply held values. Because many of these have overturned laws and practices that date back to the earliest days of the Republic, it is hardly surprising that great numbers of Americans have come to view the Court as an active player, perhaps the critical player, in the ongoing culture wars as it pursues goals which they believe to be beyond its authority. Three particularly sensitive lines of cases come to mind; namely, those in which, by narrow margins, the Supreme Court has virtually banished religion from public life, extended First Amendment protection to the most explicit pornography, and proclaimed what amounts to an unrestricted right to abortion. Aside from their dramatic impacts on American life, what these three lines of cases have in common is their creation of constitutional rights for which there is no historical or textual basis and which anyone with a feel for American history must know the authors of the Bill of Rights and the Fourteenth and other amendments cited in support of Roe v. Wade *would never have condoned.*

These and other decisions touching on deeply held values are, in my view, the root cause of the destructive acrimony that has infected so much of the Senate judicial confirmation process in recent years. Because some judges have overstepped their authority and made law, there are senators in each party who feel it is appropriate to apply political litmus tests in determining the qualifications of candidates for the federal bench. If, in 1985, the Senate had had the same approach to judicial confirmations as the one we see today, my own nomination would have been dead on arrival. I had introduced the first constitutional amendment designed to reverse Roe v. Wade *and was one of nine senators to oppose the Equal Rights Amendment, it having been my quaint belief that society ought to have the right, for example, to decide whether women should be exempted from being drafted for combat duty in Vietnam. That would have been enough to deny me even the courtesy of a hearing. I hope, though, that my service as a judge has been able to establish, if nothing else, that it is possible for a person to have the strongest views on questions of public policy and still understand and observe the sharp distinction between the constitutional role of a legislator and that of a judge.*

WW: I know you have a very strong religious background and religious sense—do you think that's had an impact on your judicial philosophy?

JLB: It is more accurate to say that I am not a religious person but that I take religion very seriously. I am utterly persuaded that the framers of the Constitution never intended to exclude religious perspectives from public life, contrary to what so many are suggesting today. If you read the writings of the founding generation, you can't help but be struck by what they saw as the relationship between religion and freedom. They believed that freedom depended on the exercise of self-control by moral people, and that morality in turn depended on religion. They would have been shocked by the idea that the state should not be hospitable to religion so long as it established none. Now, what was the question you asked me?

WW: You are answering it. The impact of your religious views.

JLB: Has religion affected the way I have conducted myself as a judge? I don't believe it has, although I could be fooling myself. As it happens, I have written an article on the place of religion in public life. For the reasons I have just recited, I say in it that it is entirely proper for a member of Congress or a president to take his religious beliefs into account when formulating public policy. At the same time I say it is improper for a judge to take his own religious beliefs into account because a judge's sole responsibility is to interpret and apply the law in a manner that is faithful to the intentions of those who had the authority to write it. I did mention an exception. Judges are quite free to take into account the hell fire that awaits those who violate their oaths.

WW: You are in remarkably unusual circumstances. You have been in all three branches of government. Looking back, which was, which is the most fun?

JLB: The Senate was, although it was becoming less and less fun because of the increasing difficulty of finding the time for serious legislative work, the work for which a senator is elected. In fact, I had privately determined that had I been reelected in 1976, I would not have gone for a third term. Another six years would have allowed me to accomplish whatever I was able to accomplish in areas that most concerned me. I have the feeling, however, that for anyone interested in the formulation of public policy, there could not have been a more glorious job in the world than to be a United States senator at any time from the founding of the Republic until relatively recently.

WW: Is that because during that period there was less media attention, fewer other things going on, so you would have had an opportunity to focus on public policy issues and make decisions based on how you felt about them where now it is difficult to do that? You think that's right?

JLB: Not really. The principal difference between the days when the Senate earned the title of the world's greatest deliberative body and the present is that in earlier days, the federal government concerned itself with relatively few areas of responsibility, namely those reasonably related to the powers enumerated in Article I of the Constitution. Each one of these involved functions that, in the judgment of the Founders, could only be effectively handled at the national level. Even through the New Deal days, Congress would usually meet for no more than seven or eight months a year, and it had the leisure to concentrate full attention on the half dozen questions at hand. There has been a vast change in the institution since then. Every morning in the Senate the leadership gets unanimous consent to waive two rules. One requires the reading, essentially, of the prior day's Congressional Record and the other prohibits the conduct of committee work when there is action on the floor of the Senate. These rules must be waived for all the obvious reasons. I once asked the Senate parliamentarian when the rule about committee work began to be waived as a matter of routine, and he said it was in the early '50s. Before that, senators would be on hand to listen to debates as a matter of course. Now, the floor is largely empty because committees are constantly having to meet to process the mountains of bills generated on Capitol Hill. That, incidentally, has affected my view of the utility of legislative history. The great majority of those who vote on bills never hear them debated.

WW: You assume they all read the Congressional Record when they were at home. They read it to their children before they went to bed. Let me ask you for a minute about writing a book. You wrote *If Men were Angels* a number of years ago, although I did not write down the dates. Tell me what inspired you to write that book.

JLB: An offer from a publisher. I thought that it could be done by assembling a bunch of my Senate speeches and articles and splicing them together. I tried that, but it didn't work; and so I had to go back to the drawing board. It was a hideous experience. So never again. [*Well, almost never. If my oral history hadn't offered me a convenient scaffolding, I would never have recorded these "annotations."*]

WW: Do you think your views have changed since then?

JLB: About writing a book?

WW: No. About what you expressed there. I must say I didn't read the whole book, but I looked through it, and it seems to be consistent with your current philosophy of government. Think that's right?

JLB: Yes.

In a debate during my 1976 reelection campaign, Pat Moynihan informed the audience that I was a fine fellow but that my feet were stuck in 18th century concrete. In response, I acknowledged that I was indeed committed to the values and political principles enshrined in the Declaration of Independence and the Constitution. My subsequent experiences in government have only reinforced that commitment. Because the Founders' philosophy of government was grounded in an accurate reading of human nature, which is the one constant we can rely on in this world, that philosophy remains as sound a guide to the creation and preservation of a free society as it was two hundred years ago. While I recognize that the complexities of modern life require a larger role for government than anyone could have anticipated in the 18th century, they do not justify the concentration of power we now see in Washington, with its potential for abuse. Nor do they require the vast number of regulations that now control so much of our lives or a welfare state that threatens to bankrupt us. (The proliferation of federal bureaus and agencies calls to mind one of the grievances against the British crown that was listed in the Declaration of Independence: "He [the King] has erected a Multitude of new Offices, and sent hither Swarms of Officers to harass our People, and eat out their substance.")

WW: So you don't need to write another book.

JLB: But I suppose I could expand on certain parts of it now that I have served in the other two branches of government.

WW: Now, because I read the *Washington Post's* "*In the Loop*" carefully every day, I did read that you had announced that you were thinking of retiring at the end of the year.

JLB: No. What I said was that it was possible that I would. There is a difference. The court schedules its work over a year in advance. I am currently set down for sittings into May of 1997. Because of the uncertainty as to whether or when the Mikva vacancy will be filled, the court has had to prepare two alternative schedules, one for an 11-judge court and another for a 12-judge court. Because it is possible that I will take senior status, I thought it a courtesy to advise the court managers that they should be considering a 10-judge alternative as well.

WW: Do you think you'll do that—take senior status?

JLB: I am thinking about it very seriously. I haven't made a precise decision yet.

My answer was disingenuous, I fear. Nineteen ninety-six was a presidential election year. Months earlier, I had decided most precisely that I would take senior status in August, before the new court term began and too late for the Senate to act before the election on any nomination Clinton might make to fill the vacancy I would be creating. For the uninitiated, a federal district or appellate judge may take senior status after serving the number of years in office proscribed by statute, the minimum being ten for those who were 60 years old or older at the time of their appointment. "Senior status" means "retired." One of the oddities of taking senior status is that it results in an increase in net income. Federal judges retire at full pay; but because they are now pensioners, Social Security taxes are no longer deducted from their pay checks. This sounds like an extremely generous retirement arrangement until one realizes that my clerks were earning more money than I did two or three years after they left my employ. (Potter Stewart told me that it was Franklin Roosevelt who engineered the current arrangement. He had hoped, apparently, to bribe superannuated Supreme Court justices into retirement so he wouldn't have to go to the trouble of trying to pack the Court. He failed to achieve his goal; but generations of federal judges owe him a debt of gratitude, whatever his motivation.)

Senior judges may volunteer to continue to perform judicial duties; and so long as they undertake at least 25 percent of the normal workload, they may continue to occupy their chambers, retain the services of a secretary, and hire the number of clerks appropriate to the workload they have agreed to assume. On taking senior status, I volunteered to assume about 30 percent of the normal appellate court caseload. I then began four years of slow-motion shuttling between our new home in Sharon, Connecticut, and the small apartment we had acquired in Bethesda, Maryland, after selling our Washington home. As time went by, I found the allure of country living more and more compelling. So, after four years of this routine, I concluded that the time had come to hang up my robe. Having attained the age of 77, I thought it would not be dishonorable to retire to my rocking chair.

WW: Are you ready to try something a little less taxing? I take it that what senior status means is that your caseload will be reduced and you could do some other things with your life.

JLB: Yes. Such as reading books instead of listening to them on tape.

WW: But not writing them.

JLB: Not writing them. I might write an article or two—I don't know. Who knows. I must confess that I find the prospect of some leisure time more and more appealing as my actuarial horizon diminishes.

WW: Any pressures from home in that respect?

JLB: No pressures whatsoever with respect to any of the exotic things I have undertaken, but I know that my wife would not be disappointed.

Befriending walruses in the Canadian arctic, 2004.

WW: As you look back over all the things you have done, which were not as some people would have thought planned out from day one, do you have any regrets in particular?

JLB: In terms of activity? I've got the standard regret of workaholics that I didn't spend more time with my children.

WW: That is the standard regret, right?

JLB: Right.

WW: Anything else?

JLB: Not regrets, no. I have had a strange life, utterly unplanned at just about every stage. I do have one regret. I regret that I don't have a memory that would enable me, when on a rocking chair in a nursing home, to recapture all of the things I have been exposed to. I just can't do it. Occasionally I bump into somebody from college who says, "Oh, do you remember such and such?" and I find I have totally forgotten some fascinating experiences. Or my children will say, "Do you remember such and such?" and I have totally forgotten the incident they are referring to.

WW: You are probably very sympathetic on the bench when you hear about witnesses who can't remember. Well, your life has been as you've described it over these last five sessions: interesting, varied, and unplanned. That is the way you have described it. You did not set out either to be a judge or to be a senator in any particular way. So what do you see ahead for yourself?

JLB: Ultimately (it is a question of timing), I will take senior status. You have heard about the income tax tail wagging the taxpayer. My wife is frantic right now because we are moving simultaneously from our home in Washington to an apartment in Bethesda and a house in Connecticut. Where does Internal Revenue come into this? We knew we would ultimately retire to the town in Connecticut where I grew up and where we raised our children. A house came on the market that met all of our specifications. Because the village is so small—about 2,800 people—years could go by before another so tailored to our needs would be available. So we grabbed it and placed it on the rental market. The magic two-year period expires next month when we have to sell our existing home in order to take advantage of the tax base rollover. So we placed our Washington house on the market last fall and managed to sell it almost immediately.

The Sharon house that caught my wife's fancy is built on one of a half dozen three-acre lots carved out of the fields above the house I lived in as a child. What especially attracted her was that ownership of the house would give us access to the large pool in which our children swam with their cousins when they were growing up. Ann thought this might be the honey that would entice them to come visit us with their own children, and this has proven to be the case. We have four spare bedrooms that are often overflowing. And so, I have come full circle—back to the original property, if not the original hearth. Life has its satisfactions.

WW: Did that have any impact on the timing of your announcement that you might take senior status?

JLB: Yes, it has. That and the fact that I am shortly going to be 73 and want to see more of my children. Also, there are places I haven't seen yet that I would like to see.

WW: Have you been to France to see your granddaughter? Is it a granddaughter or grandson?

JLB: Grandson. We have made a point of going there at least every other year. We were last there in July of 1994. It was just awful.

WW: Crowded, hot?

JLB: Crowded, very hot, and no air conditioning. In any event, our ultimate goal is for me to be a senior judge with a lot of spare time.

WW: Sounds pretty good; wouldn't be a bad thing to do. As you look ahead for this court or for the political system in this country, are you optimistic—do you think things will get better, will they change? What do you think?

JLB: They will certainly change. It will undoubtedly surprise you to learn that I found much in the elections of 1994 to give hope. [*In 1994, Republicans captured control of the House of Representatives for the first time in eons in campaigns that focused on a very conservative agenda.*] As for the future, I have had a stock speech since my late Senate days which I update and deliver periodically. It is called "Overloading the Federal Horse." It catalogs the gridlock that has been overtaking both the legislative and executive branches, underscores the philosophical virtues of assigning government responsibilities to the lowest levels of government competent to handle them, and ends with the suggestion that the gridlock may reach a point where necessity, if not philosophy, will force a return to something like the federalism we once enjoyed. The underlying themes of the 1994 congressional campaigns suggest that this thought is not entirely wild.

WW: Well, thank you very much. I think that is the exact right note on which to end this interview.

ATTACHMENT TO ORAL HISTORY

Reflections on the Oath of Office

JAMES L. BUCKLEY

WE ARE ALL familiar with that rite of passage in which an individual who has been elected or appointed to public office is asked to swear that he will defend the Constitution against all enemies, foreign and domestic. At the instant that he utters the magic words, "I do," that individual is vested with the powers of his new office, and his friends uncork the champagne in celebration. But even though that oath is required by the Constitution, I suspect that few give any thought to its implications in the larger constitutional scheme.

The requirement of an oath is to be found in the first part of the third clause of Article VI, which reads as follows:

> The Senators and Representatives . . . and the Members of the several State Legislatures, and all executive and judicial officers, both of the United States and the several States, shall be bound by Oath or Affirmation, to support this Constitution.

The balance of that clause provides that "no religious Test shall ever be required as a Qualification to any Office or public Trust under the United States."

I began to consider the implications of the oath two years ago when I was asked to participate in a symposium on "The Catholic Public Servant." As I was teamed with a former governor and a current congressman, it was obvious that I was expected to focus my remarks on the role and responsibilities of a Catholic judge. And because of the lamentable tendency these days to view members of the Supreme Court as philosopher kings who are authorized to write policy into law, I felt it necessary to focus on constitutional fundamentals.

It should be noted that the third clause of Article VI is the only provision of the original Constitution that applies to all three branches of government; the only one that applies to both state and federal officials. So it should be obvious that the Founders intended the oath to serve more than a ceremonial purpose. They were launching an extraordinary experiment in governance, and they knew it would work only if every public officer in their new Republic were to bind himself to make it work. To this end, they consciously enlisted the power of religion to ensure fidelity to the Constitution. James Madison, in fact, was to comment on the seeming paradox that such a requirement should appear in the same clause as the provision abolishing religious qualifications for public office. As he wrote in October of 1787, "Is not a religious test . . . involved in the oath itself?"

It doesn't speak well of our age that we must remind ourselves that the special power of an oath derives from the fact that in it we ask God to bear witness to the promises we make with the implicit expectation that He will hold us accountable for the manner in which we live up to them. This understanding of the meaning of an oath is as ancient as our civilization. Edward Gibbon made the point in a wry passage on the role of religion in the Roman Empire:

The various modes of worship, which prevailed in the Roman world, were all considered by the people, as equally true; by the philosopher, as equally false; and by the magistrate, as equally useful. . . . The magistrates could not be actuated by a blind, though honest bigotry, since the magistrates were themselves philosophers. . . . [But t]hey knew and valued the advantages of religion, as it is connected with civil government. . . . [A]nd they respected as the firmest bond of society, the useful persuasion that, either in this or in a future life, the crime of perjury is most assuredly punished by the avenging gods.

Like the Roman magistrates, the Founders of the American Republic took conscious advantage of this "useful persuasion" to further the interests of their new state; but unlike those magistrates, the Founders believed in both the religious nature of the oath and in the sanctions that await those who break a promise made to God. In his Farewell Address, George Washington would ask, "Where is the security for property, for reputation, for life, if the sense of religious obligation desert the oaths. . . ?" And in his diary, John Adams acknowledged his terror at the thought of eternal punishment should he ever betray his conscience and his God in order to secure political advantage.

What, then, are the implications of the oath that all public officers are required to take? What obligations does it impose on them? The answer, of course, lies in the words to which they have been asked to swear. These have been set by statute; and although the exact language will vary depending on the office being assumed, they all require that the prospective officials swear or affirm that they will support the Constitution of the United States and faithfully discharge the duties of the offices upon which they are about to enter. This undertaking demands that they determine as best they can exactly what it is their offices require of them, and what limits have been placed by law on their authority; having done so, they live under a continuing duty to meet those standards and to respect those limitations to the best of their abilities.

As my audience at the symposium was interested in the place of religion in public service, I observed that the nature of an officer's responsibilities will determine what role, if any, that religious convictions may legitimately play in his official work. I acknowledged that there are those today who will construe the First Amendment to require that public servants ignore their own religious beliefs when discharging their public duties, but suggested that this position demonstrates a profound ignorance of both the Constitution and human nature. Which brings me to the second part of clause 3 of Article VI, namely, its prohibition of religious qualifications for public office. This provision, of course, merely ensures that positions of authority in the federal and state governments will be open to persons, and therefore to influences, of every faith, and of none.

The Founders were not afraid of religion. To the contrary, they thought it essential to the success of their fledgling government. Because the Founders understood the links between religion and virtue and responsible citizenship, they emphasized throughout their writings that the Republic's survival, and the liberties it was intended to protect, ultimately depended on the morality of its citizens. In sum, we live in a society in which the importance of religion has always been recognized; and while the First Amendment forbids laws "respecting an establishment of religion," it has never required that the state be isolated from exposure to religious influences.

Thus, as I understand our constitutional arrangements, a president and members of Congress need never apologize for the fact that their views or votes may reflect their religious beliefs. As members of the elected branches of government, they are expected to engage in the formulation of public policy; and it is, quite simply, fatuous to suppose that they can check the religious components of their convictions at the door before entering the council chambers of government. The role of federal judges, however, is of a significantly different kind. As unelected officials, they can claim no mandate to reconstruct public policy. Rather, their constitutional duties are exclusively judicial. It is their job to give force and effect to the law, whether they agree with it or not; and that, I assure you, is responsibility enough.

In my remarks to my Catholic audience, I explained that in taking office, I had sworn to "administer justice . . . according to the best of my abilities and understanding, agreeably to the Constitution and laws of the United States." I then proceeded to describe this federal appellate judge's understanding of the nature and limits of his authority, more or less as follows. I said that the authority that was vested in me upon taking that oath is derived exclusively from the Constitution. Thus the justice I am sworn to administer as an appellate judge is not justice as I might see it in a particular case, but justice as it is defined by the Constitution and laws and legal traditions of the United States. And if I consciously deviate from that body of law to do justice as I see it, I violate my oath of office and undermine the constitutional safeguards embodied in the Separation of Powers. I acknowledged, of course, that a judge is no more relieved of moral responsibility for his work than anyone else in either private or public life. My duty as a federal judge, however, is to be measured by the requirements of my office. I cannot act as the impartial arbiter of the law unless I am willing to apply it.

I recognized that when it came to interpreting the Constitution, there existed a body of respected opinion that viewed that document, its nuts-and-bolts provisions aside, as essentially a depository of principles that each generation of jurists is at liberty to adapt to the exigencies of the times. I noted, however, that whatever the merits of that school of thought, I felt my own reliance on original meaning not only sounder in principle, but better designed to narrow the occasions for the ultimate judicial sin: the abuse of power. It ought to be clear, I suggested, that in a polity based on the rule of law, federal judges have no license to insert their own views of what is right or appropriate into the Constitution and statutes they are sworn to apply. To put it bluntly, no federal judge, however wise, has the moral authority or political competence to write the laws for a self-governing people; and no American should wish it otherwise. The federal judiciary is recruited from the ranks of a professional elite, and at the appellate level at least, it is isolated from the rough and tumble of everyday life.

I ended my talk by suggesting that while it is improper for any judge to use his position to smuggle religious doctrines into the law, the law may well benefit from a religious judge's approach to his work. I also said that to the degree that there is such a thing as a Catholic ethos, and I believe there is, it nurtures a respect for and acceptance of lawful authority and tradition; and it cultivates a sense of work as vocation. And to the degree that judges continue to believe that fidelity in service will be rewarded, and a betrayal of trust punished, in the next world if not in this, to that degree do they remain subject to the sanctions the Founders sought to invoke when they required the oath as a precondition to public service.

I suspect there are few positions in public life in which it is easier to keep faith with the oath than the one I now occupy. Thanks to life tenure and the cloistered environment in which appellate judges work, none of us is exposed to the temptations to depart from perceived duty that confront, for example, the members of Congress. I am persuaded that in the case of elected officials, the overwhelming temptation is to conclude that it is more important for your constituents that you be reelected than that you deal honestly with them. Hence the frequency with which legislators will yield to political pressures or expediency and vote against their convictions, especially when they can salve tender consciences by persuading themselves that a principled vote would not have affected the outcome. Given the difficulty of resisting such temptations over the longer run, a proper concern for the welfare of congressional souls may well be the ultimate argument in favor of term limitations.

In the last analysis, of course, an oath will encourage fidelity in office only to the degree that officeholders continue to believe that they cannot escape ultimate accountability for a breach of faith. In a footnote to the passage that I quoted earlier, Edward Gibbon observed that by the beginning of the Second Century A.D., the poet Juvenal would lament that the Roman world had lost the fear of punishment in the afterlife that had given oaths their special force. I suspect the same may now be said of ours. It seems that cheating no longer raises eyebrows, whether committed in a schoolroom or in bed, and such words as "sin" and "honor" and "virtue" sound quaint as we discard standards of behavior that have been rooted in our society since the founding of the Republic. Moreover, we are showing a dismaying tendency to recast God in Man's image. If enough people openly engage in conduct once considered reprehensible, we rewrite the rule book and assume that God, as a good democrat, will go along.

Still, I can't help wondering what changes there might be in the quality of public life today if more of our officeholders could be persuaded to take a truly scrupulous view of the responsibilities they assume when, with hands placed on Bible, they swear to faithfully discharge all the duties of their offices, according to the best of their abilities and understanding, so help them God.

(Published in the April 1995 issue of Crisis.*)*

Aloïse Steiner Buckley, RIP

WILLIAM F. BUCKLEY JR.

S HE BORE TEN CHILDREN, nine of whom have written for this journal, or worked for it, or both, and that earns her, I think, this half-acre of space normally devoted to those whose contributions are in the public mode. Hers were not. If ever she wrote a letter to a newspaper, we didn't remember it, and if she wrote to a congressman or senator, it was probably to say that she wished him well, and would pray for him as she did regularly for her country. If she had lived one day more, she'd have reached her ninetieth birthday. Perhaps somewhere else one woman has walked through so many years charming so many people by her warmth and diffidence and humor and faith. I wish I might have known her.

ASB was born in New Orleans, her ancestors having come there from Switzerland some time before the Civil War. She attended Sophie Newcomb College but left after her second year in order to become a nurse, her intention being to go spiritedly to the front. Over there, Over there. But when the young aspiring nurses were given a test to ascertain whether they could cope with the sight of blood and mayhem, she fainted, and was disqualified. A year later she married a prominent 36-year-old Texas-born attorney who lived and practiced in Mexico City, with which she had had ties because her aunt lived there.

She never lived again in New Orleans, her husband taking her, after his exile from Mexico (for backing an unsuccessful revolution that sought to restore religious liberty), to Europe, where his business led him. They had bought a house in Sharon, Connecticut, and in due course returned there. The great house where she brought us up still stands, condominiums now. But the call of the South was strong, and in the mid-Thirties they restored an antebellum house in Camden, South Carolina. There she was wonderfully content, making others happy by her vivacity, her delicate beauty, her habit of seeing the best in everyone, the humorous spark in her eye. She never lost a Southern innocence in which her sisters even more conspicuously shared. One of her daughters was delighted on overhearing an exchange between her and her freshly widowed sister who had for fifty years been married to a New Orleans doctor and was this morning, seated on the porch, completing a medical questionnaire checking this query, exxing the other. She turned to Mother and asked, "Darling, as girls did we have gonorrhea?"

Her cosmopolitanism was unmistakably Made-in-America. She spoke fluent French and Spanish with undiluted inaccuracy. My father, who loved her more even than he loved to tease her, and whose knowledge of Spanish was faultless, once remarked that in forty years she had never once placed a masculine article in front of a masculine noun, or a feminine article in front of a feminine noun, except on one occasion when she accidentally stumbled on the correct sequence, whereupon she stopped—unheard of in her case, so fluently did she aggress against the language—and corrected herself by changing the article: the result being that she spoke, in Spanish, of the latest encyclical of Pius XII, the Potato of Rome ("*Pio XII, la Papa de Roma*"). She would smile, and laugh compassionately, as though the joke had been at someone else's expense, and perhaps play a little with her pearls, just above the piece of lace she always wore in the V of the soft dresses that covered her diminutive frame.

There were rules she lived by, chief among them those she understood God to have specified, though she outdid Him in her accent on good cheer. And although Father was the unchallenged source of authority at home, she was unchallengeably in charge of arrangements in a house crowded with ten children and as many tutors, servants, and assistants. In the very late Thirties her children ranged in age from one to 21, and an in-built sense of the appropriate parietal arrangements governed the hour at which each of us should be back from wherever we were—away at the movies, or at a dance, or hearing Frank Sinatra sing at Pawling. The convention was inflexible. On returning, each of us would push, on one of the house's intercoms, the button that said, "ASB." The conversation, whether at ten when she was still awake, or at two when she had been two hours asleep, was always the same: "It's me, Mother." "Good night, darling." If—as hardly ever happened—it became truly late, and her mind had not recorded the repatriation of all ten of us, she would rise, and walk to the room of the missing child. If there, she would return to sleep, and remonstrate the next day on the forgotten telephone call. If not there, she would wait up, and demand an explanation.

My mother with her sons John, Jim, and Bill, 1976.

Her anxiety to do the will of God was more than ritual. I wrote to her once early in 1963. Much of our youth had been spent in South Carolina, and the cultural coordinates of our household were Southern. But the times required that we look Southern conventions like Jim Crow hard in the face, and so I asked her how she could reconcile Christian fraternity with the separation of the races, a convention as natural in the South for a hundred years after the Civil War as women's suffrage became natural after their emancipation, and she wrote, "My darling Bill: This is not an answer to your letter, for I cannot answer it too quickly. It came this morning, and, of course, I went as soon as possible to the Blessed Sacrament in our quiet, beautiful little church here, And, dear Bill, I prayed so hard for *humility* and for wisdom and for guidance from the Holy Spirit. I know He will help me to answer your questions as He thinks they should be answered. I must pray longer before I do this."

A few years earlier she had raised her glass on my father's 75th birthday, to say: "Darling, here's to 15 more years together, and then we'll both go." But my father died three years later. Her grief was profound, and she emerged from it through the solvent of prayer, her belief in submission to a divine order, and her irrepressible delight in her family, and friends. A few years later her daughter Maureen died at age 31, and she struggled to fight her desolation, though not with complete success. Her oldest daughter, Aloïse, died three years later. And then, three months ago, her son John.

She was by then in a comfortable retirement home, totally absent-minded; she knew us all, but was vague about when last she had seen us—or where—and was given to making references, every now and then, to her husband, "Will," and the trip they planned next week to Paris, or Mexico.

But she sensed what had happened, and instructed her nurse (she was endearingly under the impression that she owned the establishment in which she had a suite) to drive her to the cemetery, and there, unknown to us until later that afternoon, she saw from her car, at the edge of an assembly of cars, her oldest son lowered into the earth. He had been visiting her every day, often taking her to a local restaurant for lunch, and her grief was, by her standards, convulsive; but she did not break her record—she never broke it—which was never, ever to complain, because, she explained, she could never repay God the favors He had done her, no matter what tribulations she might need to suffer.

Ten years ago, my wife and I arrived at Sharon from New York much later than we had expected, and Mother had given up waiting for us, so we went directly up to the guest room. There was a little slip of blue paper on the bed lamp, another on the door to the bathroom, a third on the mirror. They were: love notes, on her 3 x 5 notepaper, inscribed "Mrs. William F. Buckley." Little valentines of welcome, as though we had circled the globe. There was no sensation to match the timbre of her pleasure on hearing from you when you called her on the telephone, or the vibration of her embrace when she laid eyes on you. Some things truly are unique.

Five days before she died—one week having gone by without her having said anything, though she clutched the hands of her children and grandchildren as they came to visit, came to say good-bye—the nurse brought her from the bathroom to the armchair and—inflexible rule—put on her lipstick, and the touch of rouge, and the pearls. Suddenly, and for the first time since the terminal descent began a fortnight earlier, she reached out for her mirror. With effort she raised it in front of her face, and then said, a teasing smile on her face as she turned to the nurse, "Isn't it amazing that anyone so old can be so beautiful?" The answer, clearly, was, Yes, it is amazing that anyone could be so beautiful.

(Published in the April 19, 1985 issue of National Review.*)*

Acknowledgements

THIS BOOK would be incomplete if I failed to acknowledge the special debt I owe several individuals not mentioned in the text who nevertheless played key roles at various stages of my public life, beginning with my successful campaign for the Senate. These include Phil Nicolaides, an enormously gifted, learned, and fey advertising whiz who, together with two friends, formed a mini advertising/public relations unit that did far more imaginative and effective work for me than the establishment firms I would use in my two subsequent (and losing) campaigns; and Arthur Finkelstein, an election analyst for one of the television networks who worked after hours as a volunteer in determining what questions to ask in our occasional polls and sifting out the political insights to be gained from the answers.

On arriving in the Senate, my most urgent need was for a legislative team able to analyze the flood of bills I would have to vote on while helping me with my own legislative initiatives. I was blessed at the outset with one consisting of Michael Uhlmann, who drafted my Human Life Amendment and on whom I depended for guidance on a number of key constitutional and other issues before he left to become an assistant attorney general; Jackee Schafer, who mastered the intricacies of environmental law; and Bill Schneider, whose contributions are described in the text. A senator's work, of course, is not limited to legislative duties. A major function of a congressional office these days is to help constituents affected by federal programs to deal with their intricacies. This requires an intimate knowledge of how the federal bureaucracy works combined with the arts of diplomacy. I secured these capabilities in the person of Tom Cole who had years of experience on Capitol Hill and trained the staffers in his charge in the necessary skills. And then there was the mail room. Here, I was fortunate to have Karlyn Keene (now Bowman) in charge. She combined the efficiency and political savvy required to run the complex operation of handling and answering over 4,000 communications a week.

But the key to my survival in each of my positions since leaving private life was a woman described on organizational charts as "secretary" but who played a far more important role in my life than that word implies. Each of them was highly intelligent, resourceful, unflappable, wonderfully organized, infinitely good humored, and tolerant of my idiosyncracies, and each became a valued friend. I am speaking of Dawne Cina (now Winter) in the Senate, Judith Epstein at the State Department, Maria Rerrich at Radio Free Europe/Radio Liberty, and Dee Barrack at the court. They were indispensable.

Finally, I acknowledge my debt to Peter Schweizer's *Victory* (1994), Dennis Kux's *The United States and Pakistan, 1947-2000* (2001), and Arch Puddington's *Broadcasting Freedom* (2000) for refreshing this uncertain memory on various aspects of my State Department and Radio Free Europe/Radio Liberty experiences.

Index

Index

Novak, Michael, 209
Oakes, John, 205
O'Dwyer, Paul, 111
Oil and Gas Journal, 96
Okinawa, Japan 63–66, 70–71
Oliver, Dan, 117
Olmer, Lionel, 200
O'Neill, Hugh, 79
O'Neill, Tip, 198
Oratory Preparatory School, 36
O'Reilly, Gerald, 29
Ortigas, Francisco and Nenita, 105
Ottinger, Richard, 118, 120, 122–124, 126–127
"Overloading the Federal Horse," 283
Pacific Ocean, 1, 99
Pakistan, 191–192, 193–196
Palatio Blanco, Mexico, 12
Panama Canal, 67
Pancoastal Petroleum, 95–96
Pantepec International, 95, 96
Paris, France, 26, 34, 36–38, 51, 200–201
Paris Accords, 157–159
Parr Family, 10
Patterson, Floyd, 179
Pearl Harbor, 43, 57, 60, 70
Peattie, Donald Culross, 52
Peking, China, 74, 78
Pelaez, Edith, 105
Pelaez, Emmanuel, 103, 105
Pell, Claiborne, 140
Pentagon, 190, 205
Perrier, Claude, 17
Perrier, Inez Steiner, 17, 18
Philippine-American War, 68. *See also* Philippine Insurrection
Philippine Bureau of Mines, 98
Philippine Insurrection, 68. *See also* Philippine-American War
Philippines, 63, 68–67, 74, 92, 95–96, 100–102, 105–106, 114, 190
    Congress, 102–103
    Flag, 104
    White House, 104

Pinckney, Charles, 247
Planned Parenthood International, 215
Point Hope, Alaska, 100, 205
Poland, 11, 210
Policemen's Benevolent Association, 119
Pope John Paul II, 176. *See also* Cardinal Wojyla
Port Gibson, Mississippi, 6, 20
Pravda, 162
Prince Philip, Duke of Edinburgh, 133
Princeton Plan, 117
Princeton University, 33
Puddington, Arch, 212
Puerto Rico, 68, 148
Queen Elizabeth II, 133
Rademaker, Steve, 227
Radio Free Europe and Radio Liberty (RFE/RL), 206–212, 214, 221, 228
Randolph, Jennings, 155
Reagan, Ronald, 189, 191–192, 195, 198–199, 201–202, 208, 212, 213, 216, 218, 221
Reasoner & Davis, 94
Reasoner, Dean, 94
Reefer Madness, 42
Reese, Joseph, 218, 221
"refuseniks," 162
Robinson, Spottswood, 228, 256
Rockefeller, Nelson, 114–115, 121, 124, 189
Roe v. Wade, 146–147, 216, 223, 273–274
Roosevelt, Franklin Delano, 43, 57–58, 77, 187, 279
Rostow, Eugene, 82
Republican National Convention, 115
Republican Party, 43, 107, 114–115, 121, 124–125, 130–131, 141, 170, 176, 189, 220, 283
Rochester, New York, 124
"Rule of Subsidiarity," 138
Russia, 210–211
St. Gallen, Switzerland 18, 19
St. Louis, Missouri, 20, 86, 97
Sacramento, California, 189
Saffir, Len, 161–162, 164
Saigon, 158–159